Breaking the Rules

Breaking the Rules
Liberating Writers Through Innovative Grammar Instruction

EDGAR H. SCHUSTER

Heinemann
Portsmouth, NH

Heinemann
A division of Reed Elsevier Inc.
361 Hanover Street
Portsmouth, NH 03801-3912
www.heinemann.com

Offices and agents throughout the world

The author and publisher wish to thank those who have generously given permission to reprint borrowed material:

"Rime of the Ancient Warriner's" by Robert Boynton is used by permission of Jeanne Boynton.

"Sweet Sixteen" and excerpts from student essays in Chapter 4 are reprinted from *Writing Assessment Handbook Supplement.* Published by the Pennsylvania System of School Assessment. Reprinted by permission of the Commonwealth of Pennsylvania, Department of Education.

Excerpts of student essays from *The Concord Review: Exemplary High School History Essays* are reprinted by permission of *The Concord Review. www.tcr.org.*

Excerpts of "Fox" are reprinted by permission of Northwest Regional Educational Lab, Portland, Oregon.

"Debris of Life and Mind" from *The Collected Poems of Wallace Stevens* by Wallace Stevens. Copyright © 1954 by Wallace Stevens and renewed 1982 by Holly Stevens. Used by permission of Alfred A. Knopf, a division of Random House, Inc.

"Homeless" from *Living Out Loud* by Anna Quindlen. Copyright © 1987 by Anna Quindlen. Used by permission of Random House, Inc.

Excerpts of "Reforming English Language Arts: Let's Trash the Tradition" by Edgar H. Schuster from *Phi Delta Kappan*, March 1999. Reprinted by permission of Phi Delta Kappan.

Excerpts of "Language Arts Standards and the Possessive Apostrophe" by Edgar H. Schuster from *Education Week*, April 19, 2000. Reprinted by permission of *Education Week.*

Excerpts of "Let's Get Off the Mythmobile" by Edgar H. Schuster from *The English Journal*, October 1985. Reprinted by permission of the National Council of Teachers of English.

Library of Congress Cataloging-in-Publication Data
Schuster, Edgar Howard, 1930–
   Breaking the rules : liberating writers through innovative grammar instruction / Edgar H. Schuster.
      p. cm.
   Includes bibliographical references and index.
   ISBN 0-325-00478-1
      1. English language—Composition and exercises—Study and teaching (Secondary)—United States.
   2. English language—Grammar—Study and teaching (Secondary)—United States. I. Title.

LB1631 .S285 2003
808'.042'0712—dc21   2002015855

Editor: Lisa Luedeke
Production coordinator: Elizabeth Valway
Production service: Denise Botelho, Colophon
Cover design: Catherine Hawkes, Cat and Mouse
Composition: Argosy Publishing
Manufacturing: Steve Bernier

Printed in the United States of America on acid-free paper
07 06 05 04   RRD   3 4 5

To Nancy, lifetime companion through this rich and wonderful life, and to the children, their spouses, and the grandchildren who have done so much to make it so.

In addition to my wife and family, I dedicate this book to the memory of my friend, Robert W. Boynton, a great teacher and a publisher of the best books that our profession needed to read. Bob was there at the origin of this book, in a sense, for I first met him in the very late 1950s when I joined a small band of Philadelphia-area English teachers, a "linguistics club," dedicated to finding answers to difficult questions. *Breaking the Rules* is the end product of a quest that began there.

I had just started my teaching career at Central High School (a public school that was open only to the brightest kids in the city—it's Noam Chomsky's alma mater), where they handed me a textbook and said, "Here, teach this." Having graduated from Columbia as a vagabond major, which the college permitted in those days, I quickly discovered that I was woefully unprepared to teach "grammar." My bright students asked many questions I could not answer, and when I queried fellow faculty members, they didn't know the answers either, not even veterans who had been teaching in the school for forty years.

So I joined the club. Bob was "just an English teacher" himself in those days, though a particularly energetic, outspoken, and straightforward one. I loved his wit and good humor and his antiauthoritarian stances. I still remember the Post-it note he frequently used later in his life: "Illegitimi Non Carborundum," it read— "Don't let the bastards get you down."

The world knows what Bob went on to do, but I saw much less of him once he left the Philadelphia area, until the middle 1980s, when he became my co-chair of the NCTE Committee on Publishers and English Teachers. He really energized that group, and two years in succession, we created grand all-day, postconvention workshops. The first one, however, was rejected by the program committee, which claimed we would not get a large enough audience. Feeling passionately that we would get a large audience and that we should be heard in any case, Bob refused the rejection. We began to lobby influential NCTE members, and if that hadn't worked we were prepared to put the program on *at the Convention, without Council approval*. The Program chair—or whoever it was—changed his mind. The workshop was a huge success; we had to turn people away. The succeeding year's workshop was equally successful.

That was Bob: He knew more about what the profession needed than the NCTE itself.

It was Bob, too, who first introduced to me the concept of teaching against the textbook, and the more I have learned about textbooks, the sounder this idea has become, particularly the dominant traditional school grammar textbooks, the best-sellers, like *Warriner's English Grammar and Composition* and Hodges' *Harbrace College Handbook*. When I wrote Bob, not long before he died, to tell him about this book, I was reminded of his antitextbook poem, and I conclude this dedication by giving it to you. "It's the best poem I ever wrote," Bob said, and then added with his characteristic good humor, "and the only one."

The Rime of the Ancient Warriner's

It is an ancient Warriner's
And it stoppeth every wight
From doing what is best to do
When learning how to write.

It mixes skills and drills and frills
With exhortation solemn,
And stacks itself on classroom shelves
Column after column.

Amoeba-like, it splits itself
Into scope and sequence clones,
With names alike as Mike and Ike
And wholly writ by drones.

(It transmogrifies itself with ease
Into Little, Brown, and Hodges
And Bedford, Crews and Ebbitts
And a hundred other stodges.)

It names the parts and modes and marks
It's a taxonomic rite—
And multitudes are led through it,
And still they cannot write,

And go as ones that have been stunned
And are of sense forlorn,
Much sadder and unwiser wights
Than ever they was born.

Contents

Acknowledgments   ix

Introduction: Rule Breaking and the Reflective English Teacher   xi

1. Language Acquisition and Traditional School Grammar   1

2. Traditional School Grammar: Definitions That Do Not Define   19

3. Usage: Rules That Do Not Rule (and a Few That Do)   47

4. Writing: Liberating the Student Writer   89

5. Punctuation Today   151

Appendix: An Updated Treatment of the Parts of Speech   193

References   215

Index   223

Acknowledgments

The single individual who has helped me most in this project is my friend Dorothy (Dolly) Russell, a professional reference librarian. (All my life I have said librarians were the salt of the earth; now I *really* know what that means.) Dolly was my student in a summer writing course at Lehigh University and was the best poet among the students I have taught there in over ten years. With respect to research, Dolly never failed to discover what I needed to know. Occasionally she tested ideas on her husband, her children, and her friends. I thank them as well. She has also read all of the manuscript and has made an abundance of valuable suggestions. Quite notably, she did a superb job on the index.

My son, Bill; my son-in-law, Charlie Allred; my daughter, Nina; and my wife have also read and commented on the manuscript and have helped to improve it materially. My daughter Claire has given helpful artistic advice.

Special thanks goes to Ian Michael of Bristol, UK, for his review of my history of Traditional School Grammar in Chapter 1. There is no one alive who knows more about that topic than he does, and his own *English Grammatical Categories and the Tradition to 1800* and *The Teaching of English from the Sixteenth Century to 1870* (both Cambridge University Press) deserve to be much better known in this country than they are.

Bill Varner was probably the first to suggest that an article I published in *Kappan* could be turned into a book. I thank him, too, for initially shepherding my proposal through the editorial committee at Heinemann.

For examples of outstanding student writing, I thank Will Fitzhugh, editor and publisher of *The Concord Review*, and I thank John Weiss and especially, Andrea Martine, both of the Pennsylvania Department of Education, for helping me with student writing from the Pennsylvania State Assessment. And to the editors of *Kappan*, *Education Week*, and *The English Journal*, thank you for the permission to quote from my articles.

I also appreciate the email responses of Nancy Sommers, Director of Expository Writing at Harvard, one of the very few places where they make an investment in teaching student writing that is commensurate to the task.

I particularly appreciate Jeanne Boynton, wife of Bob, who generously gave permission for me to use Bob's delightful poem, "The Rime of the Ancient Warriner's." And speaking of Warriner, I thank three people who helped me with research regarding him: Joseph Prusan, former principal of Garden City High School; Cynthia Morrongiello, a former English teacher there; and the current high school librarian, Suzanne Stuckey.

The bright, responsive, and efficient people at Heinemann were always a pleasure to deal with. I especially thank my editor, Lisa Luedeke, who made valuable suggestions to improve the manuscript, and my production editor, Elizabeth Valway. It was also a pleasure to work with Denise Botelho, who handled the production of the book.

The librarians at the Rare Book collections of the University of Pennsylvania and at the main campus of Penn State University were always cordial and helpful. These days, much primary source textbook material has been printed in facsimile, but it remains a great pleasure to hold in one's own hands books that were actually used by students and teachers of centuries ago. I thank Pat Larish, University of California, Berkeley, for assistance with translations.

Finally, without the help of my (now deceased) good friend Bill Simon, this book would probably have taken me twice as long to write. I shall always remember that gentle man.

Introduction
Rule Breaking and the
Reflective English Teacher

If you're teaching and you're not learning then you're not teaching.
—FRANK MCCOURT

Most people think students break rules aplenty. Why encourage them? The short answer: in the interest of helping them to become independent thinkers and more effective communicators. But before discussing the benefits of rule breaking, let's look at what language rules are and why some should *not* be broken.

We all feel intuitively that grammar is a *system of rules* that are to be followed. Quite so. Indeed, speakers and writers disregard these rules at their peril, usually at the cost of communicative derailment. If I were to ask you where the *office post* is, for example, communication would leave the tracks. Why? Because I would have broken a rule of English grammar that requires single-word modifiers normally to be placed *before* the word they modify.

This system of rules is acquired by native speakers mostly (not entirely) even before they enter school (see Chapter 1)—though it is a few years later before one's writing ability catches up. Let's call these the *bedrock rules of English syntax. This book does not advocate breaking these rules.*

This book also does not advocate breaking another group of rules—those that distinguish *it's* from *its* and *affect* from *effect*, for example. Breaking these usually does not derail communication, but it may delay it, and it may have the further unhappy consequence of causing the reader to think badly of the writer. In fact, you will find a glossary in the third chapter of this book that covers *how these rules can be taught effectively.* These rules have the authority of the dictionary behind them—a universally agreed upon standard.

Americans who write or edit need to know the rules of Well-Edited American Prose (WEAP)—or have an editor who knows them. These rules can be tricky, since they are not uniform across the publishing industry, which is why most publishers have their own stylebooks. People who don't write and don't intend ever to write or edit have no need to know such rules and are very unlikely to learn them. I don't mean to downplay these rules, since knowing them is empowering, but trying to teach and learn them has driven not a few teachers and students to the brink of substance abuse.

On a fourth type of rule, which might loosely be called a *usage rule*, my position is more complex, and I would rather defer discussion till the third chapter. There is no universally agreed upon standard for these rules.

Which Rules *Should* Be Broken?

What sort of rules do I advocate breaking? The answer is a host of rules that have accrued through the centuries since the first grammars of English were written and that are now so essential a part of school grammars (or English-teacher folklore) that to omit them is to foredoom any textbook or handbook to the dustbin, at least in the larger school and college textbook markets. These are mythrules, "rules" that rule no one—other than perhaps a handful of pop-grammarians and hardened purists who look for their authority somewhere in the sky rather than here on earth.

How do we know a mythrule when we meet it? I propose—with thanks to Joseph M. Williams—what I call a "favorite writer test." (It could be a favorite speaker test, if the tester were concerned with oral English.) Here is how it works.

The Favorite Writer Test of Correctness

We Catholic elementary school graduates were sure that the nuns received their rules directly from Mount Sinai, but there aren't many teaching nuns around today. Where do ordinary mortals get their linguistic commandments? Many purists will say, "From logic," but alas, even conservative linguists will tell you that—to quote one—"Language never has followed the rules of logic. There's no language on earth where mathematical logic and its grammar correspond neatly" (McWhorter, quoted in Dreifus, 2001). (In the same interview, McWhorter says he could be a purist himself—"in another universe.")

To check for correctness of the written language, try the following test. (*Note:* The test works especially well when dealing with purists, but it may also be used with anyone interested in checking for correctness.)

First, ask the interested person to name a favorite writer. It's best to use a modern writer, since real rules change from time to time. Also, to avoid the charge that "creative writers" get away with everything, it's best to choose a nonfiction writer.

Second, go to a library (it needs the business anyway) and find a book by that writer.

Third, observe whether the "rule" under discussion is observed by that writer. If it is, the other scores a point; but if it isn't, you do, and he has to back off his white charger.

Let's take an illustration. My purist friend tells me that I must not begin sentences with *and* or *but*. (My computer tells me the same thing.) One of my friend's favorite nonfiction writers is William Zinsser. Zinsser is a particularly good choice because among his books are several on how to write.

In the library, we find Zinsser's *On Writing Well* (1976), and we randomly turn to the chapter "Rewriting." The third paragraph begins with "But," and the last sentence of that paragraph begins with "And." Moreover, later in the chapter, Zinsser shows us a couple of pages that he has rewritten "four or five times." In the middle of those pages, this surviving sentence appears: "But he won't do this for long."

If my friend still insists that it is wrong to start sentences with *and* or *but*, we are, as Joseph Williams puts it, no longer debating usage but theology (1995, p. 180).

This illustration is a test of a writing mythrule, but the test works for grammar, usage, and punctuation as well.

Should Students Know the Rules Before They Can Break Them?

Most of us English teachers are aware that good writers violate "rules." Even relatively conservative handbooks, for example, acknowledge that sentence fragments may be effectively used. However, where *students* are concerned, the permission to violate is often paired with the injunction BEWARE, or "*First* learn the rules, *then* you can break them—sometimes."

Knowing certain kinds of rules can be important, as I have said, but let's keep the following points in mind before we next pass along the commonsense injunction that students have to learn rules before they can break them.

1. We need to think a great deal about *how, at what time, and under what circumstances children learn rules in the first place.* The assumption that they learn usage, composition, or punctuation rules simply by having teachers or textbooks present them is as naive as thinking that kids learn grammar by memorizing definitions. Composition theorists insist, for example, that students *do not* learn rules from English-teacher marginalia such as AWK, CS, or MM, or from teachers editing their work. Paul Diedrich, an outstanding teacher and a specialist in composition

who went on to a distinguished career at Educational Testing Service (ETS), insisted many decades ago that the best thing we teachers could do to promote growth in student writers was to make *positive* comments on the *content* of what the students wrote and *one* suggestion on how they could improve next time. This advice has been repeated by English educators thousands of times since, right up to the present day. In *Coaching Writing* (2001), William Strong suggests that after teachers read students' writing, they add *one or two* suggestions on how the kids can improve next time.

2. In initially acquiring our native language, we often *break rules before we learn them.* Composition researchers have found the same to be true where writing is concerned. Significant research demonstrates that certain kinds of errors are a sign of *growth.* In fact, to quote Constance Weaver—whose chapter "Toward a Perspective on Error" in *Teaching Grammar in Context* is an excellent discussion of this matter—"writing growth and error go hand in hand" (1996a, p. 69). I'll never forget a ninth grader's description of sitting in an empty church—the best impromptu piece of writing by a student at that level that I have ever read. It was full of punctuation errors, most of which were related to the fact that she was using participial phrases that she could not yet punctuate. Would any thoughtful English teacher prefer that this student avoid using participial phrases until she learned how to punctuate them?

3. *Overconcern with following rules may undermine self-confidence and may be the root reason why so many adults fear writing.* Not long ago, as part of a presentation, I asked a group of about seventy teachers to write to a prompt. Within a short time, all were working diligently (as was I). When I asked them to evaluate their own efforts, however, only a handful were willing to give themselves anything higher than an average grade, and many rated themselves far lower.

Why? I wanted to know. Was the environment not conducive to writing? Was the time too short? Was the topic dull? Did they not understand the task? Did they have little or nothing to say? The answer to all these questions was "no." The root problem was that they dreaded writing, and one of the main reasons was their fear of making errors. Trying to write while worrying about errors is like trying to waltz in a ballroom with loose floorboards.

It's been a long time since the early research of Donald Graves and his colleagues, but we must be ever mindful of their discovery that the second of the two most important determinants of how well kids write is their *self-confidence.* Self-confidence in writing is not fostered by insisting that students must learn rules before they may break them.

4. *Premature attention to rules may inhibit creativity and cause students to "play it safe."* Put yourself in the seat of a ninth grader (especially, perhaps, one sitting for a high-stakes writing test): "Do I use this structure [say it's some sort of verbal phrase], even though I may 'dangle' it or not know how to punctuate it correctly?" If you've had the experience of reading thousands of state essays, you probably know that her answer is frequently, "No, I'll play it safe." You may also have noticed that the papers that really come alive are often those that break rules.

5. *Finally, many of the rules aren't rules in the first place.* You'll meet a large number of these in the usage, writing, and punctuation sections of this book. For example, in spite of the fact that every textbook in print says that writers should use a semicolon before conjunctive adverbs and other transitional words and phrases, you will see in Chapter 5 that writers do *not* employ this punctuation. Even the promulgators of this mythrule regularly break it. *Why should students learn rules that no one follows?*

The Reflective Teacher

Reflective teachers are those who constantly inquire into their own practice, who are "in continual conversation with [their teaching]," as John Mayher puts it (1990, p. 283). They are experimenters, independent thinkers, and are likely to find more sense in what Mayher calls *un*common sense than in common sense. You won't find them reading from scripts or slavishly following teacher's manuals, though you might find them giving quizzes and assigning homework, maybe even asking students to memorize things.

Most important, *they will encourage students to examine rules and to break them.* Why? Because the unexamined rule is not worth keeping. Not to allow students to break rules is to deny them full access to the linguistic resources of English, resources that people need to express themselves and achieve their own voices. Huck Finn wouldn't be Huck unless he broke rules (linguistic and otherwise), and neither would his creator be the master writer he was.

"Only Look and Connect"

E. M. Forster's novel *Howards End* opens with the memorable epigraph, "Only connect." This can be modified into a motto for reflective English teachers: "Only look and connect." Look at the results of your teaching; look at the facts of language; look at practices of our best writers, both student and professional; look to see which rules really rule. Then connect what you discover to your teaching practice.

This can often be done with very little trouble. For example, earlier today I wondered just how often professional writers varied their sentence openings. Well, let's *look*. I selected a collection of essays by professional writers (*The Bedford Reader*, Sixth Edition, 1997), arbitrarily opened it to a right-hand page, and noted how the sentences in the paragraph I hit upon started. I did this five times. (I hit pages 115, 247, 377, 463, and 591.) Seventy-seven and a half percent of the forty sentences opened with the subject noun phrase. Of the remaining sentences, ten percent opened with a simple conjunction (*and, but, so*), and five percent opened with prepositional phrases. There was one adverb opening, one infinitive phrase, and one sentence opened with its object. This "research" took me five minutes. (For a more detailed look at how professional writers open their sentences, see Chapter 4, pp. 120–124.)

How does this *connect* with practice? If you teach from a textbook, you are familiar with a "rule" that students should vary their sentence openings. At the very least, this looking raises doubt about the value of this advice. I have been amazed at how many "rules" fall by the wayside when they are examined by this simple strategy.

Regularly Solicit Feedback from Students

If the purpose of teaching is to enhance student learning, a reflective teacher should solicit student feedback, often. I'm always taking pop opinion polls of my students. I do it by actually passing out ballots, rather than by a show of hands. (There's too great a chance that the sheepish and the shy will vote with the majority rather than say what they really think.) It takes only a minute to rip a piece of paper into thirty ballots, and the results can be put on the board for all to see, with a student calling out the votes and you tabulating them.

When I taught American Literature, I used six different novels. After each book, I asked my students to rate it on a scale of one to five. If a book couldn't get at least a 2.5 rating, I dropped it. That's how I learned that I couldn't teach *Moby Dick* or *The Scarlet Letter* to my eleventh graders. I stopped teaching both. (The best received novels were *To Kill a Mockingbird* at 1.6 and *The Great Gatsby* at 1.88.)

Discover What Your Students Already Know

Well before the standards mania struck, every school district I knew of already had standards. For one thing, we gave final examinations in English. We assumed that what was on the final was what students needed to learn. But we never asked whether the students might *already* know it. A few years ago, to answer this question, I gave fifty-five questions from the *final* English examination to 541 tenth graders during the *first week in October*. The average grade was 61.0 percent correct, and 30.3 percent passed the exam. Students in the honors track averaged 76.4 percent correct. A reflective teacher might ask why we're "teaching" students what they already know.

In studying individual sections of the October versus June scores, I discovered that gains were extremely modest across all tracks. For example, although the district used a textbook vocabulary program, the total gain in vocabulary for the year was only 10.4 percent. If we assume that students would have experienced some vocabulary growth from maturation alone, this percentage gain seems trivial. In all other areas, the gains were even more modest; in fact, in some areas, there were *losses*. Scores on subject-verb agreement questions, for example, went down, and there was a 7.7 percent *loss* in knowledge of "correct verb forms."

Giving parts of the final in the fall might seem a radical notion, but it has the additional benefit of revealing to the students what they need to learn. And if they don't need to learn it, you can change the curriculum and perhaps alleviate boredom.

Join or Create a Teacher-Researcher Group

As described in Marion S. MacLean and Marian M. Mohr's book, *Teacher-Researchers at Work* (1999), reflective researchers study their own classrooms or students and share their results with like-minded others. They eschew "control groups," sampling, and other sorts of statistical stuff (they're not bent on *proving* anything), but they solicit feedback from their colleagues, and they often "publish" their results, in one form or another (seven articles by teacher-researchers appear in MacLean and Mohr's book). Teacher-researchers ask significant questions, with emphasis on improving instruction and growing as teachers. The book has a chapter on forming one's own research group and an extensive bibliography. These teacher-researchers have responded to what Frank McCourt suggests in his quote at the beginning of this chapter.

Do Research on Your Own

Every conscientious public school English teacher holds the equivalent of *two* full-time jobs. The first she does during the regular work week. She does the second on weekends and evenings—and mornings, if she's an early riser. Since everyone is entitled to a life outside of work and a little leisure time, I have been suggesting reflective techniques that require relatively little time.

But a few teachers seem never to sleep. If you're one of them, you might attempt an in-depth study of one or more of your classes, on your own. That's what Finlay McQuade did in the late 1970s, examining his Editorial Skills elective. His study is a model of individual teacher research, but I discuss it here also because of its "landmark" status (Weaver, 1996b, p. 15), and because it supports an important thesis of this book—that traditional grammar traditionally taught is an utter failure (see Chapter 2).

Finlay McQuade was a young, well-qualified, energetic, popular, highly intelligent high school English teacher who taught an Editorial Skills course to eleventh- and twelfth-grade students at Sewickley Academy in Sewickley, Pennsylvania. The course was regarded as a "good" one by everybody, including the highly motivated students who enthusiastically took it and were convinced they learned a great deal from it. McQuade, furthermore, *believed* in teaching traditional grammar. I believe he taught it as well as any classroom teacher I have ever known.

Initially, McQuade made the commonsense assumption that students who had passed the course had learned something, and all was well—until the English Department decided to identify student weaknesses so that they (the weak students) could be given additional work. One of the areas examined was "mechanics." Unaccountably, some of the students who had taken and passed McQuade's Editorial Skills did not pass the departmental test and were assigned to a remedial course. McQuade was "alarmed" and decided that he had to reflect on and evaluate his own course.

If he was alarmed initially, he must have been ready to quit teaching English after his research. In fact, McQuade did quit full-time English teaching. It will surprise no one who has read his study that he subsequently pursued issues of thinking and learning.

The course was traditional. McQuade reviewed parts of speech and sentence structure and then had students apply grammatical principles to the task of finding errors. He used two traditional textbooks and lots of worksheets, tests, and exercises. He took the same approach to punctuation and diction, and to spelling, if he had the time.

Readers who want the full story are urged to read McQuade's article in the October 1980 *English Journal*, but here are the main conclusions of his research.

1. Measured by their scores on the Cooperative English Tests (at the time, a widely used, nationally normed test published by ETS), taking Editorial Skills "made no difference in student achievement" (p. 28), and students who did not take the course showed as much gain as those who did.

2. On matched, teacher-made, pre- and post-tests of course content, "The class average on the pre-test . . . was actually higher than the average on the post-test" (p. 28). The kids knew more before they took the course.

3. McQuade hoped that taking the Editorial Skills course would help students score higher than they otherwise would on the CEEB Achievement Test in Composition, and they did gain (over their SAT test scores), but "the average difference between the SAT and Achievement scores of students who had *not* taken Editorial Skills was just as high" (p. 29).

4. On essays students wrote before and after the course, the frequency of errors was reduced by almost half. But before allowing himself a small sigh of relief, McQuade looked at the specific errors and found that the improvement came from "a few students who had learned a few of the simpler skills. The number of errors involving the more complex skills of grammar and general punctuation was not reduced at all" (p. 30).

5. The pre-course essays of the students who took the course were "not spectacular," the post-course essays were "miserable." Specifically, McQuade felt that Editorial Skills graduates wrote badly after the course because they wrote "to honor correctness above all other virtues" (p. 29).

I read this study when it first appeared, over twenty years ago. I'm still waiting for a rebuttal from anyone who favors teaching traditional school grammar.

The research was based on a small sample, to be sure, and it is not without other imperfections, as McQuade himself freely and frequently admits, but it seems to me that he conclusively proves his belief that "we [teachers] must evaluate our own teaching, . . . including those features of it that we have come to value most" (p. 30).

And where did those features come from? At the beginning of the last century, the philosopher George Santayana observed that those who did not remember the past were condemned to repeat it. Read on and judge for yourself whether teachers of this grammar have been repeating the past for the last two and a half centuries.

Breaking the Rules

1
Language Acquisition and Traditional School Grammar

It is now a-days the miserable Fate of Grammar to be more Whip't than Taught; and the children like slaves, are bred up into the hatred of it. . . . the poor Boy is made dull, and then beaten for being so; because the duller Master knows neither what to teach, nor how to suit himself to the several Capacities of Children, which are as different as their Features.

—MICHAEL MAITTAIRE, THE ENGLISH GRAMMAR, 1712

No errors are so trivial but they deserve to be mended.

—HANDWRITTEN COMMENT IN LOWTH'S GRAMMAR, 1762

All grammars leak.

—EDWARD SAPIR, LANGUAGE, 1921

On a fine spring day in the late 1970s in Allentown, Pennsylvania, I was called by a principal to observe one of his veteran teachers teaching "grammar" to a first grade class. The school was an inner-city school, a large percentage of its students qualifying for the government-sponsored lunch.

The teacher—we'll call her Ms. Abbott—began the lesson by giving three children cards marked, respectively, Noun, Verb, and Adjective and sending each child to a separate corner. In the fourth corner, the other students took turns picking word cards out of a pile, after which they were expected to march their word to the correct corner.

Amy was the third; her word was *wet*. I can see her still: a pretty, frail waif with a blonde pony tail, frozen in doubt. Finally, she drifted to the Verb corner. "Amy!" Ms. Abbott thundered. "Think! Isn't 'wet' a picture word?"

By this time Amy was shaking and in tears. I have never forgotten her, nor quite forgiven her teacher. This book is for Amy. It's also for the millions of other children and older kids as well who have been victimized by this sort of myth-instruction. Traditional school grammar, traditionally taught, is a staggering, Pentagonesque waste of time and money. Moreover, since its beginnings it has scared and scarred students, as the Maittaire quote at the head of this chapter testifies.

Here's a recent grammar lesson from another classroom. This one was observed by a business executive, a man with a commitment to educational change, who considered it an exemplary lesson. I do not mean to fault him particularly, or even the teacher necessarily. His reaction would be typical of millions of observers, and the teacher may well have been following a script or a local curriculum guide or a state-mandated list of objectives.

The teacher began by asking students to give her "action words, words for something we do," and several words were suggested, all of which do indeed *sometimes* serve as predicate verbs in sentences. Next, the teacher asked for a name for all action words and elicited (timidly) "verb." Following that, she pointed to a sentence on the chalk board: "A *verb* is an *action* word."

This is of course the traditional definition (or part of it). Now consider the following sentences. In each, which word is the verb?

1. They had a fight.
2. Skipping rope is fun.
3. Do people resemble their pets?

In (1), the action word is *fight*, surely, not *had*. But *had* is the verb. In (2), *skipping* surely is an action, but *is* is the verb. And in (3), there simply is no action. The main verbs in (1) and (3), *had* and *resemble*, are *not* among those traditionally classified as state of being verbs. There are hundreds more like them.

And what about the action words that the teacher elicited from her class? Consider *go*. Is it the verb in the following sentences?

4. My mom is always on the go.
5. All systems are go.
6. Never stop at a go-ahead signal; you could cause a crash.

The teacher did not say that the words her students volunteered were verbs only, but that is the impression that the students, no doubt, got—and certainly the impression Ms. Abbott left on Amy regarding *wet*.

But here is the main point: Typical first graders can *process* and even *produce* every sentence from 1 to 6. In doing so, they prove that they know much more about the parts of speech than either the teacher or the textbook is teaching them. They *understand*, for instance, that Sentence 1 means, "they fought." They *understand* that Sentence 5 means that all systems are *ready*. Amy knows well that *wet* is not an adjective, always, certainly not in the sentence she may have heard a parent speak that very morning: "Your little brother wet his bed again last night."

Another verb elicited from the second class was *run*. Surely a verb, right? Yes, and my dictionary lists thirty-three *noun* definitions for the same word, most of which, miraculously, youngsters know without ever having been taught. How do kids gain the huge store of grammatical knowledge that all of them possess?

Language Acquisition, or What Amy Knows

It's an interesting word, *acquire*. It means *to get by one's own efforts*. We acquire our native language without being taught. We don't need teachers or books or any kind of scholastic drill.

People talk about *learning* or being *taught* a foreign language in school. But we *acquire* our native language, outside of school.

Most parents are indifferent teachers of oral language, especially with young children. The natural response to kids who overgeneralize (saying *buyed* rather than *bought*, for instance) is not correction, but "Isn't that cute?" On a weekend in June 2001, my then five-year-old granddaughter Laurel wrote a get-well card to a family friend that began, "I hop you are dancing again soon." (She had asked her father how to spell *again*, but not *hope*.) Later that day, she said of her brother, "Whitney throwed his hat." Did any parent or grandparent *correct* her—in either case? Not a chance. They were confident she would correct herself, in time.

In fact, much evidence attests to the fact that when parents do try to correct children, it doesn't work. The child persists in her *error* rather than correcting it. Here is an example from the psychologist Courtney Cazden (quoted in Pinker, 1999, p. 196):

CHILD: My teacher holded the baby rabbits and we patted them.
ADULT: Did you say your teacher held the baby rabbits?
CHILD: Yes.
ADULT: What did you say she did?
CHILD: She holded the baby rabbits and we patted them.
ADULT: Did you say she held them tightly?
CHILD: No, she holded them loosely.

That child is going to hold on to *holded* until *she* is ready to let go. Interestingly, children are sometimes conscious of the differences between their own language and adult speech. Here's my favorite illustration, an exchange between psycholinguist Tom Bever and one of his own children:

> TOM: Where's Mommy?
> CHILD: Mommy goed to the store.
> TOM: Mommy goed to the store?
> CHILD: NO! (*annoyed*) Daddy, I say it that way, not you.
> (Pinker, 1999, p. 199)

Here are two salient facts about language acquisition:

- Parents rarely correct children during their early language acquisition.
- Children are unresponsive to correction.

Facts like these have led linguist Noam Chomsky to state one of the most fascinating hypotheses ever regarding language acquisition:

> There is good reason to believe that children learn language from positive evidence only (corrections not being required or relevant). (1986, p. 55)

What a revolution if we applied that principle to the schoolroom teaching of usage and writing. And how counter it would run to the deep roots of traditional school grammar, which we will examine shortly. But first, some additional facts about language acquisition.

Think about it: Language acquisition is not something that we deliberately choose to do. Given a normal brain and a natural environment, children acquire their native language naturally. This has led psychologist Steven Pinker to posit a *language instinct*. As Pinker says in *The Language Instinct*, language is as instinctive for human beings as spinning a web is for a spider, every three-year-old is a grammatical genius, and the design of our syntax is "coded in our DNA and wired into our brains" (1994, p. 371).

We need not enter the controversy between empiricists and rationalists here. It's purely commonsensical to observe that people have an intuitive sense of the grammaticality of their native language. Certainly, if two children are raised in radically diverse circumstances, they will speak differently. One child may say, "I ain't seed my friends," and another may say, "I have not seen my friends," but neither one will say, "Seen my I friends not have." The reason is, simply, that both speakers have acquired *rules* that require them to do such things as:

- Place determiners—*my* here—before nouns
- Position the doer before the receiver

4

- Put the verb phrase between doer and receiver
- Make negatives split verb phrases

I have oversimplified the rules here, of course. The wonder is that we not only acquire such rules as "doer precedes receiver," but also acquire the exceptions; we know when *not* to follow this order—in passives, for example.

Further, the rules children acquire involve word formation as well. For example, speakers routinely *prefix* un-, mis-, and re-, but they *suffix* -ness, -ize, and -ly. There is no more chance that a child will say *nesshappyun* than it will say "Seen my I friends not have."

Even much pronunciation seems to be intuitively known. A particularly revealing illustration of what the mind knows about the parts of speech of words is such verb/nouns as *object*, which have primary stress falling on the first syllable if the word is a noun, on the second if it's a verb:

I ob**JECT** to this **OB**ject being placed into evidence.

In short, we *know* not only which is the verb and which is the noun but also which pronunciation goes with which part of speech.

The mind also knows which words do and which do not take the past-tense ending (as well as whether that ending is pronounced *t*, *d*, or *id*):

tensed (*t*)	begged (*d*)	handed (*id*)	dished	pestered
*tersed	*bigged	*harded	*densed	*pested

*In linguistics, an asterisk indicates something unacceptable for grammatical, semantic, or other reasons.

What we recognize is that *tense, beg, hand, dish,* and *pester* are all verbs (or rather, that they can be used as verbs) and that *terse, big, hard, dense,* and *pest* cannot be verbs—in spite of the closeness of pronunciation of these pairs. One might imagine that similar-sounding words would make it especially difficult for the brain/mind to distinguish one word and its part of speech from another, but apparently they do not. There appears to be a phonological component in the mind that takes care of that. We also know which words can take the *s* ending, meaning "more than one of a kind" (*girl/girls, grammar/grammars, language/languages*) and that this ending is different from the *s* attached to third-person verbs (*tell/tells, agree/agrees, develop/develops*).

Steven Pinker states the matter this way: "The most basic kind of word is a root, with a canonical sound arbitrarily paired with a meaning and a part of speech" (1999, p. 186). The part of speech of a word comes with it, as it were. Knowing a word, being able to use it, *necessitates* knowing its part of speech. To be sure, this is not equivalent to being able to *name* its part of speech, but in the world outside of the English classroom, how important is that?

Three quarters of a century ago, Edward Sapir, one of the most brilliant linguists America has ever produced, noted that the part of speech in English is "a will-o'-the-wisp." Amy, and all other children, learn this at a very early age. Would this quote were posted on every language arts bulletin board in the nation—to remind teachers and principals and business executives what children already know.

Why Do Teachers Teach *Grammar*?

Given that kids already know most of the important rules of their native language by the time they enter school, why is it that so many teachers continue to teach *grammar*, and particularly the parts of speech? An excellent list and discussion of the reasons may be found in Constance Weaver's *Teaching Grammar in Context* (1996a, pp. 23–25). I will expand on just two of her points.

First, we all feel, intuitively, that a grammar is a set of rules and that this set of rules must be followed if we are to communicate accurately with other speakers. This intuition is dead right. But these rules and grammar in this sense are *not*, in general, the rules and the grammar taught in the traditional school grammar classroom. There, too often, students are taught mythrules.

Second, teachers often teach not only what they have been taught—a point well established by educational researcher John Goodlad—but also what they think the community expects them to teach. In their book about the difficulty of effecting changes in schools (*Tinkering Toward Utopia*), David Tyack and Larry Cuban refer to "the persistence of the grammar of schooling." Briefly, this means that what gets taught in school is what feels like school. (They are not using *grammar* here in quite the same sense I have been.)

A good example in American schools is textbook instruction in spelling and weekly spelling tests. A school that doesn't do these doesn't feel like a school (to most of us). I once led an experiment that showed that fifth graders who studied spelling the traditional way did not score statistically better than fifth graders who did not use a text at all, in spite of the fact that 80 percent of the words on the final test were in the spelling book! Did this experiment change the school curriculum or culture? Not one inch. The only change was that the teacher of the nontraditional approach transferred to another building and grade level, and became a math teacher—though she had a Ph.D. in English.

Traditional grammar feels like the right thing to do (teach) in school, and so it is taught. If it's not there, something seems to be missing. Ms. Abbott's principal and Ms. Abbott herself were unwitting victims of this "grammar of schooling." The fact that she had brought the parts of speech into first grade was considered a wonderful thing. So, too, with the other teacher and the business executive who observed her. The work of school seemed to be being accomplished by these teachers, and thus they won high praise from the principal and the observer. Quite probably, not one of the four of them gave a thought to what Amy—and all other kids—already knew about language.

Although my examples are from elementary school classes, *grammar* instruction is pervasive in all schools. If you don't believe it, just look at the textbooks that sell. My favorite curriculum note of all time was written by an eleventh-grade, low-track student named Jason. When asked to express what he felt about all the years he had spent in English/language arts classes, Jason wrote, "There isn't enough variety for how there is to learn it. We wind up doing the same thing too much." When I asked Jason what *it* was, he answered in one word—*grammar*.

How Did We Arrive Where We Are?

Let's now try to discover why so many teachers, textbooks, and curriculum guides have managed to overlook what children know, confronting (and confounding) them instead with the definitions-that-do-not-define and rules-that-do-not-rule of traditional school grammar (TSG).

Traditional school grammar had its roots in *Latin* school grammar (which in turn had roots in Greek); in fact, the very first *English* grammar—published in 1586 by William Bullokar—was largely a translation of the Latin grammar attributed to William Lily (1486?–1523), which was then used widely in English schools.

It is no small irony that 1586 was the same year Shakespeare came to London; thus, our greatest playwright did not study English grammar during his own school years. Does anyone believe that he would have been a better writer if he had? I do know one person who believes Shakespeare was a great writer partly because he studied Latin grammar, but the implications of that, if true, are stupefying: If we want to improve student writing, we should be teaching *Latin* grammar to everyone. Another irony is that one of the greatest twentieth-century prose-masters of English flunked Latin grammar: Winston Churchill.

School children in Shakespeare's time studied Latin grammar because they *didn't* know it. They did not study English grammar because they *did* know it. Indeed, almost a century and a half after Shakespeare's death, Samuel Johnson indirectly acknowledged how much people already knew about their native language when, in the grammar section of his dictionary, he devoted only eighty-three *words* to English syntax—including his examples.

English grammars appeared in trickling numbers in the seventeenth century. Ian Michael, in *English Grammatical Categories and the Tradition to 1800*, lists only thirty-two for the entire *century*. About the same number were published between 1701 and 1750. Then, in sharp contrast, from 1751 to 1760—just ten *years*—twenty-five English grammars appeared; and in the next decade, there were thirty. By the time Lindley Murray published his *English Grammar* in 1795, one reviewer wrote, "The world is pestered with grammars." The boom was on, and it hasn't stopped since. We need to look carefully at the landmarks of this tradition.

The First Landmark: Robert Lowth and the *Short Introduction*

In 1762, the same year that Jean-Jacques Rousseau opened his *Social Contract* with the ringing words, "Man was born free, but he is everywhere in chains," a little noticed event occurred in England: the publication of *A Short Introduction to English Grammar*, by an unidentified author. It was an event that was to put students everywhere in England and America in chains for several decades, and ultimately, thanks to its enormous influence, for centuries.

The author of the book was Robert Lowth, the first son of Canon William Lowth of Winchester Cathedral and of Margaret Pitt, the daughter of a gentleman. Lowth's grandfather, however, was a London apothecary, and his brother became a hosier, so Robert had some climbing to do in a society in which rank was unusually important. His only biographer says, "The whole tendency of Lowth's life . . . was materialistic" (Hepworth, 1978, p. 36).

And climb he did. He was elected to the Professorship of Poetry at Oxford in 1741, a post he held until 1750, when he decided that he could best climb further by becoming a member of the clergy. He was granted a Doctor of Divinity degree from the University of Oxford in 1754 and became Bishop of Oxford in 1766 and Bishop of London eleven years later. He was offered the Archbishopric of Canterbury in 1783, but declined it on grounds of sickness, four years before his death.

A brilliant and exceptionally well educated man, Lowth knew Greek, Latin, Hebrew, and Anglo-Saxon, along with some modern languages. He was thus better qualified than most people of his century to write a grammar. However, his biographer discerns in his personality "the mark of a radical conservative" (p. 33), and *The Concise Oxford Companion to the English Language* notes that he was a man "more inclined to melancholy than to mirth." One need not look far to discover why. Born in the Winchester Cathedral close, he was admitted at the age of twelve to the "funereal environment of antique Winchester College," "a Medieval monastery for adolescents." There, he spent sixteen hours a day (except for part of Tuesdays and Thursdays), seven days a week, with no vacation except for a break of a few days after Whit Sunday—up to age nineteen.

The curriculum consisted almost entirely of studying Latin and Greek grammar and of reading Latin and Greek authors in the original. The boys were roused at five, were expected in Chapel by 5:30—school proper began at 6:00—wore "dusky" wool gowns, and were forbidden to speak English (quotes and details from Hepworth, 1978, pp. 20–27). The chief commandment of this dank and dreary place was "Either Learn, or Leave, or Be Beaten." The motto still hangs in the building called "the School" today.

It's hard not to feel a certain sympathy for a person who grew up under such conditions. But let's look at the book itself, beginning with Lowth's intentions in writing it.

Intentions and Influence of Lowth's A Short Introduction to English Grammar

In his Preface, Lowth comes across as a relatively modest man. Without revealing his identity (in England, his name was never used on the book during his lifetime), he claims his "little System" was "intended merely for a private and domestic use." However, a few lines later he says that his grammar is "calculated for the use of the Learner even of the lowest class." Finally, in the last paragraph of the Preface, he urges readers who think the book might be "worth a revisal" to communicate that opinion "through the hands of the Bookseller." Clearly, *A Short Introduction to English Grammar* was intended as a textbook. (All quotations here are from the original 1762 edition.)

What distinguishes Lowth's book from the many that preceded it is its enormous influence. According to Ian Michael, there were "more than fifty further British and American editions to 1838" (1993, p. 40). Lowth was required in such prestigious institutions as Harvard and Yale. Indeed, it was used as early as 1774 in both colleges—one year before it became the first English grammar to be printed in America—and as late as 1841. Moreover, Lowth's book was, importantly, the main influence on Lindley Murray's *English Grammar*, first published in 1795, of which there were two hundred editions, worldwide, before 1850.

Overall Characteristics of Lowth's Grammar

First of all, *A Short Introduction* is short. Omitting the Preface, the first edition contains roughly twenty-three thousand words of text. The footnotes, which are almost exclusively instances of errors by major writers, add approximately seven thousand more words. Even at that, the book is quite short by most measures, both now and then.

The book's overall plan is relatively conventional, following three of the four-part division of most grammars that had preceded it. After a brief overview, Lowth treats (1) orthography (letters and syllables), (2) etymology (words and the parts of speech), and (3) syntax (phrases and sentences). Prosody (pronunciation and versification), the fourth part of most earlier grammars, is omitted. However, Lowth adds nineteen pages on punctuation and fourteen on praxis (i.e., parsing; we would call it an *exercise*). The inclusion of punctuation is not at all unusual; Michael estimates that it is found in about 60 percent of the early grammars (1970, p. 195).

Here is a breakdown of Lowth's *Grammar*, by percentages:

Letters and syllables	2.7
Parts of speech	47.8
Syntax	31.8
Punctuation	10.3
Praxis	7.3

We see here, as we shall see in Murray, that the heaviest emphasis was on the parts of speech. In fact, Michael states flatly, "parts of speech were the most important features in a school grammar of English" (1987, p. 323). The definitions of the parts of speech are the traditional ones, by Lowth's own admission: "the known and received Terms have been retained, except in one or two instances." (For some of Lowth's explicit definitions, see page 13.)

Syntactic rules in Lowth are, for the most part, not so precisely defined as they are in Murray and some other grammars, but examples of broken rules are super-abundant. Most of these appear in the footnotes, which Lowth says "furnish a more convincing argument . . . both of the truth of the charge of inaccuracy brought against our Language as it subsists in practice, and of the necessity of investigating the Principles of it, and studying it Grammatically, if we would attain a good degree of skill in it."

Lowth acknowledges the "greatness" of those whose errors he cites, but that does not stand in his way. Among the writers of his own day that he criticizes are Pope, Swift, Addison, and Gray. Shakespeare, Milton, and Dryden are some of the earlier writers whom he takes to task. Ironically, he calls the Vulgar Translation of the Bible "the best standard of our language," yet he frequently finds "corruption" even there.

In the "second copy" of Lowth's *Grammar* in the Winchester College collection is this handwritten statement, the last in the book: "No errors are so trivial but they deserve to be mended." Although we do not know for certain who wrote this, it could well stand as the motto for Lowth's book, for he insists that one can learn much more from the study of errors than from the study of principles. This is a man as obsessed with rooting out errors as a Puritan minister with rooting out sin.

The first sentence in the body of the book defines *grammar* as "the Art of *rightly* [italics mine] expressing our thoughts by Words" (p. 1). A heavy emphasis on *propriety* and what is *right* pervades the book, but the question of how Lowth knew the rules while great writers did not is never answered. It is true that he acknowledges the power of "Custom," sometimes, but he never appears happy about it. On page 89, for example, he admits that Custom has established a particular "corruption" "beyond recovery." At another point, he says we should be "immediately shocked" by a particular usage, then adds that our ears have grown accustomed to other instances "which are altogether as barbarous." Lowth was clearly a more conservative grammarian than many other leading authorities of his time, such as his contemporary Joseph Priestley.

Lowth's "Praxis, or Example of Grammatical Resolution"

Lowth's *Short Introduction* does not contain the plethora of exercises that are universal in current textbooks, but in his final pages, he leaves no doubt that he would expect schoolmasters and -mistresses to subject their charges to extensive parsing. Lowth provides a 218-word passage from the Bible, and discusses it word for word. To illustrate, here is the second paragraph of the quotation, and Lowth's parsing of its first ten words:

> 'And he came into all the country about Jordan preaching the baptism of repentance for the remission of sins.' *And*, a Conjunction Copulative; *he*, a Pronoun, third Person Singular, Masculine Gender, Nominative Case, standing for *John*; *came*, a Verb Neuter, Indicative Mode, Past Time, third Person Singular Number, agreeing with the Nominative Case Pronoun *he*; *into*, a Prep. *all*, an Adjective; *the country*, a Subst. *about*, a Prep. *Jordan*, a Proper Name; *preaching*, the Present Participle of the Verb Active *to preach*, joined like an Adjective to the Pronoun *he*. . . .

This is precisely the kind of *activity* to which Lowth himself would have been subjected in Latin class, though he was far from unique in passing on that tradition to the English classroom. At least Lowth apparently did not favor—as an exercise for students—the correction of "false English," a grammar book activity much favored by that other pillar of TSG, Lindley Murray, to whom we now turn.

The Second Landmark: Lindley Murray's *English Grammar*

Though alike in their powerful influence on the school grammar tradition, Robert Lowth and Lindley Murray were two very different people. Unlike the Lowth family, the Murrays were very well off. In fact, Lindley's father owned more shipping tonnage (by 1768) than any other American (Tieken-Boon, 1996, p. 29), and Murray biographer, Charles Monaghan, notes that the "grand tradition of the

Murray family" was making money (1998, p. 69). The Murray Hill section of New York City is named after the family, which from 1762 occupied a mansion located at what is now Park Avenue and Thirty-Seventh Street. (A Daughters of the American Revolution commemorative plaque there celebrates one of his sisters.) Lindley was "a wealthy and privileged youth, the scion of a rich family, from a home that welcomed international travelers" (Monaghan, 1998, p. 22).

Born in 1745 in Pennsylvania (a highway marker on Route 934 just south of Route 22, about eighteen miles northeast of Harrisburg, notes the place), Lindley Murray, "the Quaker grammarian," had a very spotty education and never enrolled in college. Indeed, his formal education ended in 1756–57 at Franklin's Philadelphia academy. He was eleven. Murray did, however, read for the law, and he began practicing that profession in New York City in 1767, at the age of about twenty-two.

Lindley Murray was a lawyer and a businessman—and one thing more, a member of the Society of Friends. It was through this last association that he became a textbook author—at the age of forty.

Exiled from his native land in 1784 for his loyalist sympathies and as a family scapegoat, Murray and his wife settled just outside of York, England, in a large Quaker community. (In his *Memoirs*, Murray disingenuously claims he moved to York for his health.) He took up Quaker causes and in 1787 published his first book, *The Power of Religion on the Mind in Retirement, Sickness and Death*.

Murray also became involved with a nearby Quaker school designed for the "guarded education of young females." According to his *Memoirs*, he met with teachers of the school and they ultimately asked him to write a grammar because they were unhappy with existing ones (1827, p. 106). Though he claims to have been reluctant, he produced the book in less than a year, in spite of suffering a major depression during its composition. It was published in the spring of 1795 and was an immediate success.

Lindley Murray: A One-Man Textbook Factory

After *English Grammar*, first came two key books in establishing the school tradition as we know it today—*English Exercises, Adapted to the Grammar* and the *Key to the Exercises*, both in 1797. Also in 1797, Murray wrote an *Abridgement* of the *Grammar*, which was intended for "minor schools and those just beginning to study the language" (1827, p. 109). The *Abridgement*, incidentally, was *not* an easier book than the *Grammar*, just shorter (and far less expensive), with exercises included.

Murray then spread his quills into a wide range of other books, notably a fabulously successful *English Reader*, in 1799, which was followed by its *Sequel* (1800) and its *Introduction* (1801). In 1802, he produced a couple of French language textbooks. Two years later came *An English Spelling-Book*, and in the next year he did a *First Book for Children*. His final nonreligious work was a two-volume *English Grammar*, which included the *Exercises* and *Key* (1808).

Murray's productivity was aided by several important circumstances. First, the plant of his printers was only a mile from his home. Second, ill health made it impossible for him to engage in virtually any kind of physical activity. Indeed, according to Elizabeth Frank, his secretary, he spent upwards of (his last) sixteen years confined to his house (1827, p. 151). Finally, his religious zeal spurred him to an exceptional degree. He viewed his books as a "source of gratitude to Divine Providence."

Altogether, Charles Monaghan (1998), author of *The Murrays of Murray Hill*, estimates that during the first four decades of the nineteenth century, Murray sold a total of 15.5 million books, "making him the largest-selling author in the world" during that period (p. 135). Where the "ordinary teaching of English grammar" is concerned, Ian Michael (1970) says that only the Latin grammarians, Priscian and Lily, were on a par with Lindley Murray as influences on school grammar.

Murray and Lowth on the Parts of Speech

The largest single part of Murray's *Grammar*, as it was of Lowth's, is the parts of speech. Murray distinguishes the same nine parts as Lowth (article, noun, pronoun, verb, adjective, adverb, preposition, conjunction, interjection). Figure 1–1 provides a direct word-for-word comparison of some of their definitions.

Lowth	*Murray*
Noun: . . . the Name of a thing; of whatever we conceive in any way to subsist, or of which we have any notion.	Noun: . . . the name of any thing that exists, or of which we have any notion.
Pronoun: . . . a word standing instead of a Noun, as its Substitute or Representative.	Pronoun: . . . a word used instead of a noun, to avoid the too frequent repetition of the same word.
Adjective: . . . a word joined to a Substantive to express its Quality.	Adjective: . . . a word added to a substantive, to express its quality.
Verb: . . . a word which signifies to be, to do, or to suffer.	Verb: . . . a word which signifies to BE, to DO, or to SUFFER.

Figure 1–1. *Parts of Speech Definitions in Lowth and Murray: A Comparison*

Murray sometimes refers to himself as a compiler, rather than an author. (Some consider him a plagiarist, since he almost never cites a source.) From these definitions, it's easy to see why. It's also obvious that not much change occurred in traditional definitions over a fifty-year period.

Murray's Syntax

A major *difference* between Murray and Lowth is the former's codification of the rules of syntax: With a simplicity that belies the facts, Murray lists precisely twenty-two rules. What a long way we've come—in only forty years—from Samuel Johnson, who handled the matter in eleven *lines*.

All in all, Murray's twenty-two rules take sixty-eight closely printed *pages* to cover. The one ray of salvation for students was that only the main rules—which were printed in a larger typeface—were to be committed to memory. Michael cites two grammars from the nineteenth century whose authors required students to memorize about twelve thousand words (1987, p. 347). Murray's count can't be far behind that.

Parsing in Murray

Lindley Murray's treatment of parsing may seem brief compared with Lowth's, but there are three major differences. One is that Lowth parses a single long passage, while Murray gives twenty distinct sentences. Another is that Murray published an entire book of exercises, meant to accompany the *English Grammar*—a book nearly as long as the *Grammar* itself. Finally, Lowth's parsing exercise is complete in itself, but Murray's exercises always require additional work of the students. Here, for example, is a typical parsing exercise. Note Murray's parenthetical instructions.

'Virtue ennobles us.'

Virtue is a common substantive, of the neuter gender, the third person, the singular number, and in the nominative case. (*Decline the noun.*) *Ennobles* is a regular verb active, indicative mood, present tense, and the third person singular. (*Repeat the present tense, the imperfect tense, and the present participle.*[†]) *Us* is a personal pronoun, of the first person plural, and in the objective case. (*Decline it.*)

[†]The learner should occasionally repeat all the moods and tenses of the verb.

Anyone believing that I exaggerated when I drew a parallel between the lot of the traditional school grammar drudge and Rousseau's remark about mankind being everywhere in chains might wish to reconsider in the light of such a typical parsing exercise as this.

Conclusion: The Lowth-Murray Tradition

Robert Lowth and Lindley Murray, through the huge demand for their grammars, became the chief architects of TSG, the tradition that has enchained students ever since. No doubt both of these men thought they were doing good work; indeed, Murray thought he was doing the work of the Lord. Everywhere, he praises virtues and castigates vices like an evangelist let loose in Purgatory. Though one grows weary of his pieties, I admit I prefer them to the following, used by Samuel Kirkham: "The boy was beaten by his father" and "I saw the boy abused" (*English Grammar in Familiar Lectures*, 1843, pp. 157, 189). (In America, Kirkham, who was used by Abraham Lincoln, was Murray's greatest competitor.)

In fairness, it should be said that Lowth's and Murray's texts are not without merit. Many of Lowth's criticisms of great writers would be made by most competent grammarians today. Murray had considerable organizing abilities, and his text is much less complex and much easier for school children than those of Lowth, Noah Webster, or a number of other grammarians.

Nevertheless, there is far more wrong than right with the tradition these men helped establish. Here are some of their main faults:

1. They seemed wholly unaware of the intuitive grammatical knowledge of the native speaker.
2. They believed that the best way to learn was by studying errors, memorizing definitions, and drilling.
3. They relied on definitions that did not define grammatical terms in ways that were truly helpful to students (see Chapter 2).
4. They created—in grammar, usage, composition, and punctuation—rules that did not rule, rules that educated writers and speakers did not observe.

That they were so successful in spite of these shortcomings says a good deal about their buyers. Institutions, teachers, and individual purchasers of their books were interested in being told what was *right*, and Lowth and Murray didn't hesitate to tell them. TSG was and is a "compacted and overwhelmingly authoritative tradition" (Michael, 1970, p. 9), in large measure because that is what the public and most teachers wanted.

TSG was the prevailing grammar from the middle of the nineteenth century to the middle of the twentieth. There, we meet the two greatest American stalwarts of our own time, to which we next turn.

John E. Warriner: A Latter-Day Lindley Murray

Warriner is the name both of a person and an institution. The person, John E. Warriner, spent most of his professional life teaching high school English and chairing the department at the public school in Garden City, Long Island. At the time he wrote his first texts, Warriner's students were almost exclusively white, Anglo-Saxon Protestants—and highly privileged. Nevertheless, they made errors in spelling, capitalization, and punctuation, so Warriner and his colleagues administered a test to all at the end of tenth grade. The forty lowest scoring students (out of a class of approximately 175) were required to take a special eleventh grade course designed to remediate them—regardless of how high they scored. (See Warriner, 1946, apparently his only published article.)

Though this could not have endeared him to some students, Warriner the person seems to have been a respected teacher and colleague. The 1953 Garden City yearbook contains a photograph of him lecturing a class. The caption reads, "Great White Father speaks (who listens?)." It seems a disrespectful thrust, unless one knows that Warriner himself was the yearbook sponsor.

With a "practically complete" manuscript, John Warriner approached Harcourt Brace in the fall of 1945, and that company published *Warriner's Handbook of English*, Book One, meant for ninth and tenth grades, in 1948. It was followed in 1951 by a second volume for eleventh and twelfth grades. They were accompanied by workbooks, one each, for grades nine to twelve. The total package, originally called the *English Workshop Series*, was highly successful, and the aggressive, astute head of the School Division of Harcourt, James M. Reid, then created what I am calling the Warriner Institution: three series of six books each (grades 7–12): *Warriner's English Grammar and Composition*, *English Workshop*, and finally, *Composition: Models and Exercises*.

Obviously, a large team of editors and authors was required to bring this forth. Of the basic texts, Warriner himself wrote only the twelfth- and the tenth-grade books, and had assistance with the latter. Other authors included the distinguished English educator, Joseph Mersand; Mary Whitten, a text-writing workhorse, who taught at a Texas teachers college at the time (she later became the chief author of the *Harbrace College Handbook*); John H. Treanor, then a principal of a Boston Intermediate School; George Shaftel, "a sparky free-lance writer"; and Bill Frankel, "free-lance writer extraordinary" (Reid, 1969, pp. 119–120). The series became "the best selling textbook series in the history of American education" (Flood et al., 1991, p. 327).

From the outset, even the main books featured a superabundance of exercises. In the original *Handbook*, for instance, the twenty-five-page · first chapter ("Spotting the Parts of Speech") contained twenty-seven exercises and five review exercises, a good deal more than one exercise per page. In all, 40.5 percent of this book was text and 59.5 percent exercises. Warriner justified this by claiming that the teacher himself would provide the "motivation" for his students. Whether the teacher did or did not, it is questionable whether stodgy exercises based on definitions that did not define and rules that did not rule had any efficacy at all.

John E. Warriner died in 1987, but the institution continued. Even today, Warriner is listed as the Program Author for the Grammar, Usage, and Mechanics "Instructional Framework" of the *Elements of Language* series, published by Holt, Rinehart and Winston (a Harcourt Classroom Education Company) in 2001. The editors of this series note that "teaching remained [Warriner's] major interest . . . throughout his career" (p. iii). Actually, Mr. Warriner retired in 1962, at the age of fifty-five, after the sales of the series named after him climbed into the stratosphere. Here is how the publishing magnate James M. Reid puts it: "Success did not spoil John Warriner. He finally felt it was safe to retire from his $10,000 a year teaching job and live on his fat, well-gotten gains" (p. 120).

Altogether, Harcourt sold some thirty million copies of *Warriner's*. People who credit *A Nation at Risk* (1983) with bringing schools back to basics should know that the "Back to Basics" movement started about a decade earlier, and the new edition of *Warriner's* that appeared in 1977 rode the crest of the wave, breaking all sales records (Flood et al., 1991, p. 328). If schools were "at risk" in 1983, it could be said that the emphasis on basics put them there.

John C. Hodges' *Harbrace College Handbook*: Robert Lowth Revisited

I have before me as I write the revised thirteenth edition of the *Harbrace College Handbook*, published in 1998. It still bears in first position the name of its original author, John C. Hodges, who died in 1967—the date of the *sixth* edition. This single text could not have matched the Warriner series for total sales, but it dominated the Freshman English field for decades. Reid says it was selling over 250,000 copies every year in the middle 1960s, and further notes that it was the best college-division seller of all time at Harcourt. Connors and Lunsford (1988) note that it was still "the most popular handbook of writing" in 1988.

Like Robert Lowth, John Hodges was a mighty hunter of the error. He based his handbook on twenty thousand student papers—mostly from the University of Tennessee, where he was director of Freshman English—marked by sixteen different teachers. (The research was done in 1938–1939; the first edition—which was called *Harbrace Handbook of English*—was published in 1941.) On the basis of this research, which he never published, Hodges formulated "the rules," for which Reid and others developed "a drastic new design": They printed them "in the boldest of bold black type" (p. 104). Hodges' was the same sort of "no nonsense" approach that Warriner used, and it clearly was what the market craved.

The exercise density in Hodges is much less than in Warriner. (Chapter 1 of the 1982 edition, for example, has only eleven exercises in its thirty pages.) However, teachers had an assortment of several workbooks that they could order independently. And Hodges seemed even more driven by an error-correction mentality than Warriner: His prefaces stressed that his was a "system for the correction of student papers" (1982, p. v). The four-point indictment (page 15) of TSG applies to both of these best-sellers.

The Countertradition and This Book

In spite of the power and prevalence of TSG, there has always been a lively countertradition. William Bullokar's *Bref Grammar* of 1586, for example, shows in places a sensitivity to student needs that is not found in Lowth or Murray. After his definition of nouns, for example, this schoolmaster adds that nouns may further be known by the fact that *a, an,* and *the* can easily be set before them (p. 1). The notion that children learned parts of speech by means of definitions was challenged as early as 1670, by Mark Lewis, a follower of Comenius; and in his grammar of 1712, Michael Maittaire commented on the great difficulty of defining everyday grammatical terms (p. viii, quoted in Michael, 1970).

Dozens of other early grammarians were not of the tradition and often actively opposed it. In fact, at the conclusion of his *English Grammatical Categories*, Ian Michael states that our respect for the Tradition has been misplaced. We should instead have trusted, he says, the "dissatisfied, protesting, and sometimes perceptive schoolmasters who were making the first attempts to give English a grammar of its own, and to teach English children how to control the English language" (1970, p. 518).

But we didn't. Indeed, Michael notes a narrowing of points of view as time went on. For example, after Maittaire, the failure of the traditional definitions to define was not noted by grammarians through nearly the whole of the eighteenth century (1970, p. 283). In addition, the two main systems of classification of the parts of speech (differing only in how they treated the participle) had been used in only 35 percent of the classifications between 1568 and 1800; but in the period from 1800 to 1825, these two accounted for 90 percent of all grammars. Eventually, of course, the one of the two favored by Lowth and Murray prevailed. How many different classifications of the parts of speech does one find in school grammars today?

This book is not a school textbook, of course, but I like to think that it is part of the countertradition. I am more of a teacher than either a grammarian or a linguist, and I share with Michael Maittaire (1668–1747), a fellow teacher (though he was far more distinguished than I), the desire that grammar be "taught" rather than "whipped" and that students enjoy it rather than hate it. And, like Maittaire, I believe children should be treated as the born-free persons they naturally are.

2
Traditional School Grammar: Definitions That Do Not Define

. . . in consequence, after all his labour, he [the schoolmaster] often ends by possessing of the science of grammar nothing but a heap of terms jumbled together in inextricable confusion.

—MATTHEW ARNOLD, 1853

If there is one thing I dislike in grammar, it is definitions (of parts of speech) too often met with in our textbooks. They are neither exhaustive nor true; they have not, and cannot have, the precision and clearness of the definitions found in textbooks of mathematics, and it is extremely easy to pick holes in them. . . . And thus we might go on to the definitions found even in the best grammars: they are unsatisfactory all of them and I do not think they are necessary.

—OTTO JESPERSEN, "THE TEACHING OF GRAMMAR,"
THE ENGLISH JOURNAL, 1924

Even in Latin and Greek brief definitions had always been inadequate. Partly for this reason, . . . most parts of speech were submitted to elaborate and sometimes grotesque subdivision.

—IAN MICHAEL, *THE TEACHING OF ENGLISH*, 1987

This chapter is devoted to illustrating that traditional school grammar (TSG) definitions do not define, that they do not offer meaningful help to students, neither to students like me, when I was in tenth grade (see section, Pronouns), nor to students like the sixteen-year-old boy in the South Bronx, who Jonathan Kozol reported to be "in a dark mood" because (among other things) he had to know the parts of speech to pass final examinations, and he didn't have a clue (*Savage Inequalities*, 1992, p. 111).

Well, of course, that young man *did* know the parts of speech. He wouldn't be able to communicate if he didn't. What he did not know was how to apply particular labels in particular instances. What is more, there is every chance that neither his teacher nor his textbook would offer him any help. He'd been told, no doubt, that nouns name persons, places, or things; he'd been told that verbs express action or state of being; he'd been told that a sentence expresses a complete thought; and on and on. He'd been "taught" these definitions probably in every grade since early elementary school. Telling him again would not make any difference. (The fact that many standards movements mandate that such terms shall be taught will not make any difference either, not unless the mandaters can also direct us to a usable, enlightened pedagogical grammar, and train teachers in its use.) In the first line of a report made at the 2001 NCTE Convention in Baltimore, the Assembly for the Teaching of English Grammar wrote, "Traditional grammar is a broken part of the curriculum" (Hausmann, 2001). And the members of this group *strongly favor* the teaching of grammar in the classroom.

It's vitally important to see that TSG definitions do not define, because until we do see that, we will simply be chasing our own grammatical tails. We'd be better off to totally scrap current practices. On the other hand, it is *possible* to do a better job teaching grammar, and in places in this chapter and in the Appendix, I offer some modest suggestions. Others have also proposed solutions to the terminology problem that is pointed up in the three quotations at the head of this chapter.

- Linguist Rei R. Noguchi (in *Grammar and the Teaching of Writing*) argues that we can teach writing perfectly well using a mere handful of grammatical terms. He would not even use some of the simplest terms, such as noun, verb, or adjective.
- Sentence combining typically uses *no* grammatical terminology, yet it requires students to manipulate phrases and sentences in such ways that they in fact make wide use of the grammatical resources of our language. (See particularly William Strong's latest book, *Coaching Writing*.)
- In *Image Grammar*, middle school teacher Harry R. Noden uses plenty of grammatical terms but he does not worry about their definitions. While occasionally offering a sketchy definition, basically he defines by example rather than by definition as he "teaches grammar in an artist's studio."
- Educators have attempted to create a solid pedagogical grammar, perhaps most notably in recent years some of the members of the NCTE Assembly for the Teaching of English Grammar. To my knowledge, the group itself has

not yet produced a consensus grammar for students. However, see their website (ATEG.org) for some interesting materials.

- Finally, there are legions of writing instructors, both within and outside of the field of education (Donald Murray, William Zinnser, Tom Romano, Peter Elbow, to mention only a few), who help people improve their writing with little or no recourse to grammatical terminology. It can be done; indeed, it is being done in Freshman English courses across the country, since the teachers of these courses are confronted every semester with students, most of whom, as the instructors say, "can't tell a noun from a verb."

But back to the issue at hand: TSG, taught traditionally, does *not* help students understand grammar. In fact, to the extent that kids actually pay attention, their efforts at understanding will often be undermined, their intuitive knowledge contradicted. By "taught traditionally," I mean by means of the traditional grammar paradigm:

Definition
Examples
And
Drill

Here is an example, from the first edition of *Warriner's Handbook of English*:

1b. A pronoun is a word used in place of a noun.
    You ask your teacher, "Is there any *ink* there?" Your teacher looks into the empty ink bottle and replies, "No, *it* is all gone." In place of the noun *ink*, the teacher has used the pronoun *it*.
    A friend says to you, "I am looking for *Harry*. Have you seen *him*?" Here your friend has used the pronoun *him* in place of the proper noun *Harry*.
    EXERCISE 4. By filling in the blanks in the following sentences. . . . (1948, p. 4)

Not only is this *deadly*—especially when it is repeated year after year from first grade on—it also doesn't work. As I will show, the definitions of TSG do not define, the examples are typically simpleminded, and the drill is mindless and unengaging.

Pronouns

Of all the misdefinitions of the parts of speech, I have a special fondness for the pronoun. In the middle of tenth grade, I transferred from a Catholic to a public high school, where I met with an examination known as the Minimum Essentials

Test, or the MIMS, for short. I had had lots of grammar in Catholic elementary school (which doesn't mean I learned any). I was taught by nuns and was a champion sentence-diagrammer in seventh grade. Nevertheless, I was all mimsy about the MIMS.

Students took the test at the end of every semester, until they succeeded in rising from "D" to "A" English—if they ever got that far (most didn't). I desperately wanted to be in "A" English because that meant no grammar and lots of writing, and I liked to write. So I worked very hard to learn the things one needed to know to succeed on the MIMS.

Among those was how to recognize a pronoun. The book and the teacher were united in defining this part of speech as a word that "takes the place of a noun." I didn't just memorize that definition, I *used* it.

It was a fatal mistake.

Take this sentence: "The author wrote a new novel." It seemed obvious to me that one could replace *author* with *writer* and that *novel* could be replaced by *book*. In short, it was clear that words rather general in meaning—like *writer* and *book*—had to be pronouns. There were lots of nouns they could replace. I truly believed and acted on this logical conclusion. To the detriment of my grade on the MIMS, I concluded that all nouns of general meaning were pronouns. *Animal, person, boy, girl* were pronouns. *Thing* was the quintessential pronoun in the language; consider how many nouns it can replace. (Why does it never occur to textbook writers that *synonyms* are words that "take the place" of other words, and thus must all be pronouns?)

Moreover, *using the definition*, we can readily prove that words that truly *are* pronouns are not. In the sentence just mentioned, try substituting *she* for *author* and *it* for *book*. You get "The she wrote a new it," which didn't sound like good English to me when I was in tenth grade.

What's the problem here? The definition is inadequate. An improvement would be "A pronoun is a word that takes the place of a *noun phrase*"; that is, it takes the place of a noun *and* all its modifiers. When you substitute a pronoun for the complement in my sentence, it takes the place of "a new novel," not of "novel" alone. Below is a sentence that contains much longer noun phrases. Notice that *he* replaces *all* the words, from *the* to *clouds*; *it* (or *one*) replaces *all* the words from *a* to *France*.

> *The curious guy whose mind was always in the clouds* became
>   He   became

> *a flight attendant for Air France.*
>   it/one.

Why don't the textbooks make a slight correction in their definition? It's probably because *noun phrase* is a term the tradition does not recognize (though this is gradually changing). Suppose a textbook author used it and her competitors did not? Which text would the school district buy? Thus, the tradition calcifies.

In truth, the traditional definition could profit from further correction. Consider the pronouns *I* and *you*. What noun do they replace? If I say to my wife, Nancy, "I love you," she is not likely to ask what nouns *I* and *you* replace. However, if I said, "Ed loves Nancy," she might wonder whether I was talking about another couple. *I* does not truly replace the speaker's name, anymore than *you* replaces the name of the person spoken to.

The case is even plainer for the so-called *indefinite* pronouns—such words as *everyone, something,* and *anybody*. They do not necessarily "stand for" anything in particular. For example, what noun phrase does the pronoun *anything* stand for in the sentence I have just written? Similarly, in "A pansophist knows everything," it would be silly to try to find a noun phrase substitute for *everything*.

There isn't any question that the human mind recognizes pronouns and, basically, knows how to use them. They are stored in its lexicon as pronouns and are known to function as replacements for noun phrases. The only thing students may not know is which particular words are *called pronouns*. That's quite a different matter, and much less consequential.

Activity 2–1: Basic Personal Pronoun Lesson

Goal: To demonstrate that students already intuitively know a great deal about pronouns.

Here's a lesson on the personal pronouns. Through it, you can demonstrate to students how much they intuitively know about these pronouns, as well as a few things they may yet need to learn. I've taught this lesson fruitfully in a wide range of classes, from a third-grade class in a Latino school in Philadelphia to college Freshman English classes.

Procedure

Begin by making a transparency of the chart in Figure 2–1, by drawing the chart on the chalkboard, or by passing out copies of it. The ultimate aim is to fill this chart with the appropriate personal pronouns, as shown in the final version in Figure 2–2.

1. Referring to the sentences at the head of each column in Figure 2–1, ask a question that will elicit from the class the correct pronoun to fill each of the blank spaces. For example, for the space in Row 1, Column 1, you would ask, "What word would you use if you were referring to yourself?"

A Personal Pronoun Chart				
_____ saw the cats.	The cats saw _____.	_____ snack was good.	The snack is _____.	(self/selves)
SINGULAR				
PLURAL				

Figure 2–1. *Basic Personal Pronoun Chart*

For the sixth space in the same column, you would ask, "What word would you use if you were referring to yourself and another person?"

2. For the first three columns, proceed from the top to the bottom, but for the fourth column, proceed from the bottom to the top—beginning with *theirs* (see Figure 2–2). When you get to the top of this column, point out that the word *mine*, unlike all the other words in the column, does not end in -*s*. Thus, it breaks a rule that words in this column are formed by adding -*s* to the Column 3 word (unless the word already ends in *s*). Why wouldn't the correct word be *mines*? The short answer is because that's not the form speakers of standard English use.

It is, however, a more *logical* form, a form that *follows the rule*. It is speakers of *standard* English who violate the rule, and the kid who just blew in from Ecuador, whose native language is not English and who

A Personal Pronoun Chart				
_____ saw the cats.	The cats saw _____ .	_____ snack was good.	The snack is _____ .	(self/selves)
SINGULAR				
I	me	my	mine	myself
you	you	your	yours	yourself
she	her	her	hers	herself
he	him	his	his	himself
it	it	its	its	itself
PLURAL				
we	us	our	ours	ourselves
you	you	your	yours	yourselves
they	them	their	theirs	themselves

Figure 2–2. *Completed Basic Personal Pronoun Chart*

says *mines*, has more right to criticize us than we have to criticize him. (Forms such as *hisn* and *ourn*—analogous to *mine*—were once used by our best writers because the words in this group originally ended in *-en*.)

3. For the last column, begin at the top again, asking students simply what *self* word belongs in the blank space. Note that *myself, yourself,* and *herself* all follow a *rule*: Take the word from the third column and add *-self*. (*Her*, of course, is a second- and first-column word.) With the masculine pronoun, however, most standard speakers pick up *him* from the *second* column and use *himself*. (There are places in the United States where *hisself* is heard in the speech of well-educated people.)

In the area of the country where I live, *himself* is well established for educated speakers, but this is much less the case for the final pronoun on the chart. The standard is *themselves*, but *theirselves* is frequently heard, and written. The reason seems to be that we hear *himself* far more often than *themselves*, so the former is more solidly in the memory bank than is the latter.

What actually goes on in the human mind when it is confronted with a choice, say between *themselves* and *theirselves*? It can do one of two things: (1) Go by the rule: add *-selves* to the third-column word (result: *theirselves*), or (2) consult the memory bank, which may or may not have stored *themselves*.

You may wish to call attention to the fact that the words in the *fourth* column do not contain any apostrophes. They are possessives, but they become so without the benefit of an apostrophe.

Note: I generally do not label the columns. If you prefer to use labels, *subject* and *object* are probably the best for Columns 1 and 2. The third and fourth columns could be labeled *first possessive* and *second possessive*, respectively. The *-self* pronouns are typically called *reflexive* or *reflexive/intensive*.

If it's really important for students to know that these words are called pronouns, you might magnify a chart, laminate it, and post it on a bulletin board. (A similar chart hangs somewhere in the human brain, perhaps.) If you prepare such a chart, you could label the whole thing A Personal Pronoun Chart and add the headings Singular and Plural. Your chart would then look like the completed chart in Figure 2–2. Having a view of a chart like this in my classroom would certainly have helped me pass the dreadful MIMS. For an extension of this lesson as well as additional activities related to pronouns, see the Appendix.

Nouns

The TSG definition of a *noun* is semantic (i.e., based on meaning): "A noun is a word used to name a person, place, or thing" (Warriner, 1948, p. 1). (See also the Lowth and Murray definitions on page 13.) Frequently, the term *idea* is added (Warriner and Treanor, 1959, *Grade 8*, p. 26). (*Harbrace* expands the list even further, adding "animal, quality, or action.")

Anyone who has actually tried to identify nouns by determining whether words name persons, places, things, or ideas knows how frustrating it is. The first exercise in Warriner's first book contains such items as *jumble, side, collection, haste, departure*, and *carelessness*, all of which are expected to be identified as nouns, whereas *hockey* (in "hockey sticks") is not. Students who do well in these exercises typically respond to clues *other than* the semantic definition. (See the Appendix.)

Even more revealing, here are the opening and final sentences from a randomly chosen story. *Using* the definition of *noun*, find all the nouns:

> Long ago, there lived an old woman. She had a pig. One day at sunset, the pig would not go home.
>
> All of a sudden, the old woman turned. There was her pig by her feet. She giggled with glee and went home with her pig.

Is *pig* a noun? (Does it name a *person*, a *thing*?) Is *woman* the name of "a person"? What about *day* and *sunset*? Things? *Home*, used twice, which may obviously (to students) seem to name a place, is used adverbially in the story (as is *day*).

Continuing, is *sudden* a noun? Does *feet* refer to "a thing," *glee* to "an idea," "a thing"?

We are talking about the beginning and end of a *primer* story. Kids are expected to be able to read this in *first grade*, and no doubt many can read and understand it. *Some* older kids may be able to identify the nouns in these sentences, but once again, *not by using the definition*. Rather than applying it, they are better off ignoring it, just as I was better off ignoring the definition of *pronoun*.

Activity 2–2: The Failure of a Definition

Goal: To demonstrate that the TSG definition (person, place, thing, or idea) of *noun* does not work.

Procedure

To demonstrate that "person, place, thing, or idea" does *not* define the term *noun*, try the following activity with your students. All sixteen of the words listed *were used as nouns* in an article on adapting to college life (*The New York Times* Education Life Supplement, Section 4A, August 6, 2000, p. 12). Give the TSG definition, and ask your students whether they would be able to identify the words as nouns. (*Thing* is so vague that some students might substitute it for some of the words in the list. But the "things" below are not physical things, like *office* or *guitar*. *Idea* is equally vague as a defining criteria.)

year	mistake	war	anxiety
rate	awareness	advice	recordkeeping
variety	majority	transition	self-doubt
exercise	life	stigma	commitments

Next, have students apply the same definition-test to the following sixteen words, which appeared on the same page of the same article:

American	residence	office	high school
freshman	peer	hall	faculty

27

telephone	campus	radio	theatre
student	ice cream	guitar	team

These words, which *do* name "persons, places, or things," were *not* used as nouns in the article. (Most were modifiers or adverbs.) Thus, we have demonstrated the paradox that students who *use* the definition may actually be misled.

Verbs

As with nouns, the TSG definition of verbs is semantic: "A word which expresses action or state of being" (Warriner, 1948, p. 9). (*Harbrace* adds "occurrence.") Lowth and Murray use the same definition, essentially: "to be, to do, and to suffer." (They included "to suffer" to account for "passive verbs," such as "was advised.")

Teachers have long been aware that this definition was particularly "rubbishy" (to use Ian Michael's characterization of all TSG definitions). A great many verbs do not denote action of any kind. Consider these:

1. Dad made an angry reply.
2. Mountain climbing is a dangerous sport.
3. Do people weigh more today than they did last century?

In each case, if you *use* the definition, you get either no answer at all or the wrong one. When asked, many kids say *reply* is the verb/action word in the first sentence. And only older kids who have learned to call *is* a verb would ever deny that *climbing* is the verb/action word in the second. (Most kids pick *climbing* anyway.) In the third, there are three verb forms (*do, weigh,* and *did*), none of which have anything to do with action.

The notion of a "state of being" verb invariably leaves students in a state of confusion. As well it might. Any dictionary is replete with *noun* definitions that begin: "The state of being. . ." For example, in my dictionary, the first definition for *motherhood* is "the state of being a mother." Is *motherhood* a verb? Can we blame students if they—*using* the definition—think that it is? It's another case of the user being a loser.

Textbook writers know this, too, which is one of the reasons why almost in the same breath that they first use the term *verb*, they list the "state of being" verbs. Here is the list from *Warriner's* original Book One and Book Two:

be, become, seem, grow, appear, look, feel, smell, taste, remain, sound, stay

In a giant leap into the twenty-first century, the Warriner clone, *Elements of Language, Sixth Course*, while listing precisely the same words, adds *turn*.

The main ideas of textbook authors here, I think, are two. First of all, the list is short enough that it can be memorized. Second, the list has a feel of finality: There, now, we have precisely twelve state-of-being verbs. (In most contemporary textbooks, including *Elements*, they're called "linking verbs.") But, of course, the list *isn't* complete, *even* as a list of the most common items. Some others are *make*, *prove*, *rest*, and *stand*.

Many attempts have been made to elaborate the definition of *verb*. One popular one is to say that verbs denote "mental action"—*believe* and *think* are examples. Another is to say that they express "occurrence"—"things *happen*"/"the holiday *fell* on a Tuesday."

Apart from their enormous vagueness, these do little to make the verb category truly inclusive.

Activity 2–3: Verb Lesson Plan

Goal: To demonstrate that one learns the part of speech of a word automatically, at the same time one learns its meaning.

Procedure

Duplicate the following group of sentences and give a copy to individuals, pairs of students, or groups. Ask them to discuss the meaning *and* the part of speech of the word *run* in each sentence. Then ask them to discuss *how* they know its part of speech.

1. The quarterback made a *run* around left end.
2. We had several good *runs* down the ski slopes.
3. I'm going to make a quick *run* into town for some groceries.
4. My mother is always on the *run*.
5. The first press *run* of the yearbook was two thousand copies.
6. Fred finally lost, but he gave Dave a *run* for his money.
7. Donna had two *runs* in her new stockings.
8. I need a four-foot *run* of hose to reach the end of the lawn.
9. Do you think there will be a *run* on the bank tomorrow?
10. We'll have to have a *run*-off election.

Note: If students have never met some of these *runs*, they still may make good educated guesses about the part of speech of the word. They may do so by responding to "clues," such as the fact that a word follows *a/an* or *the* or the fact that it names more than one thing. Ask students who have never met a given word to speculate on its meaning.

Activity 2–4: Definition of Verb as Action Word

Goal: To help students see for themselves that traditional definitions of verbs as expressing physical or mental action ignore a wide range of commonly used verbs.

Procedure

Duplicate the following group of sentences and give a copy to individuals, pairs of students, or groups. Ask students if they can discover the verb by determining whether it expresses physical or mental action. Then ask what clues they *do* use to identify the verbs.

1. She ignored the teacher's advice.
2. Her point of view deserves to be respected.
3. That pleases me very much.
4. I mean what I say. [Note that there are two verbs here.]
5. That newspaper belongs to my father.
6. Certain foods do not satisfy hunger.
7. Our fence needs a second coat of paint.
8. Our dog weighs eighty pounds.
9. How much money do we owe?
10. The lawyer charged too little money.

Activity 2–5: Definition of Verb as State-of-Being Word

Goal: To demonstrate that many verbs other than those typically listed as "state-of-being" verbs are main verbs in sentences.

Procedure

Duplicate the following sentences and give a copy to individuals, pairs of students, or groups. Ask students if they can discover the verb by determining whether it expresses "state of being." Then ask what clues they *did* use to identify the verbs.

1. Grammar makes me ill.
2. The students ran wild.
3. My dream came true.
4. The milk went sour.
5. You can rest content now.
6. We had a fight.
7. The boys were proved innocent.
8. The machine stood idle.
9. We need to get ready now.
10. I hope that you will keep silent.

Adjectives

Considering how much we English teachers care about parallel structure, it's remarkable that we ignore the fact that the TSG definition of the adjective (and adverb) is not parallel to its definition of the noun and verb. The latter pair are defined semantically, as we have seen; the former, functionally. The adjective, for example, is defined functionally as "a word that modifies a noun or a pronoun." (Lowth and Murray were more consistent, using semantic definitions of these parts of speech. For them, an adjective is a word that expresses the *quality* of a thing. See page 13.)

To understand the problem this presents, consider the following italicized phrase:

Susan made *a wonderful career choice.*

A, *wonderful*, and *career* are all modifiers of *choice*, and based on the functional definition, they are therefore all adjectives. But doesn't *career* also name a "thing"? (Actually, *career* is more clearly a thing than *choice*, at least in the minds of the students I have taught. And indeed it is obviously related to the verb *to choose*.)

Activity 2–6: Types of Modifiers of Noun Headwords

Goal: To teach the difference between true adjectives and other single-word modifiers in noun phrases.

Procedure

1. Write on the chalkboard or overhead the following sentence:

    _____ witnesses _____ are not ready to testify.

2. Next, give students the following five words, and ask them to fit all of the words in the preceding sentence, either before or after *witnesses*.

    three   defense   here   anxious   the

    The resulting sentence will be:

    The three anxious defense witnesses here are not ready to testify.

3. Try to elicit the following observations from your students:
    *   *The* must be the outermost (left-hand) word in the noun phrase.
    *   *Defense* sticks like glue to *witnesses*, and must stand directly before it.
    *   *Anxious*, a true adjective, fits between *the* and *defense*.
    *   *Three* occurs between *the* and *anxious*.
    *   *Here* fits after *witnesses*.

We may label the order of modifiers: Determiner/Article, Numeral, Adjective, Noun, [Noun Head], Adverb. Since the behavior of these words varies so significantly, it makes good sense to distinguish them, although it is also true that all are *modifiers* of the noun headword.

Note 1: Determiners are recognized as a distinct class by every linguist we've ever read. In setting numerals apart from adjectives and determiners, we are following Quirk et al., *A Comprehensive Grammar of the English Language*.

Note 2: Students will often try to find a place for *here* other than the position immediately following the headword. Perhaps this is because this position is normally reserved for word-group modifiers (such as clauses and prepositional phrases), or it may be that they have learned that adverbs "do not modify nouns." In reality, however, many adverbs that signify place or time do postmodify nouns. That is a fact.

Note 3: Nouns serving as premodifiers of other nouns differ from adjectives in that they correspond to prepositional phrases with the noun as complement: "a defense witness," for example, is "a witness for the defense." Adjectives don't do this: "an anxious witness" is not *"a witness for the anxious."

Activity 2–7: Commas in Series

Goal: To demonstrate when commas are and are not needed within a series of modifying adjectives.

Procedure

1. Write on the chalkboard or an overhead, the following sentence:

    The _____ witnesses were not ready to testify.

2. Give students the words *anxious*, *cowardly*, and *timid*. Ask them to place all the words in the blank space before *witnesses*. Then ask whether they could change the order they used. Ask how many different orders are possible. You should find that all of the following are natural:
    the anxious, cowardly, timid witnesses
    the timid, anxious, cowardly witnesses
    the cowardly, timid, anxious witnesses
    the anxious, timid, cowardly witnesses

Ask students whether they would use commas between the modifiers. Since no commas were used in Activity 2–6, try to elicit what the difference is between the modifiers in that activity and the modifiers here. The answer is that the order here makes no (grammatical) difference because all three of the modifiers are in the same subclass of adjectives.

Note: There has been a tendency in American publishing for some time to use fewer commas, even in well-edited prose. For example, in the phrase "shiftless loquacious alcoholic father" from Frank McCourt's *Angela's Ashes*, no commas are used. Since McCourt was a long-time high school English teacher and his publisher is among the best, we are on very shaky ground if we mark students wrong for omitting commas in series such as these. See the Appendix for an extension of this activity.

Adverbs

As with the adjective, contemporary school grammars typically give a functional definition of the adverb as a word that modifies verbs, adjectives, and other adverbs. (This was common, even in the eighteenth century.) However, as just noted, adverbs can modify nouns, and indeed, they *often* modify *sentences*, as in, "*Tomorrow*, let's play tennis together."

From the earliest times to the most recent, grammarians have been aware of the complexity of this part of speech. (Quirk et al. call *adverb* "the least satisfactory of the traditional parts of speech" (1972, p. 267).) Dionysius Thrax had twenty-eight kinds of adverbs in Greek; Priscian had twenty-six in Latin. *The English Accidence* of 1733 recognized forty-one kinds of adverbs. John Collyer, the schoolmaster author of *General Principles of English Grammar* (1735), declared that we put many words in the adverb class "because we do not know what else to call them"; and in 1786, the quirky grammarian Horne Tooke called the adverb "that common sink and repository of all heterogeneous unknown corruptions" (quoted in Michael, 1970, p. 444).

In *A Comprehensive Grammar of the English Language,* Quirk and his colleagues list seven *main* categories of adverbs: space, time, process, respect, contingency, modality, and degree. However, they go on to identify subdivisions within most of these seven and wind up with a total of twenty-eight "semantic roles" of adverbs (1985, p. 479).

In spite of the "sink and repository of corruptions" charge and the complexity of adverbs, it is nevertheless true that native speakers regularly use them effortlessly.

It is probably best to identify adverbs by the information they provide. Here is a partial list:

Information	Examples	Question Word
Time	today, tomorrow, now	When?
Place	here, outside, anywhere, home	Where?
Manner	slowly, urgently, swiftly	How?
Frequency	often, always, sometimes	How often?
Duration	weekly, hourly, yearly	How long?
Direction	northward, away, here	In what direction?
Concession	yet, still	Under what conditions?
Sequence	first, last, next, afterward	In what order?

Note: An *adverbial* may be defined as a word or group of words that functions like an adverb; that is, one that answers questions like those in the preceding list. The following italicized phrases are all adverbials.

They left *Sunday afternoon.*
We will be there *the day after tomorrow.*
The girls were standing around *outside of the house after the game.*
To find the answer, consult the index.
Leave *whenever the clock strikes twelve.*

The well-worn opening of so many elementary stories—*once upon a time*—is an adverbial phrase. It tells *when.*

Activity 2–8: Basic Lesson Plan on Adverbial Mobility

Goal: To teach students that adverbs are useful stylistically, for we can alter the rhythm of sentences by moving them from one position to another.

Procedure
The adverbs or adverbial phrases in the following sentences have been italicized. Let students experiment with moving them to various other positions. What might be their reason(s) for preferring one position to another? Also, can students discover some limits on the mobility of some adverbs, or other special characteristics of them?

1. *Carefully* we go out late at night.
2. We go out late at night *occasionally.*
3. We *regularly* go out late at night.
4. *Just once* we went out late at night.
5. We will go out late at night *tomorrow.*
6. We will *still* go out late at night.
7. We will *afterward* go out late at night.
8. *Seldom* do we go out late at night.
9. We *never* go out late at night.
10. We *hardly ever* go out late at night.

Prepositions

The preposition is traditionally defined as "a word that shows the relationship of a noun or a pronoun to some other word in the sentence." But isn't *every* word in a sentence related in some way to one or more other words? In the definition itself, the word *that* shows a relationship between the noun *word* and some other word in the sentence, *shows*. Yet *that* is not a preposition.

Like so many definitions, this one may be described as COIK: *Clear Only If Known*. (I have borrowed this term from an article by Patrick Hartwell.) But too many of our students don't know it, and for them, applying the definition only sinks them further into confusion.

Given this inadequate definition, traditional school texts show good sense when they follow it with a list of words commonly used as prepositions. However, the list is apt to be much too lengthy to be useful—usually forty or more words, even at an elementary level. (*Warriner's* offers fifty-one in tenth grade [1977]; *Writers INC* has sixty-three one-word prepositions.)

Pedagogically, it is much better to cast a sharp focus on the most commonly used prepositions, and perhaps gradually add to the list. We know, for instance, that just three prepositions are far more widely used than any others: *of, to,* and *in*. According to the *American Heritage* survey of published materials for students in grades three to nine, these three are the second, fifth, and sixth most commonly used words in the English language.

If we add just six more words, we will have the nine prepositions that account for 92.6 percent of all prepositional phrases. (The statistic comes from Fries' *American English Grammar*, and is based on the prepositions used in letters written by speakers of standard English.) The remaining six words are *for, on, with, at, from,* and *by*. (Some of these words function sometimes as other parts of speech. See the Appendix.)

All of these are among the twenty-seven most commonly used words in the *American Heritage* list. In addition, they are much more frequently used than the next three in popularity: *about, up,* and *into*.

Activity 2–9: Test Frames for Prepositions

Goal: To show students that they can generate large numbers of prepositions by trying to fit words into test frames.

It's easy to devise test frames into which words that are prepositions will fit. Here are some:

The message ____ our principal was friendly.
The store ____ the street is open.
Something was moving ____ the woods.

Procedure
Divide the class into groups and encourage them to find as many words as they can to fill in the preposition blanks.

Conjunctions

According to the TSG definition, conjunctions are "words that join words or groups of words." As we have just seen, that's also what prepositions do. Indeed, all sorts of words join words or groups of words, as the following illustrate:

the children *and* their pets   (conjunction)
the children *near* their pets   (preposition)
the children *walked* their pets   (verb)
the children *stroking* their pets   (participle)

Once again, the definition does not define and is clear only if known. Students who learn which words are called *conjunctions* do so, in effect, by memorizing them. Ian Michael says this about the conjunction:

> By the time of Priscian, at the beginning of the sixth century, the category of conjunction was formed: it was indeclinable, and it joined. The question was just what exactly did it join: or rather, for everyone knew that it joined, how to express in a definition what everyone knew. (1970, p. 62)

We are still searching for that definition. The question may never be resolved.

Activity 2–10: Two Distinct Groups of Conjunctions

Goal: To help students distinguish the coordinating conjunctions from another group of conjunctions, the so-called *conjunctive adverbs*, and appreciate what implications this difference has for punctuation.

Usually, handbook lists of the coordinating conjunctions contain these seven words: *and, but, for, or, nor, yet,* and *so*. Typical conjunctive adverbs include *however, therefore, in addition,* and *nevertheless*. The two groups of words often communicate very similar, if not identical, meanings; for example:

> There will always be death and taxes, but death doesn't get worse every year.
> There will always be death and taxes; however, death doesn't get worse every year.

Because the sentences are so similar in meaning, students have great difficulty understanding why we English teachers say that a comma is acceptable before *but* but not before *however*.

Procedure

Ask students to try to move *but* to another position in the sentence. Then ask them to try to move *however*. The former will not move, the latter will. It is because *however* can be moved that we need stronger punctuation after the last word of the previous sentence. Try to read this without strong punctuation after *taxes*:

> There will always be death and taxes, death, however, doesn't get worse every year.

Note: The *typical* punctuation before words like *however* is a period. See pages 176–179.

The Appositive

Traditionally, an appositive is defined as "a noun or noun phrase placed next to or very near another noun or noun phrase to identify, explain, or supplement its meaning" (1998, *Harbrace*, G-17). That this is another good instance of a COIK definition can be seen from the simplest of simple sentences. Why is *our first president* not an appositive in the following:

George Washington was our first president.

Our first president clearly is a noun phrase. It clearly is placed "very near" another noun phrase (only one word away). It clearly "identifies" or "supplements the meaning of" that other noun phrase. It fits the definition precisely. But it's *not* an appositive. Traditionally, it's called a *predicate noun*; that is, a noun that comes after a linking verb (*was* here) and renames the subject.

An appositive *immediately* follows a noun (or noun phrase), and it has the same function as that noun/noun phrase:

subject noun phrase   *appositive*
George Washington, our first president, was one of our best.

                    object noun phrase   *appositive*
Ms. Gregory holds an important position, director of marketing.

Activity 2–11: The Versatile Appositive

Goal: To help students see how useful appositives may be.
Appositives are one of the most useful and versatile ways of embedding one sentence within another. Their range and variety may be seen in the following excerpts in *The New York Times* from a single article about a ceremony dedicated to the 9/11 tragedy (March 11, 2002).

Procedure
Students may be encouraged to study and discuss these uses and imitate them in their own writing. The appositives are italicized.

1. Workers in bright orange vests put the finishing touches on what quickly became the newest stop in the tour of somber reminders: *a large brass spherical sculpture that once stood in the World Trade Center plaza.* [The appositive is in apposition to "somber reminders." Note that it is separated from the main clause by a colon.]

2. "I don't know what it looked like before, but it gives you the chills now," said Joni Moore, 41, *a visitor from Southlake, Tex.* [The appositive is in apposition to the name of a person who has just been quoted.]

3. Moments of silence will be observed just before and just after 9 a.m., *the times six months ago to the day when the two hijacked jetliners crashed into the towers.* [The appositive is in apposition to an adverbial of time—"just before and just after 9 a.m."]

4. A second ceremony is planned during the unveiling of "Tribute in Light," *a temporary memorial consisting of two parallel light beams created by 88 searchlights.* [The appositive describes the memorial, "Tribute to Light."]

5./6. The switch powering the pair of luminous towers is to be thrown by 12-year-old Valerie Webb, whose father, *Nathaniel, a Port Authority police officer,* was killed on Sept. 11. [The first appositive names Valerie's father; the second further identifies him.]

7. Mr. Bloomberg said that two brothers, *Philip and Peter Raimondi,* who lost their father in the attack, would read a poem. [We usually think of appositives following proper nouns, but here, the proper nouns are in apposition to "two brothers."]

8. "The real surprise was how heavy it still feels," said John R. Pinheiro, 40, *a sergeant in the Air Force Reserve who took a break from a training session to visit the viewing platform.* [This is identical to the appositive in Sentence 2 above, but notice that it is a great deal more expansive.]

9. There is one New Yorker clutching a plastic shopping bag bearing the red-lettered logo of Century 21, *the discount department store across the street from the World Trade Center.* [This appositive describes a place rather than a person.]

10. "Missing: Streetscape of a City in Mourning," *a special exhibition of shrines and memorials to victims of the World Trade Center attack,* opens at the New York Historical Society. [Here, the appositive specifies the nature and content of a title of a special exhibit.]

The Sentence

Of all the terms in the grammar lexicon, perhaps none has caused more definition problems than *sentence. The Concise Oxford Companion to the English Language,* which devotes over five columns to *sentence,* states, "Contemporary linguists tend not to worry over the definition of a sentence" (p. 837). Quirk, in his comprehensive study, observes that the term "cannot be given a clear-cut definition"

(1985, p. 47), and he doesn't try. Even college handbooks, including *Harbrace*, do *not* use the classic, "a word group that contains a subject and a verb and that expresses a complete thought."

Although this TSG "definition" is over two thousand years old, it is inaccurate, misleading, and of no help to any student who does not know in the first place what a sentence is. To see the problem, compare these two sentences, the first of which was written by a college freshman in a theme about attending her first mixer:

   A. I really hoped I'd meet a nice guy, it was about time I had a date.
   B. I really hoped I'd meet a nice guy because it was about time I had a date.

What is the difference between A and B, in terms of their *completeness of thought*? For the student, there was none. By the sentence she wrote (A), she meant precisely what the B sentence says. I think most readers would read her sentence precisely that way. Semantically speaking, the sentences are identical.

The difference in "completeness" is not semantical, it's grammatical. The TSG definition would be on firmer ground if it read, "A sentence is . . . that expresses a *grammatically* complete thought." Why don't textbook writers amend it? Some do. The current *Harbrace*, for example, calls a sentence a "grammatically independent unit of expression." A speculation about others is that they don't care to attempt to define *grammatically*. And who can blame them?

Most English teachers want students to see that there are *two* "complete thoughts" in the example sentence:

   1. I really hoped I'd meet a nice guy.
   2. It was about time I had a date.

In terms of grammatical completeness, they are right. The verb *hoped* requires a complement, and "(that) I'd meet a nice guy" provides one. In the second sentence, "It was about time" is grammatically incomplete, until we specify what *time*; namely, I-had-a-date time.

Try asking your students how many "complete thoughts" are contained in my former student's sentence. I've asked the question often and gotten everywhere from *one* to *four*. It's easy to see why. There are four subject-verb combinations (*I hoped, I'd like, It was,* and *I had*). One could also argue that there are four distinct propositions or *kernels* in the utterance.

The fact that it is so difficult to define *sentence* doesn't mean we can't teach grammar. (If it did, linguists would have closed shop long ago.) Basic concepts in many disciplines elude definition. *Atom* and *gene* are two examples; but physicists and biologists have moved forward nevertheless.

In fact, even our least academically able students seem to have a good *intuitive* grasp of what a sentence is, at least where the oral language is concerned. This was brought home to me dramatically several years ago when I was experimenting with sentence-combining activities in what was perhaps the lowest-of-the-low classes in the public schools in the city of Allentown, Pennsylvania—which had a rigidly tracked system at that time. The students had to combine groups of sentences into single sentences and write their answer. Sometimes, they would come up with ungrammatical *written* solutions, but when the teacher and I asked them *to read their "sentences" aloud*, the author himself was usually the first to recognize his sentence as ungrammatical—and want to change it.

Activity 2–12: Distinguishing Full Sentences from Fragments

Goal: To help students eliminate ineffective sentence fragments from their written work.

Procedure

If you have students who write (rhetorically ineffective) sentence fragments, duplicate some of them, and ask the student to read his sentences aloud. This activity works even better if you include some full sentences written by the same author(s). If a student wants his written work to be read and understood, encourage him to read his work aloud before submitting it to his intended audience.

The Subject

The *subject* of a sentence has been traditionally defined as the part that tells what the sentence is about. Try applying that definition to these:

1a. The quarreling lovers buried the hatchet.
2a. The hatchet was buried by the quarreling lovers.

Since the sentences mean the same thing, how can one be about quarreling lovers and the other be about a hatchet?
Or try this one:

3a. Ed loves his new printer.

The sentence is about Ed? When I said it the other day, I thought I was speaking about my printer, not myself.
Finally, consider the following sentence. Is it about *I, Mary, Mary's wedding date*, or *being wrong*?

4a. I couldn't have been wrong about Mary's wedding date.

Intuitively, it seems that "all of the above" is the only logical answer.

Yes, the *subjects* of the respective sentences (1a–4a) are *lovers, the hatchet, Ed,* and *I,* but to say that these are what the sentences are *about* only stirs up sand. Sentences are *about* their subjects *and* their complements and frequently about other parts as well.

Activity 2–13: Identifying Subjects

Goal: To give students a key to the identification of subjects.

Procedure

How does one recognize the subject of a sentence? One possibility is to use a tag question. Have students try this on the following sentences. (I have provided the tag questions for each sentence.)

1b. The quarreling lovers buried the hatchet, didn't *they?*
2b. The hatchet was buried by the quarreling lovers, wasn't *it?*
3b. Ed loves his new printer, doesn't *he?*
4b. I couldn't have been wrong about Mary's wedding date, could *I?*

If students can find the noun (or noun phrase) to which the italicized pronouns are referring, they will have found the subjects of the sentences. (Here, these are *the quarreling lovers, the hatchet, Ed,* and *I.*)

Objects and Complements

TSG handbooks generally have used *complement* as a cover term that includes the following five items:

- Direct objects

    The Diamondbacks won *the Series.*

    In this instance, the verb may be called *transitive.* A transitive verb requires a complement that does not refer to the subject of the sentence.
- Predicate nouns (also called *subject complements*)

    She became *my best friend.*

- Predicate adjectives/subject complements

    The fruit was *luscious.*

    In both of these cases, the verb is called a *linking* verb. The complements of linking verbs do refer to their subjects, either by further identifying them or by describing them.
- Indirect objects

The lawyer gave *the judge* her word.

In this case, the verb may be called a *two-place transitive* verb (*give*-type), which require a direct object *and* an additional noun phrase, called an *indirect object*. (Throughout this section, I am following the schema of Max Morenberg, in *Doing Grammar*.)

- Objective complements

We considered the manager *our leader*.

Here, the verb is called a two-place transitive verb of the *consider*-type. In these cases, the first complement is the direct object; the second is called an *objective complement*.

It is not the complement categories of TSG that fail, but, once again, the definitions. Direct objects are described as words that "receive the action" of the verb. This is a seriously inadequate definition. Large numbers of transitive verbs express no action at all. Thus, in sentences like the following, there is no action for the objects to receive:

We have no money.
She resembles her mother.
My father weighs two hundred pounds.

Even with verbs that do express action of some sort, the matter may be tenuous at best, quickly tying any student who *really* tried to apply the definition into semantic knots. Compare these two sentences:

The Diamondbacks beat the Yankees.
The Diamondbacks won the World Series.

The Yankees were indeed receivers of the beating, but in what sense did the World Series receive the winning?

Of course, with passives, the "receiver of the action" will be the subject, thus introducing yet another element of confusion:

The Yankees were beaten by the Diamondbacks.

TSG defines the more general term *complement* as "a word or words used to complete the sense of the verb." While it's true in some sense that complements complete the sense of verbs, so do many other structures that are *not* considered complements in TSG, such as many sorts of adverbials:

Don't talk *like that*.
The escapees went *that way*.

I will leave now *if you insist.*

Furthermore, "complete the sense of" is maddeningly vague. In the sentence, "The fruit was luscious," how does *luscious* "complete the sense of" the verb *was*? *Luscious* describes *fruit*; *was* does little more than link the adjective with the noun. (Indeed, in many languages such verbs may be omitted in sentences such as this.)

Note: Verbs can change categories. This is especially true for transitive and intransitive verbs. Huge numbers of English verbs are both intransitive and transitive: "The submarine sank"/"The submarine sank many ships."

Activity 2–14: Verbs and Their Complements

Goal: To deepen students' appreciation of the verb-complement relationship.

Procedure

Give students the following sentences, which contain verbs without their complements. Ask *why* the sentences sound incomplete and what needs to be done to make them complete. (The answer, basically, is that verbs that require complements are not given them.) Students ordinarily would not speak or write sentences like these precisely because they have a good intuitive feel for the various types of verb-complement relationships.

1. At the shopping mall, the teenagers bought.
2. For many years, my elementary school friends remained.
3. Enemies of the state are often called.
4. After the performance, opera lovers sent James Morris.
5. The person ringing our doorbell is.
6. Someone said.
7. Our baseball club postponed.
8. A majority of the voters elected.
9. In America, do dreams often come?
10. Jason has.

Postscript: A speaker doesn't ordinarily say, "Jill mailed her mother" (unless Jill has an unusually small mother or she has found an unusually large mailbox). What about a verb that has recently entered the language, *email* (from the noun of the same name)? We *can* say, "Jill emailed her mother." Why should *emailed* be different from *mailed*?

A Final Note on Grammar

How often have you heard someone—including English teachers— say, "I didn't learn English grammar until I studied Latin" (or some other foreign language)?

What could they mean by this? Let's take a look at some grammar rules that people would indeed learn if they learned a particular foreign language.

In Latin class, students would learn that objects can precede verbs:

Latin: Caesarem interfecit Brutus.
Literal: Caesar   killed   Brutus.
English: Brutus killed Caesar.

(For those who may have forgotten, *Brutus* killed *Caesar*, in fact; and that is precisely what the preceding Latin sentence says—through the proper case-marking endings.)

In French class, one would learn that both direct and indirect objects come *before* the verb:

French: Elle me   les   donne.
Literal: She (to) me them   gives.
English: She gives me them/She gives them to me.

In studying Italian, a student would discover that speakers commonly omit the subjects of their sentences:

Italian: Ne   ho   bisogno.
Literal: Of it have need.
English: I need it.

In Hebrew (and Russian, and Chinese, and many, many other languages), learners would discover that it is unnecessary to use the verb *to be* when using the present tense:

Hebrew: Hī   chachām.
Literal: She wise.
English: She is wise.

In Romanian, students would learn that one places articles *after* nouns, not before them:

Romanian: omul
Literal: man the
English: the man

Those who study German would discover that the speakers of that language typically place the content verb after its complement:

German: Wir haben den Geburtstag gefeiert.
Literal: We have the birthday   celebrated.
English: We have celebrated the birthday.

Finally, consider the fact that Spanish has more verb forms that Sandra Bullock has movies—some fifty different forms. Compare this with English, which has only three live verb inflections: *-s, -ed,* and *-ing.* To conjugate a verb in Spanish is meaningful; to conjugate a verb in English is a waste of time. We merely need to know its principal parts.

This is but a tiny fraction of the illustrations that might have been used, illustrations that the grammars of other languages are *different* from the grammar of English. If students really learned English grammar from studying foreign languages, they would be hopelessly inarticulate in English. How does one explain, then, the statement that someone has "finally" learned English grammar by studying a foreign language?

First, note that this statement implies that students *did not learn* English grammar from their English teachers or English textbooks. Did they not use English textbooks? Did their teachers not teach "grammar"? Not much chance of that. (See Chapter 1, page 17.)

All right, *what did they learn* in Latin or Spanish, French or German, about English grammar? My guess is that they finally learned how to apply terms to the grammar they already knew. They learned a metalanguage; they learned how to talk about grammar. They'd always known that X was a noun and Y was a pronoun. They did not know that word X was *called noun* and word Y, *pronoun*. Is this knowledge worth having?

It's worth having if you're an English teacher, to be sure. It *could* be worth having in courses such as Freshman English, particularly in instances where the teacher used such terms. I suspect, however, that one of two things happens in *most* Freshman English classes. First, the teacher herself isn't very sure about the language, most such courses being taught by part-timers or graduate assistants whose main strength is not grammar. Consequently, they avoid grammatical terms themselves. Or second, the instructor does not use the language because she knows that most students do not understand it. (For the record, that's what I do.)

Beyond Freshman English, knowledge *about* grammar has very limited utility, even for people who write as part of their lives. Of course, this is not to deny that it may be intellectually satisfying to possess such knowledge. It's intellectually satisfying to know all sorts of things—to know about music, for instance, or algebra. I'm very happy that I know as much as I do about English grammar, even though it is very little compared with what linguists know. I'd also be happy if my students knew much more than they do, but their knowledge about grammar, or lack of it, is not going to stop me from attempting to help them communicate better.

One thing I am certain of is that if you teach TSG traditionally, you are not helping anyone. Those students—and they are very, very few indeed, if I may judge by the college students I have taught over many years—who seem to have learned some rudiments of "grammar" from the traditional approach have done so *in spite of* rather than because of the teaching to which they have been exposed. I hope this chapter has proved that. Indeed, I agree with Alfie Kohn when he says that "nothing bears a greater responsibility for undermining excellence in American education than the success of the back-to-basics movement [which brought a resurgence of TSG] and the continued dominance of traditional instruction" (*The Schools Our Children Deserve*, p. 185). Our children do deserve better.

And now we move on to usage, and writing, and punctuating—important, real-world concerns, and concerns with which we English teachers can help our students, whether or not they know *about* grammar.

Postscript

Traditional school grammars should be distinguished from traditional scholarly grammars. The latter are represented by the works of such people as Otto Jespersen (see the quote at the beginning of this chapter), of the early to middle 1900s, and Randolph Quirk, closer to our own time. They, and others, have written distinguished descriptive grammars of the English language. The existence of traditional scholarly grammar in our best-selling school textbooks, however, has never been more than a whisper. This in itself is a fact worth pondering—and testimony to the persistence of the grammar of schooling (see page 6).

3
Usage: Rules That Do Not Rule (and a Few That Do)

Scholars have always consistently averred that good usage is the only conceivable criterion of good English, but most people still clamor for a heaven-sent standard to measure their words by.

—George Lyman Kittredge, Some Landmarks in the
History of English Grammar, 1906

Until we recognize the arbitrary nature of our judgments, too many of us will take bad grammar as evidence of laziness, carelessness, or a low IQ. That belief is not just wrong. It is socially destructive.

—Joseph M. Williams, Style: Toward Clarity and Grace, 1995

In his article, "The Usage Industry," Tom McArthur (1986) traces the origin of the notion of good English back to 1604, when schoolmaster Robert Cawdrey published his *Table Alphabeticall of Hard Usuall English Words*, which was designed for "the linguistically insecure" (says McArthur). Cawdrey specifically addresses himself to "Ladies, Gentlewomen, or any other unskillfull persons" (doesn't that make your blood boil?), yet according to McArthur, it was not only women who bought the book but members of the rising middle class generally, a group anxious to better themselves by learning "the King's English." McArthur contends that such people were prone to be followers and were preyed upon by publishers eager to make money with all kinds of self-improvement books (1986, p. 8). Just visit the language section of your local bookstore and you'll see that the usage industry is very much alive today and still preying on the insecure. (The most revealing title among the books is *Woe Is I*, by former *New York Times Book Review* editor Patricia T. O'Connor. It's also one of the best and best written of the guides.)

Traditional school grammar (TSG) has left a heritage of prescriptive rules that have little or no basis in the realities of everyday spoken or written language. Put another way, usage—what good writers and speakers actually do—rules too little. But let's begin by examining the concept of *rule* in language.

Two Fundamental Kinds of Rules: Descriptive and Prescriptive

As a way of distinguishing two basically different kinds of rules, consider these sentences:

1a. Where is the teacher biology?
1b. Where is the biology teacher at?

No native speaker of English with a fully functioning brain and not under the influence of a medication, say, or lack of sleep, would speak or write a sentence like 1a. The reason is that our brains are wired with rules (see Chapter 1), one of which tells us that modifiers generally *precede* the headword they modify. This type of rule is often called a *descriptive* rule, a rule that *describes* what native speakers of a language customarily do. There are a large but unknown number of such rules. They are used by all native speakers of English. (Some of us are better wired than others: I've rarely taught a group of teachers without finding someone who was better wired than I am; and I've rarely observed a grammar class in which some students weren't better wired than their teacher.)

In contrast, no descriptive rule prevents us from speaking sentences like 1b, and indeed, the sentence would be used by many native speakers of English. Those who disapprove of it do so because it "doesn't sound right" or because they have been taught that it is wrong to end a sentence with a preposition. The rule that prohibits 1b is known as a *prescriptive* rule. Prescriptive rules tell us what we *should do*. They are *not* observed universally.

Here are four basic characteristics of descriptive versus prescriptive rules:

Descriptive Rules

1. Universal: Observed by all native speakers of a language
2. Learned unconsciously, wired into the brain
3. Tell what native speakers do in fact
4. Violation causes lack of understanding or misunderstanding of the *message*

Prescriptive Rules

1. Limited: Observed by some native speakers, not by others
2. Learned from various environmental sources
3. Tell what speakers *should do*
4. Violation causes no misunderstanding; may focus on the *messenger*

48

Activity 3–1: Sense versus Nonsense

Goal: To help students appreciate the nature of descriptive rules and the fact that they have so many in their heads.

Procedure

Write on the chalkboard or overhead projector duplicate pairs of sentences such as these:

A. Dug a has carpet our in cat hole the.
B. Our cat has dug a hole in the carpet.

Clearly, A is ungrammatical, B is grammatical. Ask students why they routinely produce sentences like B and never produce "sentences" like A. The answer is that they have descriptive rules built into their heads. No native speaker ever says he learned to produce sentences like B from a textbook.

Next, list (and discuss, if you wish) some of those descriptive rules by contrasting the two "sentences." Your rules might include:

1. *our, the,* and *a* must precede nouns (*cat, carpet, hole*).
2. *has* must precede the verb (*dug*).
3. *in* introduces a noun phrase (*the carpet*).
4. Prepositional phrases (*in the carpet*) follow verb phrases (*has dug*) or noun phrases.
5. Subjects (*our cat*) must precede verb phrases (*has dug*).
6. Objects (*a hole*) must follow verb phrases.

With the exception of the glossary of commonly confused words at the end, the remainder of this chapter is devoted to a discussion of prescriptive rules, beginning with the issue of a *standard* for judging linguistic rights and wrongs.

The Search for a Standard: On Whose Authority?

If we want to declare something is wrong or incorrect, we need some standard by which to measure. The standard for descriptive rules is clear enough: accurate communication of the message. ("Where's the teacher biology" is *wrong* because it does not communicate the intended meaning of the speaker.) What is the standard for prescriptive rules? Early grammarians were conscious of the need to answer this question.

A Linguistic Academy

One way to distinguish "correct" speech and writing from incorrect is to institute an academy, a group of linguistic scholars who would be empowered to decide such matters. Such an academy had been instituted in Italy in 1582 and in France in 1635 (founded in 1634). Although Cawdrey's work was published in 1604, the effort to correct and improve *English* didn't really gain momentum until around 1660, when it gathered the backing of some of the most eminent literary figures of the age, including John Evelyn, John Dryden, Daniel Defoe, Joseph Addison, and Jonathan Swift. Perhaps the two best known documents were Defoe's *Essay upon Projects* of 1697 and Swift's *Proposal for Correcting, Improving, and Ascertaining the English Tongue*, which appeared in 1712. But nothing significant was done; indeed, fifty years after Swift's *Proposal*, Bishop Lowth opened his *Grammar* (1762) with the lament that "no effectual method hath hitherto been taken to redress the grievance which was the object of it [i.e., of Swift's *Proposal*]" (p. iv).

By Lowth's time, literary figures such as Samuel Johnson and Joseph Priestley had weighed in *against* this means of establishing authority, but perhaps the most eloquent statement against it was made much later by the Danish grammarian, Otto Jespersen, who wrote in *Growth and Structure of the English Language* (1905)

> . . . the English [language] is like an English park, which is laid out seemingly without any definite plan, and in which you are allowed to walk everywhere according to your fancy without having to fear a stern keeper enforcing rigorous regulations. The English language would not have been what it is if the English had not been for centuries great respecters of the liberties of each individual and if everybody had not been free to strike out new paths for himself.

One wonders how Shakespeare would have fared with an academy peering over his shoulder. And how liberty-loving Americans of the seventeenth and eighteenth centuries would have reacted to an academy proposal. At any rate, the proposal died.

The Lexicographer as Authority

Although the English did not institute an academy to rule on usage matters, they got a good dictionary in 1755. Samuel Johnson's *A Dictionary of the English Language* did establish standards where spelling, pronunciation, and word meanings were concerned. (Noah Webster's *American Dictionary* did the same in this country in 1828.) Dictionaries *are* authorities on these matters because there is widespread agreement to abide by them. Also, most dictionaries do not prescribe spellings and pronunciations; they merely describe those that exist. My dictionary, for example, lists five distinct spellings and three pronunciations for *bogeyman*.

But is a dictionary a valid source of authority for correctness in usage?

Samuel Johnson and Noah Webster no doubt knew a great deal about usage, but was there good reason to trust them beyond all others? Suppose they disagreed with each other? And they often did: Webster, for example, approved of *noways*, but Johnson said it was used only by "ignorant barbarians."

What if they disagreed with themselves? Johnson approved of *learn* for *teach* in his 1755 edition, but reversed himself, declaring it "obsolete" in his 1785 edition. (Obsolescence apparently can take forever; see the treatment of "learn, teach" in the 2001 *Elements of Language, Sixth Course*, p. 769.)

What if they were way out of the mainstream, and swimming against the current? Johnson, for example, defended double comparisons and comparison of incomparables—such as *perfect*—but thought *banter* was "barbarous" and *con* (*against*) was "despicable cant." Webster defended *you was* and *who is it for?* He also accused Shakespeare of using barbarisms and "the grossest improprieties."

In fact, Webster once stated that the people of America "spoke the most pure English now known in the world." (Had Johnson been alive at the time, one can imagine his roar crossing the Atlantic.) As this comment itself well illustrates, lexicographers of the age were no more likely to be objective in matters of usage than anyone else.

The Authority of Custom or Usage

We have already seen (in Chapter 2) that Bishop Lowth, in particular, had no compunctions about criticizing the best writers of his own and earlier times. Nevertheless, he and other grammarians often cited the authority of "usage" or "custom," by which they meant what educated writers or speakers actually wrote and said. Here, for example, is Lindley Murray's tribute to what is often called "the doctrine of usage":

> The practice of the best and most correct writers, or a great majority of them, corroborated by general usage, forms, during its continuance, the standard of language; especially, if, in particular instances, this practice continue, after objection and due consideration. Every connexion and application of words and phrases, thus supported, must therefore be proper, and entitled to respect, if not exceptionable in a moral point of view. . . . With respect to anomalies and variations of language, thus established, it is the grammarian's business to submit, not to remonstrate. (1795, p. 144)

Though there are more hedges here than in a formal French garden, Murray finally seems to come down on the side of good usage. But as Sterling Leonard notes in his chapter, "The Appeal to Usage and Its Practical Repudiation," no eighteenth-century grammarian except Joseph Priestley "made the appeal to usage with anything approaching consistency," and indeed, "the appeal to usage . . . resulted in a complete repudiation of usage" (1929, p. 165).

To What Authority Did the Eighteenth-Century Grammarians Appeal?

If even good usage was not truly an authority for the eighteenth-century prescriptive grammarians, what was? According to Leonard, these were the main appeals:

1. Ipse dixit appeals to authority
2. Appeals to supposed parallels in the Latin language, chiefly; sometimes to Greek, French, or Anglo-Saxon
3. Appeals to "reason and analogy" (i.e., logic or grammatical regularity of any kind)

The weakest of these is the first: It's right because I say so; for after all, who are you? And why should I obey your commandments? But questions like these never seem to trouble true prescriptivists. Goold Brown, for example, who wrote a monumental *Grammar of Grammars* in 1851, purported to have all the answers, and clearly saw himself as the "heaven-sent standard" Kittredge refers to in the quote at the beginning of this chapter. Pooley notes that Brown excoriated every well-known grammarian who preceded him and saw himself as "the messiah to lead the way to a correct and perfect grammar" (1957, p. 28).

The second appeal—to other languages—pitches one upon a very slippery linguistic slope. For example, we might demonstrate through an appeal to the French language that infinitives should not be split (since French infinitives are single words). On the other hand, French routinely uses double negatives. What is the rationale for following the French language for one rule and ignoring it for another? (See other examples of where this appeal would pitch us, at the conclusion of the previous chapter.)

Finally, the third appeal—to reason and grammatical regularities—is full of the deepest pitfalls and potholes. Nothing is truer of languages than that they change. And they change often in unpredictable, irrational ways. Consider the pronoun set:

I	me	my	myself
you	you	your	yourself
we	us	our	ourselves

Then compare these:

| he | him | his | *himself* |
| they | them | their | *themselves* |

If grammatical regularity were a reliable guide, *himself* and *themselves* would have to be *hisself* and *theirselves*. *Mine* is another irregularity; the other pronouns in its set all end in *-s*. Consider also subject-verb agreement in tag sentences like this: "I'm right about that, *aren't I?*" I *are?*

If analogy truly ruled, English teachers would long ago have accepted *alright*, on the analogy of *already* and *altogether*, but even though James Joyce, Flannery O'Connor, and Langston Hughes used it, teachers (and lexicographers) have not accepted it. For a demonstration of the falsity of appeal to logic, see the next activity.

Activity 3–2: Do Two Negatives Make a Positive? Always?

Goal: To demonstrate first-hand that language is not necessarily logical.

Procedure

I was always taught that it was wrong to use double negatives, not because it would label me as a person of low socioeconomic status, but because "two negatives make a positive." Two negatives do make a positive in mathematics, but language is often not logical. The reality in the English language is that two negatives *sometimes* make a positive but more often do not.

You can dramatize this interestingly in the following way. Select two students from the class as "actors" (one will be no more than a prop). Tell everyone in the class to imagine that it is a swelteringly hot mid-summer day and that the first actor is dying of thirst. She is desperate for a soft drink, and happily, there is a drink-dispensing machine nearby. However, she has only a dollar bill and the machine is insisting on the right change.

Instruct the actor with the dollar bill to behave normally at all times. You are standing closest to the machine; the other student is farther away; there is no one else on the scene. If the actor behaves normally, after trying the machine, she will ask you if you have change for a dollar. You respond by saying, "I don't have no change." The student will move on and ask the same question of the student who is standing farther away from the machine.

The point is that, although you have violated the double-negative rule, the student understands perfectly well that you are denying her request; that is, the violation of the double-negative rule causes no misunderstanding. That's because it's a prescriptive rather than a descriptive rule. Point out, if necessary, that if two negatives *really* made a positive, the student would offer you the dollar bill, expecting change. (I have tried this experiment many, many times and have *never* had a student act this way, not even in jest.)

Of course, it is true that two negatives *sometimes* make a positive. If you altered the intonation of your voice: "I don't have NO change," it might be interpreted as a positive. The remarkable thing is that the human mind is capable of deciding when two negatives do make a positive, and when they do not. Most of the time, it's the latter.

Standard English

In the search for authority, perhaps nothing has been more final and yet more controversial than the notion of *standard English*. We know, of course, that that band of people who invaded England in 449 A.D. and rapidly spread their language (Old English) across the island in all directions did not arrive speaking standard English. In fact, what is called *standard English* developed from the East Midlands dialect that William Caxton used in his publications. It evolved alongside dialects that eventually became relegated to regional status. It was merely one of many dialects. And it still is. If it is superior to others, it is so because of its prestige, not because of any innate superiority.

Defining *standard English* is not easy, and quarrels about what is and what is not "standard" appear to be endless. But according to the editors of *The Concise Oxford Companion to the English Language*, linguists agree on these three things about the standard:

1. It is most easily identified in printed materials.
2. It is generally used by English-language news broadcasters.
3. It relates to social class and level of education, and is often considered to "match the average level of attainment of students who have finished secondary-level schooling." (1996, p. 903)

Standard English, then, in America, would be the English of Well-Edited American Prose (WEAP); that is, the English of editors at such institutions as Alfred A. Knopf and *The New York Times*. Especially when we are referring to the spoken standard, it is the English of our major news broadcasters. Broadly, it is the dialect of educated speakers, of those who "run things."

In no other respect is it more important for English teachers to "only look (or listen) and connect." If standard English *is* the language of *The New York Times* and Alfred A. Knopf editors and radio and television news broadcasters, then that is it. Sure, even a broadcasting dean or a *Times* editor may slip occasionally, but if we hear or read words or expressions on a regular basis in these media, then they *are* standard English, whether we like it or not. There is no higher appeal, no academy here, no Pope of the Word.

In our looking and listening, we English teachers may often need to be more conscious than we sometimes are of two basic principles:

1. There are significant differences between *written* and *spoken* standard English, and we should not hold speakers to the same standards as writers.
2. There are major differences between relaxed standard and more uptight standard English. Even Edwin Newman must loosen his tongue along with his tie after work.

Is standard English, then, the certainty grammarians have long sought? Is any given word, phrase, or structure *correct* if it can be found in the standard English dialect and *incorrect* if it cannot?

So many people think so that it would be foolish to ignore them. Nevertheless, a little thought should convince anyone that it is not always simply a matter of correct versus incorrect. (Sometimes, it is. See the glossary of commonly confused words at the end of this chapter.) There are often *degrees* of correctness, and they run in a continuum, from what have been called *status-marking errors* on the one extreme to "errors" recognized as erroneous *only* by those who get their authority from celestial spheres on the other. Consider the following by way of example:

2a. I seen them yesterday.
2b. I've got the latest CD.

The rule violated in Sentence 2a is, of course, that *saw*, not *seen*, is the standard past tense form of the verb *to see*. When a word or phrase sharply differentiates educated from uneducated speakers, we will call that expression a *status-marking* error.

A linguist once observed that there is not two cents worth of difference between "I seen them yesterday" and "I saw them yesterday"—except the I-saw-them people run the schools. It's a clever remark, and it's true that both sentences mean the same thing. But the fact that the I-saw-them people run the schools (and a good deal else besides) is of no small consequence.

We can bewail the fact that there are expressions that divide native speakers of English from one another (I do), but it is impossible to escape that fact. It's impossible to escape the fact that regular use of nonstandard English in the larger society is likely to handicap the user, economically and socially.

Sentence 2b uses a contracted form of the phrase *have got*. That this is *not* a status-marking error may be established by listening to the daily speech of *any* educated person. You will find *have got* in WEAP sources as well. (See the glossary of mythrules later in this chapter for further comment on this item.) To outlaw this is to play messiah. I call it a *mythrule*. Specifically, a usage mythrule is a rule that someone believes should be followed by educated speakers of the language, but which is generally *not* followed by them.

Characteristics of Nonstandard English

We have said, borrowing the term from Maxine Hairston (1981), that the sharpest divergences from the standard may be characterized as status-marking errors. It is appropriate to describe some of them. They have been given various names, but *nonstandard* seems the most neutral.

1. *Nonstandard verb forms.* Some of these are nonstandard past-tense forms of irregular verbs, such as *brung* for *brought*; and nonstandard past participial forms, such as *had went* for *had gone*. Also nonstandard is using a regular ending on an irregular verb, such as *growed* for *grew*. We are not talking here of items like *lie/lay*, which sometimes make even well-educated people throw up their hands; and of course, we are not talking about cases where either of two forms may be used by educated speakers, such as the past tense of *sing*, which may be either *sang* or *sung*.

2. *Double negatives and comparatives.* It's true that double negatives and double comparatives were defended by Samuel Johnson and were once used by our best writers: Chaucer and Shakespeare, for example. It's also true that two negatives very often do *not* make a positive—the second merely intensifies the first (see Activity 3–2). Nevertheless, this is one area where the prescriptive grammarians have prevailed. For the last two centuries, speakers and writers of standard English have eschewed both the double negative and the double comparative (*more better*, *most unkindest*). Quasi double negatives such as *can't hardly/scarcely* should probably also be listed under this heading.

3. *Some subject-verb disagreements.* If we listen carefully to the speech of well-educated persons, perhaps even to ourselves, we will hear subject-verb disagreements from time to time, particularly when the verb is distant from its subject. But when verbs immediately follow their subjects, speakers of standard English rarely disagree. We would list as status-marking errors such items as *we was* for *we were*, *she have* for *she has*, and *he don't* rather than *he doesn't*. The dropping of the *-s* on most third-person, present tense verbs probably also belongs here, though this usage is deeply ingrained in some dialects, and it poses a special problem for many Asians, who have no such inflectional endings in their native languages.

4. *Some incorrect pronouns.* In standard English, object pronouns are not used as subjects, for the most part, and vice versa. The use of *them* as a substitute for *these* or *those* is another example of nonstandard speech: "I'd like one of them books."

5. *Some adjectives for adverbs.* When a sentence ends with an adverb that modifies the whole predicate rather than the complement alone, standard English speakers use the adverbial form: "We go to soccer games regular*ly*." Most English teachers also claim that *really* (not *real*) should be used as a modifier of adjectives.

6. *Miscellaneous words and phrases. Ain't, ways* attached to words like *any* and *some, this here, learn* for *teach,* and perhaps *had ought, hisself,* and *irregardless,* though some would consider some of these regional rather than nonstandard (see comments below), are often considered nonstandard English. *Could of, should of, would of,* and so on, are nonstandard in writing, but the pronunciation *of* for *'ve* is common in everyone's speech.

Further Observations on Nonstandard English

As stated, there are degrees of correctness within standard English and, as noted, large differences exist between standard written and spoken English and between relaxed and uptight standard. What about nonstandard English? Can the same things be said about it? More importantly, do speakers of standard English sometimes use nonstandard?

If some of the following comments appear irreverent, I can only plead the irreverence of observation.

Ain't

From time to time, people get into a huff about certain words or phrases and try to ban them from the language. *Hopefully* is a recent example of a failure to win a ban, but sometimes, as with *ain't,* the ban succeeds. Though it was used for centuries by educated speakers—*ain't* can be found, for example, in written texts from the seventeenth and eighteenth centuries, and "Mystery Theatre" watchers have heard it in the speech of the ultra-sophisticated Lord Peter Whimsey—it has been stigmatized "beyond any possibility of rehabilitation," according to the *American Heritage Dictionary.*

One might observe, however, that this judgment applies to the *unselfconscious* use of *ain't.* When we know that a speaker "knows better," many of us do not necessarily find the word objectionable. (I once sat for an hour listening to a nationally famous authority in the field of reading who must have used *ain't* at least three dozen times. He was clearly using it as a sort of folksy emphatic, but he did it so often that, frankly, I grew quite tired of it—and of him. But I didn't for a moment judge him illiterate.)

Ain't is also more common in some sections of the country than in others, and appears to be more acceptable in everyday conversation in those areas—though probably not at afternoon tea parties. It is also informally used in England, as a substitute for *am not.* It is common in popular music—and we're not talking only about rap or country. Golden Oldies and show tunes use it frequently. Finally, it is common in phrases such as "You ain't seen nothing yet" (used often by Al Gore in the 2000 presidential campaign), "If it ain't broke, don't fix it," "You ain't just whistling Dixie," and others.

Anyways

I insert this item—which the original (1941) *Harbrace* labeled as a *vulgarism* for *anyway*—not because I wish to contradict the notion that it is nonstandard, but because it was used *regularly* in speech by a highly intelligent and well-educated daughter of highly intelligent, well-educated parents. She was, furthermore, a great editor for a major publisher. I don't know how or why it became a staple of her speech, but it certainly did not brand her as a speaker of nonstandard English. We are all entitled to some eccentricities.

Irregardless

In some people's minds, the prefix *ir-* in *irregardless* must mean *not*, the suffix *-less* must mean *without*, and on that basis, they argue that *irregardless* is a double negative. But is it? If someone said to me in a conversation, "I don't believe you, irregardless of your credentials," I doubt very much that I would think the speaker was saying something positive about my credentials. Two of the most sophisticated, literate, and well-educated people I know use this word. One used it in a lengthy article, as recently as 1999; he is a long-time college English professor. The other, a writer by profession, says he learned it in his childhood and will never give it up. (I grew up in the same neighborhood, but didn't learn it. Figure that.)

I suppose all dictionaries label *irregardless* as *nonstandard*. The OED (Second Edition, 1989) says it's "chiefly North American" and "in nonstandard or humorous use." Some might say this shows how little they know about what's happening on this side of the Atlantic, but I won't quarrel with that characterization, in spite of my friends. However, those who fly into a rage over it and claim, "There is no such word," are clearly misguided.

Real for Really

"You're a *real* good friend" is supposed to be nonstandard English, but keep your eyes and ears open on this one. On March 22, 2002, in *The New York Times*, I read: " . . . best news to hit this city in a real long time." This was written by the reporter; it was not quoted dialogue.

Me and My Friends Are. . . .

The expression "me and my friends" (and variants, with nouns other than *friends*) as *subject* of a sentence really upsets many speakers of standard English—especially older speakers, who often reject it outright as an illiteracy. I know this well, since I was one of them. (No good English teacher objects to "me and my friends" as an *object*—"The coach gave me and my friends a reward"—though some might prefer to reverse the order: ". . . my friends and me.")

I modified my position when, at the urging of my friend and colleague, Hans P. Guth, I *listened* to the speech of well-educated people—particularly of young people. Hans argued that it was perfectly good *informal* English. Well, I did listen, and I heard object pronouns in subject territory frequently in the speech of a wide range of people, including Ivy League college graduates. When I recently reminded my son that he used it after graduation from college, this is what he wrote:

> The phrase came into my mind, completely separate from our discussions, just last night when I was describing some of the antics my friends and I were involved in years ago. My first impulse was actually to say "me and my friends" but I halted myself because I knew it did not sound proper with an educated audience (our friends Jeff and Julie, who went to good schools in Boston). If I was with other people last night I might actually have used the phrase, and that is at age 45 with hopefully a university professorship in my near future! Old habits die hard.
>
> I do feel that I first and most often used the phrase with Bobby and Tommy years ago and knew even then that it was not proper English. But kids, particularly in conversation with each other, couldn't care less about using proper English. And yes, although I do not remember the instance you recall, I expect that my Columbia friends (Tim, Charlie, Mark) and I did use the phrase frequently in informal conversation. They probably grew up using it in their neighborhoods; it was widespread kidspeak. I clearly remember a Columbia classmate who eventually became a nuclear physicist often bragging, employing one-upmanship, starting sentences with "Oh yeah, well me and my friends . . .".
>
> I was startled last night to find that the phrase was actually still stored in the back of my head!

Notice that Bill *wrote* (twice) "my friends and I." There seems to be a disjuncture between the phrase in speech and in writing—at least for users of standard English. "Me and my X" is in the air, so to speak, and it has been for a long time. Do you remember the song, "Me and My Shadow," in which the structure is used as a subject in many lines? It was written in 1927, by Billy Rose, with music by Al Jolson and Dave Dreyer. More recently (2002), the distinguished editor, Herman Gollob, published *Me and Shakespeare*. Novelist Jane Smiley entitled one of her *New York Times Magazine* articles, "The Dream Factory: Me and My Product." (Within her article, however, Ms. Smiley wrote "The skirt and I did talk about engineering a takeover," *not* "The skirt and me" [March 12, 2000, p. 36].)

Some linguistic justification for this usage has been offered by Steven Pinker (1994), who observes that *me and my friends* is an example of a *headless* structure. It is not the same as any of its parts. The fact that *me and my friends* is the subject of a sentence does not mean that either *me* or *my friends* is a subject. The whole phrase is the subject. T. S. Eliot used a similar headless structure in his famous line, "Let us go then, you and I." Here, the headless *you and I* is presumably in apposition to *us*: "Let us [you and I] go then." Since *us* is an object case pronoun, should Eliot have written *you and me*? I think most English teachers would agree that he should not.

To test for pronoun correctness, textbook authors and teachers often recommend that students drop *and* and the other words in the subject and try the pronoun by itself. Note how this might work:

Sentence tested: Me and my friends are walking together.
Deletion test (A):   Me are walking together.

Since we would not say this, it supposedly proves that *Me* is incorrect. However, look what happens when we try *I*:

Deletion test (B):   I are walking together.

This doesn't work either, proving that "*I and my friends* (or *My friends and I*) are walking together" is also incorrect—even though it isn't.

I believe WEAP editors would not let a *me and my friends* subject noun phrase get by, even if an Ivy League graduate did write it, but in the oral language, the structure remains "widespread kidspeak," as my son put it (though I've caught adults using it, too), and judging by the college freshmen I've been teaching during three decades, it is peculiarly resistant to change.

The Double Negative

Although the unselfconscious use of double negatives is characteristic of nonstandard English, there is a lot more at the bottom of this issue than one might suppose. Let's stir it up.

Robert Lowth was the first, I believe, to maintain that "Two negatives in English destroy one another, or are equivalent to an affirmative." He gives several illustrations of double negatives from Shakespeare in his footnotes, and calls the latter's usage a "relique of the antient style," which is "now obsolete" (1775, p. 93). What a small distance into the future he saw.

In Activity 3–2, there is one situation in which two negatives were not perceived as making a positive. Here is another:

Assume you are checking student homework. If one of your students casually says, "I didn't do no homework," you immediately understand that he did none, and grade him accordingly. (Two negatives do not make a positive.) But with a different inflection of his voice—something like, "I didn't do NO homework"—he would be denying that he did none, implying that he did at least some. (Two negatives do make a positive.)

I'm a Sinatra fan (and wish that all of us articulated as well as he did). One of my earliest memories of his work is the ballad "All or Nothing at All," which he recorded with Harry James in 1939. It contains a line in which he says there *is* no in between. When he recorded the song again in 1966, he sang, there ai*n't no* in between. Did Sinatra change his mind about there being an in between? Obviously not. In this case, the added *ain't* strengthens *no*; it does not negate it.

Another example of one negative intensifying another is seen in such sentences as these:

No, I didn't commit the crime.
No judge would think the speaker was pleading guilty.

Or consider an angry lover who says, "I never, never want to see you again." Any rejected lover would not treat this as a positive, nor would she be likely to correct the speaker by saying, "You mean you never *ever* want to see me again."

Here's a similar pair (borrowed from usage experts Bergen and Cornelia Evans). Is there any difference between the double negative of the first sentence and the single negative of the second?

He couldn't sleep, not even with a sedative.
He couldn't sleep, even with a sedative.

On the other hand, two negatives—even without any special inflection— often *do* make a positive, as in these examples from *The Concise Oxford Companion to the English Language*:

It's not unlikely [i.e., it's likely] that I'll come.
You can't not admire them. [i.e., you must admire]

The fact is that the line between standard and nonstandard English rules for negation can be very slight. What's the difference, Steven Pinker asks, between

I didn't buy any lottery tickets and
I didn't buy no lottery tickets?

The slim difference is that standard English adopted *any* as the agreement element, whereas nonstandard adopted *no*. The French went a different route. In standard French, the double negative is used routinely: "Ce n'est pas mal" means "It's not bad," but it translates literally: "It not is not bad." "C'est pas mal" is nonstandard French. (For a good discussion of how the double negative arose in the French language, see McWhorter's *The Power of Babel* (2001), pp. 26–27.)

None of this is meant to deny that the unselfconscious use of most double negatives is nonstandard. If you want to be categorized as ill educated, few things would get you there quicker than consistent use of double negatives.

The Double Comparison

When declining adjectives and adverbs, it is standard either to prefix *more/most* or to attach the suffixes *-er/-est*. To use both is to be guilty of the double comparison error: "I like swimming more better now."

But recall the speech of Shakespeare's Mark Anthony, referring to Brutus' stabbing of Caesar:

That was the most unkindest cut of all.

It is, even today, a memorable and moving line, and I suspect that no one but a very narrow minded grammarian would find it otherwise. The *most* before the superlative *unkindest* simply intensifies its force. It did so in Shakespeare's time. It does so today.

Yet many decades after Shakespeare, grammarians found such structures to be "double comparisons" (technically, it's a double superlative here) and legislated them out of existence in standard English. They did so on the ground that it was illogical to do the same job twice. It *should* be "most unkind cut" or "unkindest cut." No need for *both* "most" and "-est." The problem with this apparently solid conclusion is that, once again, a natural language is not necessarily logical, nor need it be.

What Should Teachers Do About Nonstandard Speech?

I speak a dialect, you speak a dialect, all God's children speak dialects, because as linguist John McWhorter (2001) says, dialects are all there is/are/be. I grew up speaking a Philadelphia dialect, one that has several nonstandard features ("Yo, youse guys, how 'bout them Iggles!"). Although I went to a Catholic elementary school where I was taught by nuns for eight years and went on to a fine public high school, several elements of the dialect remained with me. Then, in college, I promptly fell in love with a professor's daughter, and she literally kicked the dialect out of me within days. Every time I would use a nonstandard expression, she'd boot me in the shins. "*We* don't talk like that," she'd say. In short order, *I* didn't talk like that either.

Today, I speak standard English, most of the time (not on the golf course). Yet some years after I had graduated from college, when I was driving a cab in Philadelphia, the dialect came in handy. I shifted from my standard English whenever my fare spoke Philadelphian—and got much better tips as a result.

I tell this story as a prelude to the following observations about ways of dealing with kids who don't "know the rules."

1. Regardless of the dialect someone speaks, his language will have far more *in common* with standard English than differences from it. He will put determiners in front of nouns; he will put phrasal modifiers after nouns; he will put subjects before verbs and objects after them; and so on and on. In other words, he will follow bedrock grammar rules. The job of learning standard English is not necessarily difficult. It's not a foreign language, after all. And many of the kids who don't know it already speak at least one foreign language.

2. *However*, I was instructed by good people for *twelve years*, without much effect on some aspects of my dialect. Within about *two weeks*, Christine had done the job. This points up the powerful influence of motivation (see my comments about court reporter students before the glossary of commonly confused words later in the chapter), and perhaps it also says something about the *social* nature of learning. (For some good activities designed to promote motivation for students to learn the standard dialect, see Larry Andrews' *Language Exploration and Awareness: A Resource Book for Teachers*.)

3. *We must begin by respecting the students' own dialect.* During what some chose to characterize as the Eubonics plague a few years back, you'd have thought that African-American Vernacular English was some kind of disease, but it isn't, and those who use it communicate perfectly well with others who do. The notion that any dialect is rule-less is absurd.

It's difficult enough to change habits learned at the mother's knee and reinforced by everyone in the child's home environment; we must not make it even more difficult by acting as if our students were linguistic failures for not having learned "proper English." Our students must respect their own linguistic aptitude, as Mina Shaughnessy (1977) insisted, and see that mastering standard English is a matter of staking a claim to the language of public transactions—educational, civic, and professional. It shouldn't be seen as disloyal to or destructive of their native culture.

Activity 3–3: Code Switching and Respecting Students' Dialects

Goal: To promote the use of standard English in students who speak other dialects.

Procedure

Code switching refers to changing one's dialect, depending on circumstances. As I have pointed out, as a cab driver, *I* switched codes depending on my passengers.

Some good work to encourage code switching in elementary school students is being done by Rebecca Wheeler (2001) and teachers who work with her in the Virginia Peninsula. (Some similar activities are used in various urban school systems.) Rather than follow the *correctionist* approach, they observe the contrast between the *rules* of the students' dialect (called *home speech*) and the rules of standard English (*school speech*). Here are two examples of contrasting rules, from third-grade teacher Rachel's class:

Example One: Possession

Home Speech: Christopher family moved to Spain.
(*Rule*: The possessor appears next to and before what is possessed.)
School Speech: Christopher's family moved to Spain.
(*Rule*: Possession is shown by adding 's to the possessor.)

Example Two: Plurality

Home Speech: I have two sister and two brother.
(*Rule*: Plurality is shown by numbers before the nouns.)
School Speech: I have two sisters and two brothers.
(*Rule*: Plurality is shown by adding *-s* to nouns. *Note*: The standard English rule here requires the speaker to be redundant.)

Students are not expected to use school speech on all occasions—we all vary our speech somewhat, depending on the occasion. But they are taught to code switch when the occasion demands it. Taking state tests is one good example of such an occasion.

You can easily make up your own activities along these lines, always beginning by noting that the dialect of your students does follow rules. Linguist Johanna Rubba comments on this method:

> An approach to teaching that recognizes students' home speech as rule-following and valuable in its own context, and compares it with standard English as an equal rather than as an inferior, makes the children feel valued as well. When their native intelligence is not denigrated by suggesting that they have learned English poorly, their confidence about learning another variety is boosted. (personal email communication)

Activity 3–4: Third-Person, Present Tense Subject-Verb Agreement

Goal: To help students learn standard English subject-verb agreement in the third person, present tense.

Procedure

Begin by writing on the board or duplicating a number of relatively "bare-bones" sentences, such as those that follow. In each case, I have italicized the subject and the part of the verb phrase that controls agreement. You may or may not wish to do that.

Our TV *set works* now.
Our TV *sets work* now.
The *boys stand* on the corner every afternoon.
The *boy stands* on the corner every afternoon.
The new *teachers don't* like interruptions.
The new *teacher doesn't* like interruptions.
My *aunt has* come to visit.
My *aunts have* come to visit.

Invite your students to divide each sentence in half, at the most natural place. You should get

Our TV *set / works* now.
Our TV *sets / work* now.
The *boys / stand* on the corner.
The *boy / stands* on the corner.
The new *teachers / don't* like interruptions.
The new *teacher / doesn't* like interruptions.
My *aunt / has* come to visit.
My *aunts / have* come to visit.

This separates the subject part of the sentence from its predicate, and since we have excluded modifiers after the subject and before the verb, the subject will be the word directly to the left of the slanted line and the verb or the auxiliary that carries agreement will be directly to the right.

Ask the students what observations they can make about these two words. The expected answer is that when the subject ends in *-s*, the verb or auxiliary does not; and when the subject does not end in *-s*, the verb does. I call this the *-s, no s; no s, -s* principle of standard English.

You might ask students to pronounce carefully pairs of sentences, like these:

Our set works.	The boy stands.	The teacher doesn't like.
Our sets work.	The boys stand.	The teachers don't like.

To conclude, ask students to substitute pronouns for the noun subjects. They will find that the -s verb goes with the pronouns *she*, *he*, and *it*; the uninflected verb goes with *they*.

LESSON EXTENSION

As you know, the -s, *no s; no s*, -s principle works only if the subject noun has an -s plural form (which means that it works for probably ninety percent of all the nouns in the language). For nouns with irregular plurals—*man/men*, *child/children*, *mouse/mice*—the speaker has to learn that the singular form calls for a verb in -s; the plural form calls for a verb without the -s.

LESSON FOOTNOTES

1. Students who regularly use nonstandard verb forms may have special difficulty *pronouncing* verbs that end in certain consonant clusters—*asks*, *expects*, and *takes*, for example—and may avoid the added -s for that reason.
2. Teachers interested in a superb discussion of this and similar problems of nonstandard speakers or writers will find it—along with a great deal of good exercise material—in Mina Shaughnessy's *Errors & Expectations*. See her Chapter 4 especially.
3. With past-tense verbs (except *be*) and with modal auxiliaries, subject-verb agreement is automatic:

Past Tense	**Modal Auxiliary**
Our TV set work*ed* yesterday.	Our TV set *will* not work.
Our TV sets work*ed* yesterday.	Our TV sets *will* not work.

The Overwhelmingly Negative and Arbitrary Attitudes of the Tradition

One of the problems with the TSG tradition is that it finds usage errors in every kitchen cabinet and corner, making the task of learning standard English seem almost insurmountable, even for speakers whose dialect is much closer to the standard than are those of many of our students. Moreover, the *attitude* toward those who use less than "proper" speech is appallingly negative. Here, for example, are Hodges' comments on the 280 usage errors in the Glossary of the first edition (1941) of the *Harbrace Handbook of English*:

absurd	faulty	not proper
avoid	illiterate	overworked
bad	illogical	provincial
careless	impermissible	questionable

a contradiction	impropriety	redundant
colloquial	incorrect	should be restricted
corruption	misused	slang
crude	needless	superfluous
dialectal	never use	vague
don't use	no longer used	vulgar(ism)
do not confuse	not recognized	wrong

Talk about sinners in the hands of an angry God (see Chapter 4). One can only wish our vocabulary of praise were half so extensive.

Yet in the 1998 Glossary of the same handbook, this huge 280-item catalogue has dwindled to 156 errors. That's a reduction of 124 errors, or forty-four percent. However, ninety-one of the 156 are new errors, errors not recognized in the 1941 edition. This means that from mid-century to end-century only sixty-five errors survived.

Does the reduction mean that speakers stopped making the other errors? Yes, in a few cases, assuming they were errors in the first place. In 2003, we don't often hear *gent* for *gentleman* (which *Harbrace* labeled "a vulgarism" in 1941), but for the most part the "errors" of 1941 have become standard English in 2003.

Here is a little quiz. How many usage errors do you find in the following sentences?

- The philosopher was born in the second century A.D.
- Did you put the ad in the newspaper?
- After having eaten his dinner, he left.
- All of the trees were bare.
- They bought bread and also butter.
- Every place I go, I see her face.
- We are not as young as we used to be.
- The bus arrived at about noon.
- Park your auto in the lot.
- My dog was awfully sick yesterday.

Most people, given this "test," find few or no errors. Yet the 1941 *Harbrace* found one in every sentence. And these are from the entries under "A" only. The "errors" in the ten sentences were labeled, respectively, absurd (because it means "in the second century in the year of our Lord"), colloquial (should be *advertisement*), redundant (cut *after*), colloquial (should be *all the trees*), weak (cut *also*), vulgar (*every place* should be *everywhere*), careless (the first *as* should be *so*), redundant (cut *at*), not proper in formal writing (should be *automobile*), and slang (*awfully*).

The sixty-five errors that survive into this century are a mixed bag. Some are distinctly nonstandard items, such as *ain't* and *learn* for *teach*. Some are confusing pairs, such as *accept/except* and *affect/effect*. Some others are perennial difficult-to-master verbs, such as *lie/lay*, *rise/raise*, and *sit/set*. And finally, there are miscellaneous items like *and etc.*, *fewer/less*, *good/well*, *like*, *as*, *as if*, and *try and*.

Although they are talking about the written rather than the spoken language, Connors and Lunsford (1988) make this cogent observation about teachers' ideas about errors, "[They] have always been absolute products of their times and cultures" (p. 399).

The list of errors in the original *Warriner's*, by the way, is very similar to *Harbrace's*, though they are fewer in number. Several of these items are discussed in the sections that follow.

I will say more about the rules-and-error mania in Chapter 4, but whenever I think about spoken usage, I get a sick feeling. Notions like *superiority* and *inferiority*, *security* and *insecurity*, and all sorts of ideas related to *class* flash in my mind. "What good is learning a rule if all we can do is obey it?" Joseph Williams (1997, p. 20) asked some time ago, and the question has haunted me for years. Too many of us want not simply to learn rules, but to enforce them, to lord ourselves over others.

I don't want to do that, and I don't want the profession to which I have devoted most of my adult life to stand for that. In that spirit, I offer my Glossary of Bêtes Noires and Mythrules, all of which deal with "rules" that are largely ignored by educated and careful writers, and even more so by educated and careful speakers. My *On the Other Hand* comments speak to the fact that the whole matter of usage is far more subtle than TSG makes it out to be.

I do not mean to suggest that people who react against certain uses of language are necessarily ill tempered or ill willed. Even more so, I am aware that people do abuse language and should be criticized for it. If you want to consider language abuse, look at the National Council of Teachers of English Doublespeak Awards, which are given out each November at the annual convention of the organization. The Committee might criticize the Pentagon for glamorizing war ("Operation Desert Storm") or for attempting to defend the indefensible—for example, by calling napalm bombs "anti-personnel ordinance," or naming the killing of innocent children "collateral damage." These are linguistic abuses that ought to be criticized. I'm not aware of Doublespeak *ever* giving an award to someone who wrote *like* for *as* or who used *irregardless*.

A Word About Usage Guides and Textbooks

I've long believed that every practicing English teacher ought to have an up-to-date usage manual right next to her dictionary. Modern dictionaries append usage notes to entries and have usage panels, but individual books often go into more detail.

Up-to-date is a critical modifier, since usage changes, sometimes on relatively short notice. A good example would be the word *hopefully*. In 1969, this word used as a sentence adverb was accepted by forty-four percent of *The American Heritage Usage Panel*. In 1992, only twenty-seven percent of the Panel accepted it. It's my best guess, based on listening to well-educated speakers, that the percentage will turn sharply the other way the next time a poll is taken.

Probably the most famous usage guide is the first one organized as a dictionary and the first that used the term *usage* in its title: H. W. Fowler's *A Dictionary of Modern English Usage* (1926). An American-English usage guide, "based on" Fowler's, written by Margaret Nicholson, appeared in 1957. (This has been out of print for some time.) The original Fowler was lightly edited by Sir Ernest Gowers and published in 1965. While certainly not a reliable guide to contemporary usage, it remains an interesting book, and it contains some historical information not always found in current guides.

Usage guides go in and out of print so often that I hesitate to recommend any specific one. I look for authors who have spent much of their lives in the study of usage. It's also interesting to compare usage guides with one another.

It is particularly important that English teachers below the college level *not* rely on their *textbooks* for usage opinions. As the contrast between the backgrounds of Robert Lowth, with his many advanced degrees, and Lindley Murray, who left off schooling at age eleven, dramatically illustrates, textbook writers have always been a very mixed lot. In today's market, moreover, major publishing houses frequently farm out large sections of textbooks to what are called "development houses." In these places, an editor is hooked up by telephone, fax, FedEx, or whatever, to anonymous worker bees who produce manuscript at x-dollars per page. This farming out is probably more often done with the grammar, mechanics, and usage sections of texts than with others because these parts are perceived as fixed or unchanging. Development-house editors themselves may be well-qualified individuals in many respects (I know a couple who are very well qualified), but they are not likely to be usage authorities, and those who work under them are often even less likely to possess up-to-date knowledge of usage or grammar.

All this is not to say that a decent textbook can't be produced in a development house, an even better book perhaps than comes from the hand of a named author. But where the named author fails, at least we have someone to blame for the failure. To whom do we look if a book produced in a development house fails?

Of course, that's *assuming* the author actually wrote the book. Unfortunately, we can never tell for sure from the cover who wrote it. As we have seen, most of the books bearing Warriner's name were not written by him, and this "tradition," while by no means universal (Hans Guth *always* wrote his textbooks), is not at all uncommon. I once asked Theodore Hornberger, who was on my dissertation committee and who was a long-time chief author of *The United States in Literature* volume in the best-selling Scott Foresman series, how much he had to do with the book. He responded, "I make a few suggestions, now and then." The book was mainly written by Foresman editors. And James Reid at Harcourt had at various times more editors in his stable than Pimlico has horses.

A few years ago, I met a young man at an NCTE convention who was a "writer" on a well-known series of books dealing with composition. He told me he had been ordered to "stay away from the authors." It was clear that the "authors" were not expected to write, and the writers were not authors. Welcome to textbook publishers' Wonderland.

A Glossary of Bêtes Noires and Mythrules

In his discussion of usage, Joseph M. Williams (1995, 1997) creates a special category of error that he calls a *bête noire* (literally "black beast" in French). He defines it as a so-called rule that is "largely capricious, with no foundation in logic or linguistic efficiency," but that nevertheless arouses a particularly fierce ire in many people. It is the ferocity that the word or phrase generates that is the chief defining condition distinguishing bêtes noires from other usage errors. Perhaps the most common bête noire during this generation is the word *hopefully*. Around the time I graduated from college, we had *finalize*.

And of course there have been others. I remember a time while my children were still in secondary school that the phrasal verb *sleep over* became a local bête noire. So strenuously was the English Department—or at least several members of it—against it that teachers swore on their red pens to slash it out of existence. The regional newspaper took up the cause as well, maintaining that only the cartoon character Snoopy truly slept over. Children might sleep overnight at one another's houses, but *sleep over* by itself made no sense. Sleep over *what?* the crusaders demanded to know.

The dust has long since settled on this bête noire, but it settled over a little corner of the English Department, not the tomb of the expression. *Sleep over* is recognized as a phrasal verb in current dictionaries without any usage label, leaving one wondering what all the fuss was about. In the list to follow, the first three items qualify as bêtes noires; the rest are what I call *mythrules*.

Different From/Than

Not all bêtes noires die as quickly as *sleep over* did. The question of whether one should say or write *different from* or *different than* has been with us since the mid-eighteenth century at least, and it still survives in the most recent *Harbrace*, in the following form:

> Both [*different from* and *different than*] are widely used, although *different from* is generally preferred in formal writing (1998, G6).

The condemnations seem to be growing softer, however, and perhaps this distinction will finally go the way of *sleep over*.

Like, As, As If

I'm old enough to recall the cigarette ad, "Winston tastes good like a cigarette should," and to remember what a tizzy that *like* caused. It went on for a couple of decades, as I remember, and though the slogan is long dead, many still mightily object to conjunctive *like*.

This is all the more curious because writers from Chaucer's time on have used *like* as a conjunction and no eighteenth-century grammarian condemned this usage.

Here is a passage from an essay published in *Harper's*, one of our most reputable magazines. Furthermore, the article was written by David Foster Wallace, who is a self-confessed SNOOT (Syntax Noodnicks Of Our Time) about language. He is talking about Bryan A. Garner, the author of *A Dictionary of Modern American Usage*.

> His argumentative strategy is totally brilliant and totally sneaky, and part of both qualities is that it doesn't seem *like* [italics mine] there's even an argument going on at all. ("Tense Present," p. 57)

The phrase "like I (you, she, he) said," in particular, is as standard in the speech of educated Americans as standard gets. "As I said" identifies one as stuffy or overly self-conscious.

On the Other Hand

Although my advice would be to ease up on *like* for *as if* in speech, it is a different matter in writing. The famous *New Yorker* editor William Maxwell once advised an author, "Write as if you wish to be understood by an unusually bright 10-year-old." It is unlikely that he would have written, "Write like . . .". I find myself as a writer often asking whether my *likes* would sound better as *as ifs*, and if they would, I change them.

Hopefully

Hopefully is supposed to be used only as an adverb, meaning "in a hopeful manner." It is not to be used to replace a phrase like "I hope" or "It is to be hoped." But consider these sentences:

Thankfully, she stepped on the brakes in time.
Fortunately, she stepped on the brakes in time.
Blessedly, she stepped on the brakes in time.
Happily, she stepped on the brakes in time.
Hopefully, she stepped on the brakes in time.

Does anyone really believe that the last must mean that she stepped on the brakes in a hopeful manner? The force of analogy does win, sometimes, in language, and it seems to be winning on this one.

Split Infinitives

Mythrule: Do not insert other words between the infinitive marker *to* and the verb form that follows it. Example: *to deny* is the infinitive form of the verb *deny*; to *actually* deny or to *forcefully* deny are deemed split infinitives.

Curiously, Sterling Leonard (1929) found no objections to the split infinitive among eighteenth-century grammarians, and he calls it "both a discovery and an aversion of nineteenth century grammarians" (p. 95). The rationale for this non-rule is supposedly that the infinitive is considered a single word—as it is in fact in such languages as Latin, French, and Spanish—and that one should not cleave this word in two. Historically, the infinitive marker *to* was actually a preposition meaning "toward," and thus there was nothing to split. However, the prepositional force of the infinitive *to* was lost as early as the fourteenth century, and today there remains no prepositional force at all.

While literate writers and most editors now split infinitives remorselessly, many language watchers still take this mythrule seriously. In a 1986 survey of letters sent to the BBC radio series *English Now*, the split infinitive ranked number two in a list of listeners' complaints. (Number one was the *I* in *between you and I.*) Randolph Quirk comments, "There is no feature of usage on which critical native reaction more frequently focuses" than the split infinitive (1985, p. 497). However, Quirk also points out that infinitives often *should be split*, particularly when not to split them leads to artificiality or ambiguity.

Closer to home, in the 1959 edition of *The Elements of Style*, Strunk says the split infinitive "is for the most part avoided by the careful writer," but in the fifth chapter of the same edition, which was added by E. B. White, we read that "some infinitives seem to improve on being split." In the 2000 edition, White's comment is retained, but Strunk's is modified, allowing for splitting if "the writer wishes to place unusual stress on the adverb."

Try the following little "test" with the English teachers on your staff—after trying it yourself. Insert the word given in brackets in the sentences below into the most natural place next to or inside of the italicized infinitives. How many infinitives did you split?

> I want you *to tell* it like it is. [*really*]
> I'd like *to know* an opera star. [*actually*]
> He's the last person *to consider* being dishonest. [*ever*]

On the Other Hand

Perhaps precisely because infinitives are split so commonly, we can sometimes achieve a nice effect by *not* splitting one. On page xvii, I purposely wrote, "A few teachers seem never to sleep." For me, it is notably more emphatic than "A few teachers seem to never sleep." Students who really care about writing style ought to be made aware of this option.

Have Got

Mythrule: Avoid using *have got* in the sense of *possess*. Use *have* instead. According to this, we should write, "We have many friends here," rather than "We've got many friends here."

Have got in the sense of "possess" has been good conversational English for a long time, according to the conservative usage expert Sir Ernest Gowers' revision of H. W. Fowler's A *Dictionary of Modern English Usage* (1965). Gowers furthermore notes that many careful writers—including Samuel Johnson, Jonathan Swift, and John Ruskin—approved of this usage. After quoting Philip Ballard, who concluded that *have got* is "not a real error but a counterfeit invented by schoolmasters," Gowers adds, "Acceptance of this verdict is here recommended."

At times, *have got* is essential. Consider the following responses to the question: "Have you received it yet?"

> A.   Yes, I already have it. (present tense)
> B.   Yes, I've already got it. (present perfect tense)
> C.   *Yes, I've already it.

The (C) response is not English. The (B) sentence is the *natural* contracted *perfective response* to the question and, it seems to me, is much more likely than (A).

Some people harbor the notion that there is something vaguely vulgar about the verb *got*, but this is clearly not so. It is the past tense of *get*, and my dictionary lists forty-five distinct uses of that verb. Only three of these are labeled "informal."

Henry James, as scrupulous and sophisticated a writer as we have ever had, wrote: "[She] had mastered the sovereign truth that nothing in the world is got for nothing" (*The Portrait of a Lady*, p. 80).

This one is from Strunk and White's *The Elements of Style*:

Later, when the reader has got his bearings, shorten them.

In William Gass' latest collection of essays, *Tests of Time*, he uses the heading, "I've Got a Little List." Few people in our time have a greater mastery of standard English than Gass.

On the Other Hand

Do you remember Myrtle Wilson, Tom Buchanan's mistress in *The Great Gatsby*? Fitzgerald establishes her character early on, partly by filling her dialogue with *got*'s:

I'd like to get one of those police dogs; I don't suppose you *got* that kind?
I'm going to have the McKees come up. And of course I *got* to call up my sister too.
I *got* to write down a list so I won't forget all the things I *got* to do.

This use of *got*—for *have got*—may be nonstandard. It may also be the source of that anti-*got* feeling in the pit of some stomachs.

Ending Sentences with Prepositions

Mythrule: Do not end a sentence with a preposition.

This mythrule has been the butt of ridicule as early as John Milton, who wrote regarding it, "What a fine conformity would it starch us all into!" The origin of the rule has been traced to Bishop Lowth, yet the latter does not formulate a rigid rule. Rather, he comments that placing a preposition at the end of a relative clause (as opposed to *before* the relative pronoun) is less graceful and doesn't agree with the "solemn and elevated style." Lindley Murray copied Lowth almost verbatim.

Many textbooks maintain that prepositions are *always* followed by their objects, but it is much harder to find one that explicitly forbids ending sentences with prepositions. (*Harbrace*, indeed, says sentences *may* end with prepositions, and offers examples.)

If Shakespeare had followed this rule, Prospero's lovely, "We are such stuff as dreams are made of," would have to be revised to something like, "We are such stuff of which dreams are made." And simple, straightforward questions like, "What am I guilty of?" would become the much stiffer, "Of what am I guilty?"

Where day-to-day speech is concerned, the best "rule" is to forget about this one.

On the Other Hand

Compare:	Ask not for whom the bell tolls.
With:	Don't ask who the bell tolls for.

As a writer seeking a formal tone, is there any doubt which you would select?

Placement of Only

Mythrule: Only should be placed as close as possible to the word(s) it modifies. "I only have eyes for you" *should* be "I have eyes only for you," according to this mythrule.

I still remember correcting this error on student papers—back in my greener years—over and over again. Why couldn't students see that "I only have eyes. . . ." meant that *eyes* are the only thing I have? No arms, legs, head, torso? Well, they couldn't see it because it isn't so. "I only have eyes" doesn't mean that at all, and *every* reader—except dunderheaded English teachers such as I was—knows that perfectly well.

Even in a relatively formal register, we commonly find *only* placed before the verb when it "ought" to go after. For example, Nathan Hale was presumably using his best English as he was about to be executed, yet he purportedly said, "I only regret that I have but one life to give to my country," not "I regret only. . . ."

On the Other Hand

Sometimes, the cause of precision is better served—and ambiguity avoided—by careful placement of *only*. Sterling Leonard cites an author who wrote, "I will only mention another instance," and then went on to supply a lengthy paragraph about a single instance.

Less/Fewer

Mythrule: We're supposed to use *less* with nouns that can't be counted: less sugar, less paper, less money; and we are supposed to use *fewer* with nouns that can be counted: fewer students, fewer cars, fewer minutes.

The real situation is much more complex. For one, many of our nouns are countable in some meanings, uncountable in others. *Liberty*, for example, is often a mass noun, as in Patrick Henry's "Give me liberty, or give me death." But we often hear such uses as, "Since her fall, she takes (fewer or less?) liberties in the skating rink."

We runners regularly count laps around a track, but would you say, "I did fewer laps today than I did yesterday"? Or how about *minutes* in the same context? Should it be *fewer* or *less* minutes? I don't think I've ever said that I ran fewer minutes than on a previous occasion, but one can certainly count minutes. Colin Powell—who speaks a pretty good standard English—recently said something about "less people than ever." Should he have said "fewer"?

If one has to pause in mid-sentence to decide whether *less* or *fewer* is the "right" choice, it's a sign that the choice is not worth the trouble.

On the Other Hand

In writing, we can usually take the time to choose among alternatives, and one might find it more elegant to use *fewer* rather than *less* in some instances.

> The National Assessment of Educational Progress has found fewer errors in student papers than they did a decade ago. That is good: the fewer errors students make, the better.

Activity 3–5: What Really Is Standard English?

Goal: To engage students in discovering the rules of standard English.

Procedure

Have your students select public figures whose standard English credentials are impeccable. Then ask the kids to select words or expressions from the bêtes noires and mythrules (or from any other source) and track that person's speech habits over a period of time. I ask students to avoid speakers who read their words from hard copy or teleprompters, since such material is likely to be written by others in the first place.

To give an example, I once chose Christie Todd Whitman, who was governor of New Jersey at the time. She is well bred, intelligent, well educated, and she certainly "ran things." (Besides, I liked her.) Other good choices are mayors, local congress people, senators, and of course national political figures.

Individual reports may be made at the end of the project, or a class project could be a dictionary of standard expressions. Note how this contrasts with what is normally done by usage police. They *start with* the "rules."

Twenty-seven Commonly Confused Words: A Glossary with a Difference

Thanks to spell-check programs, many erstwhile spelling problems have vanished, but thanks to the same programs, our confidence that we are spelling incorrectly spelled words correctly may also be at an all-time high. The chief villains of the piece are commonly confused words.

Lists of such words may be found in nearly all textbooks and handbooks, and on websites as well. Some of these sources offer useful advice; many are virtually useless. In textbooks, particularly, rare is the list that gives more than a minimum of information, usually couched in technical jargon. The list that follows no doubt has its own imperfections, but I think you will find that it offers many fresh solutions to perennial problems, and it avoids technical terms almost entirely. My selection of items is based on my long experience as a teacher of Freshman English. The items have been common errors among my college freshmen.

However, I developed most of my teaching suggestions while I was an adjunct professor in the Court Reporter Program at Temple University. Most of my students there had graduated from Philadelphia public or parochial schools and had to work hard to succeed in an English course in which the *passing* grade was eighty-five percent correct on the final examination. They weren't brilliant scholars, but they were highly motivated (a $40,000 job was waiting at the other end of my course). I will never forget them; they motivated me to work as hard as I have ever done as a teacher.

For each item, I first offer practical, nontechnical information that will help most students *get the item right*. This part is addressed directly to students. The notes that follow some items make additional comments or suggestions; they are addressed to the teacher and to more intellectually curious students.

Note: References are made to the Collins Cobuild corpus. This is a huge corpus of modern English text, which is used to analyze language usage. You can reach it on the Internet at titania.cobuild.collins.co.uk. I also make some references to the Kantz/Yates survey. These two teachers ranked the seriousness of usage errors, based on their survey of faculty in all disciplines at Central Missouri State. This survey may be accessed at the website of NCTE's Assembly for the Teaching of English Grammar, a site worth visiting for several reasons. Just go to ateg.org and enter "Kantz/Yates."

Advice/Advise

To Get It Right: Associate *advice* with the sound and spelling of *vice*, as in *vice principal* or *vice president*. If the word sounds that way, spell it that way. Remember: "The *vice* principal gave good *advice*."

Affect/Effect

To Get It Right: If you need a verb, write *affect*. If you need a noun, write *effect*. A useful memory device (mnemonic) is the acronym VANE (Verb–Affect, Noun–Effect).

The new policy will *affect* all students. [verb, following *will*]
The *effect* will be profound. [noun, following *the*]

Notes

1. In determining whether the word they need is a verb or a noun, students are helped by looking for signal words—mainly auxiliaries and determiners—that precede the word in question. (See Chapter 2.) Here are the statistics from the Collins Cobuild corpus:

   > The verb use of *affect* is preceded by a modal auxiliary (*will/would, can/could, may/might,* etc.) or by the infinitive marker *to seventy-eight percent* of the time.

   > The noun use of *effect* is preceded by an article *sixty-two-and-a-half percent* of the time and by *in* (in the phrase, *in effect*) *seventeen-and-a-half percent* of the time.

2. *Affect* may be a noun; *effect* may be a verb. In the first forty American English illustrations from the Collins Cobuild corpus, however, there are *no* instances of *effect* as a verb and only three instances of *affect* as a noun. The odds, therefore, are very much in favor of the preceding *Get It Right* advice.

3. As a verb, *affect* means, broadly, "to influence"; *effect*, broadly, means "to cause, bring about." These synonyms work well for most students. However, they do not work invariably. For instance, the first meaning of the verb *effect*, in my dictionary, is "to bring into existence." Taken literally, that would mean the sentence, "My mother effected my baby brother," is correct, but it is not.

   Some students are helped by the observation that *affect* often takes an animate object: "Cold weather affects *me*," whereas the verb *effect* usually does not: "The new government effected many *changes*."

4. I tell students that they should associate *affect* as a noun with the field of psychology. "Emotional response" is perhaps the best brief synonym. Here are the examples from the Collins Cobuild corpus:

   > his distant, depressed affect
   > The flat, unresponsive affect of her depression
   > an individual whose affect ranged from

5. Textbooks and handbooks nearly always totally ignore the use of *affect* as a noun, spending all their space on distinguishing the verb uses of this confusing pair. Frankly, both the noun use of *affect* and the verb use of *effect* are uncommon in the student papers I have read; but it's ill advised to pretend they do not exist.

A lot/Alot

To Get It Right: Ask yourself what an "alot" is. If you don't know, then don't write it.

Note

1. I introduce this item by walking around the class, asking students if they have ever heard of an "alot," and I follow up with the preceding suggestion. Incidentally, although I have occasionally seen *alright* in print, I have never seen *alot*.

Are/Our

To Get It Right: Remember the sentence: "They *are our* best friends." Articulate it carefully, and you will hear the difference, a difference that the separate spelling of the two words reflects.

Note

1. Even well-educated people usually do not distinguish these two words in normal speech. It doesn't make a great deal of difference in speech, but in writing, the error is an embarrassment.

Brake/Break

To Get It Right: Associate *brake* with the slowing or stopping of motion or with the device that has that effect. Otherwise, use the *break* spelling.

Notes

1. The *American Heritage Dictionary* has six different entries for *brake*. Most of them, however, are rarely used words. *Break*, in contrast, runs for two full columns and has dozens of meanings.
2. *Break* is very common as a word initiator in compound words: *breakage, breakdown, breakout, breakup,* and so forth. In *breakfast,* it has an uncharacteristic sound.

Capitol/Capital

To Get It Right: Capitols usually have domes. For all other meanings, write *capital*.

Cite/Site/Sight

To Get It Right: *Cite* is related to *citation*, which you may be familiar with through research papers—or the traffic court. *Site* is a *place*, such as a *website* or *campsite*. *Sight* refers to one of the senses and to seeing, which we do with that sense.

Compliment/Complement

To Get It Right: Try remembering *I complimented Ida.* Use the *e* spelling in the middle of the word for all other uses.

Note

1. A compliment is an act of courtesy or praise. Complement has a wider range of meanings, which is why we suggest students remember the former.

Could of, Would of, and Others

To Get It Right: The word you use in conversation after *could, would, should,* and so on, sounds like *of,* but it is actually a contracted form of *have.* When you write, always use *have* (or *'ve*).

Wrong:	You should of warned me.
Right:	You should have warned me.
Informal:	You should've warned me.

Notes

1. Some might consider this error, which Hairston (1981) labels "very serious," a status-marking error. I remember clearly making it myself until about eleventh grade; I simply never realized that it was an error. (Or perhaps I wasn't ready to learn that it was one.) At any rate, I vividly recall my eleventh-grade English teacher telling me that I should *never* use *of* after words like *could, should,* and *would,* and I never did it again. (The fact is that one could of course use *of* after a word like *could.* I just did it.)

2. Here is the lesson plan I use to teach this item:
   Begin by telling your students that they have in their minds a list of nine words, all of which do the same job of work. I take the risk of saying that if I give them just two of them, they will be able to generate the other seven, and I offer them *will* and *would.* Sometimes, I get a word that does not belong to this list of what grammarians call the *modal auxiliaries.* It's invariably an auxiliary of another ilk, such as *do.* I compliment such answers, without listing them on the chalkboard, where I put the others. My students have never failed to generate the following words:

   will, would, can, could, shall, should, may, might, must

   (For a complete list of modals, one would add *ought to, used to, dare,* and *need,* the latter pair being more common in the United Kingdom than in the United States. However, only the ones listed above—and some of them only in restricted circumstances—are followed by *of* in student writing.)

Next, I point out that these words are normally followed by verbs in their base form and let the students fill in the examples:

will write	shall find	can sing	may listen	must finish
would go	should stop	could win	might end	

Now, inserting the word *have* between the modal and the verb we obtain:

will have written
would have gone   could have won
shall have found   may have listened
should have stopped   might have ended
can have sung   must have finished

You might wish to call attention to the fact that the form of the main verb changes here, but the important next step is to ask students to pronounce these combinations, as in rapid speech. The answers are, truly:

will of ('ve) written
would of ('ve) gone   could of ('ve) won
?shall of ('ve) found*   may of ('ve) listened
should of ('ve) stopped   might of ('ve) ended
?can of ('ve) sung*   must of ('ve) finished

*These are more common in the negative: shall not of ('ve) found, can't of ('ve) sung.

The *'ve* sounds exactly like *of*. Thus, it's easy enough to write that word.

When students *see* this *of/'ve* confusion, they are more likely to correct themselves in the future. Sometimes, I have found students subsequently writing "would've" in their papers. If it's in dialogue, that's perfectly all right, but I tell them that most of us English teachers prefer *have* in other kinds of writing.

Council/Counsel/Consul

To Get It Right: *Council* refers to a governing body of some sort, such as a city council (or a student council). *Counsel* refers to advice, the kind of thing a guidance *counselor* gives. A *consul* is an officer in the foreign service of a country.

Except/Accept

To Get It Right: If you pronounce these carefully, you will never confuse them. Remember: "Everyone *except* me must *accept* some blame."

Notes

1. Normally a preposition, *except* is sometimes used as a verb meaning "to exclude." We've all seen those signs that warn "No twenty or fifty dollar bills excepted," meaning that they are accepted. This is an interesting double negative.
2. *Except* has the noun form *exception*.

It's/Its

To Get It Right: If in context you mean "it is" or "it has," write *it's*. If you do not mean one of these, write *its*. (NB: Never write *its'*.)

(It's/Its?) time to leave.	The cat ate (it's/its?) dinner early.
(It is) time to leave. (Yes)	The cat ate (it is) dinner early. (No)
Therefore: *It's* time to leave.	Therefore: The cat ate *its* dinner.

Notes

1. Sentences must always be read *in context*.
   It's the truth. (It is the truth. Right!)
   Its truth is obvious. (It is truth is obvious. No way!)
2. If students are unsure what meaning they intend—for instance in a sentence like "It's true"—ask them to make the sentence emphatic by stressing the *-s*:
   (It's/Its) right. *Means*: It *is* right. *Therefore*: It's right.
   (It's/Its) right hand is hurt. *Does Not Mean*: It is right hand.
   Therefore: *Its* right hand . . . is correct.
3. Nearly all textbooks and handbooks ignore the fact that *it's* sometimes means "it has." But ignoring this fact won't make it go away. Consider the following sentences. Isn't the second as natural as the first?
   It's difficult to pass algebra. [It's = It is]
   It's been difficult to pass algebra. [It's = It has]

Know/No and Knew/New

To Get It Right: *Know* and *knew* are the present and past forms, respectively, of the verb *to know*. If you're talking about knowing, write them. If you write *no* and *new* instead, your audience will think you are illiterate.

Led/Lead

To Get It Right: *Led* refers to the action of leading performed in the past. It is also the form to use after *has*, *have*, and *had*. For all other uses, regardless of pronunciation, use *lead*.

Notes

1. The l-e-a-d spelling has multiple meanings and two distinct pronunciations. That is why we focus attention on *led*.
2. Students sometimes miss the contracted form of *have*. Note the following:
   a. She's led us well. (She *has led* us.)
   b. You've led me astray. (You *have led* me.)

Loose/Lose

To Get It Right: Remember the phrase, *loose laces*, and whenever you need to decide whether to write *loose* or *lose*, let the pronunciation of *loose* in the phrase guide you. (The eyelets in the shoes suggest the double *o* of *loose*.) "Loose laces lose races" is a terrific mnemonic sentence.

Notes

1. *Loose* is the opposite of *tight* and has an *s* sound. *Lose* is the opposite of *win* and has a *z* sound. *Lose* also means "to have no longer."
2. This is an extremely difficult item for many people. I once had an editor of a professional magazine change my perfectly correct *loose* to *lose* (in the phrase, "turn the students loose").

Past/Passed

To Get It Right: Remember that *passed* is the past tense of the verb *pass*. Use it when you need a verb in that tense or after the verb markers *have*, *has*, and *had*. At all other times, write *past*.

Precede/Proceed

To Get It Right: To precede means "to go or come before," as in *a* precedes *b* in the alphabet. If you mean anything other than this, spell the word with two *e*'s in succession.

Notes

1. *Precede* has three *e*'s, one after each consonant except the first.

2. *Precede* can mean to go or come before not only in space or time but also in rank or position.

3. *Proceed* is often jargon and can be omitted: We proceeded to meet for three hours—We met for three hours.

4. It's a fact that the root of both these words is the Latin word for *go* (*cedere*). Thus, the real difference between them lies in their respective prefixes.

Principle/Principal

To Get It Right: If the word you want refers to a ru*le* in some way, write princip*le*. Also, use the *-le* spelling for the idiomatic phrase, *in principle*. For all other uses, write *principal*.

Notes

1. Focus is on the *-le* spelling because that is the more restricted term. The *-al* spelling is used for both nouns and adjectives in a wide range of meanings.

2. Elementary students are commonly taught, "The Princi*pal* is your *pal*"— whether she is or not, presumably. This is fair enough, but it doesn't go very far. A good single-word synonym for *principal* is "main." The principal of a building is the main person in the building. The principal in a bank account is the main sum. The principal in a trial is the main contestant, or one of them. One's principal reason for doing or thinking something is one's main reason.

Stationery/Stationary

To Get It Right: Remember that station*ery* is what we write a lett*er*s on (or a place where we can buy such material). If this is not your meaning, write *-ary*.

Note

1. *Stationery* is somewhat more limited in its meanings than *stationary*; therefore, we focus on it. Students may be familiar with *stationary*, however, from such common terms as *stationary bike* or a *stationary front* in weather.

Than/Then

To Get It Right: Pronounce aloud the sentence in which *than* or *then* is used, putting emphasis on the word. You should be able to hear the difference and thus write the correct form.

Example Sentences: 1a. I'd rather spend time with my friends *than* go shopping.

                           1b. I'd rather spend time with my friends, *then* go shopping.

                           2a. We first had waffles, *then* cereal.

                           2b. I like waffles better *than* cereal.

                           3a. If you work hard, *then* you will succeed.

                           3b. She worked harder *than* she had ever worked before.

Notes

1. In general, *then* means "next." In general, *than* is used in making comparisons, where it typically expresses an alternative.

2. In my experience, the *if . . . then* (conditional) relationship is particularly difficult for students; they often write *if . . . than*. Encourage them to remember that it's always "i before e"—*if . . .* then. If they know the abbreviation *i.e.,* it could serve as the memory aid: i(f) . . . (th)e(n).

They're/Their/There

To Get It Right: "Test" the word, in the order shown, beginning with *they're*, which means "they are." Test next for *their*, which is a word like *the* and must be followed by a word it is working with (usually a noun). If the word you want passes neither of these tests, write *there*.

Example Sentences: 1. _____ always welcome here.

                           2. The students began _____ homework early.

                           3. I found my homework over _____.

                           4. _____ are bugs in our mugs.

Example 1 passes Test 1; therefore, *They're* is the right answer.

Example 2 does *not* pass Test 1: One cannot say, "The students began they are homework early."

Example 2 does pass Test 2: The students began their homework. Therefore, *their* is the correct answer. (*Homework* is the word *their* is working with.)

Examples 3 and 4 cannot pass either Test 1 or Test 2. Therefore, *there* is the correct answer for both.

   N.B. for poor spellers: All three words begin t-h-e. Thus, *thier* must be a misspelling.

Notes

1. The words are in order from least to most complex. It's useful for students to memorize this order.

2. In the Collins Cobuild corpus, *their* is immediately followed by the noun it is working with 67.5 percent of the time. In nearly all other cases, only one modifier separates *their* from its noun.

3. *There* is two words. *There-1* is an adverb, roughly meaning "in that place." *There-2* has no lexical content; it's just a way of getting a sentence started when one does not wish to begin with its subject. For example, in Example 4, *in our mugs* tells where the bugs are, not the word *there*. Indeed, one can write "There are bugs there," which even more clearly demonstrates the distinction between the two *there*'s.

4. Although *there-2* is sometimes not recognized as a separate entity in grammar books, it is actually slightly more common than *there-1* in the Collins Cobuild corpus.

5. This error ranks third in the Kantz/Yates survey.

Threw/Through

To Get It Right: *Threw* is the past tense of the verb *to throw*. Use *through* for all other meanings. Remember "The pitcher *threw* the ball *through* the strike zone."

Two/Too/To

To Get It Right: Always first ask if you are referring to the number. If so, *two* is always correct. Next, be aware that *too* is two distinct words. It may mean "also." Alternatively, it may be used simply to intensify the degree of the word that follows it. In that use, you can often substitute *very* for it.

too-1: Are your parents coming, too? (*too* = also)
too-2: I was too busy to call. (*too* = very)

If neither the number nor either meaning of *too* is involved, write *to*.

Notes

1. In everyday speech, we commonly distinguish *too* from *to* by pronouncing the former with a long "u" sound. Indeed, we *must* pronounce it that way. *To* is normally pronounced with a schwa sound. However, if *to* is stressed for any reason, it, too, may receive a long "u" sound.

2. *To* is actually two words. Its most common use is as a preposition, but it is also frequently used as an infinitive marker. Here are both uses in the same sentence:

We expect to [infinitive marker] go to [preposition] school today.

We're/Were/Where

To Get It Right: Pronounce the word distinctly, and you will easily distinguish among these three.

Note

1. The *were/where* pair ranked as the eighth most irritating error in the Kantz/Yates survey.

Who's/Whose

To Get It Right: If in context you mean "who is" or "who has," write *who's*. If you do not mean one of these, write *whose*.

Someone (who's/whose) friendly makes friends easily.
Someone *who is* friendly makes friends easily. (*Right*)
Therefore: Someone *who's* friendly makes friends easily.
No one (who's/whose) seen the Rockies can forget them.
No one *who has* seen the Rockies can forget them. (*Right*)
Therefore: No one who's seen the Rockies can forget them.
Anyone (who's/whose) car is double parked will get a ticket.
Anyone *who is* car is double parked will get a ticket. (*Wrong*)
Therefore: Anyone *whose* car is double parked will get a ticket.

Note

1. This item directly parallels *it's/its*. It may therefore be good to teach them together. See additional notes for *it's/its*.

Write/Right

To Get It Right: Remember "Did you *write* the *right* answer?" Writing is something we do with our *w*rists.

Notes

1. *Rite* also rhymes with this pair, but it has a specialized meaning.
2. *Wright* has an even more specialized meaning (one who makes or builds something), but it comes into play in compounds like *playwright*, which must be distinguished from compounds like *copyright*.

You're/Your

To Get It Right: *You're* means "you are." If that is the intended meaning, write *you're*. Otherwise, write *your*.

Notes

1. This is a very easy item for anyone who stops to think about it. Alas, many of us do not, including me. I find I must constantly monitor myself. (I use my own test.)

2. In the Kantz/Yates survey, this item ranked second in the list of errors that most irritated college teachers. Only nonstandard verb forms out-ranked it. Don't ask me why.

4
Writing: Liberating the Student Writer

I can't write five words but that I change seven.
—DOROTHY PARKER

Learning to write is learning to use all one's mind in making.
—JAMES SLEDD

Errors count, but not as much as most English teachers think.
—MINA SHAUGHNESSY

James Gray (former director of the Bay Area Writing Project and of the National Writing Project) once said that writing is the hardest thing we ask kids to do in school. Teaching writing may well be the hardest thing we ask teachers to do. And measuring how well students write is probably the hardest thing we ask assessors to do. In this chapter, I begin by discussing these topics, then move on to treat a number of composition myths, with the hope that dispelling them will free student writers to focus on meaning.

The Myth of a Golden Age

Let's take a close look at issues relevant to the teaching, learning, and assessment of writing, beginning with the following comments on student writing. Can you guess when each one was made?

Statement A

Every year the complaints become louder that the investment in English teaching yields but a small fraction of the desired returns. Every year teachers break down, resign, perhaps become permanently invalided . . . every year thousands of pupils drift through the schools, half-cared for in English classes where they should have constant and encouraging personal attention . . . to emerge in a more or less damaged linguistic condition, incapable of meeting the simplest practical demand upon their powers of expression. Much money is spent, valuable teachers are worn out at an inhumanly rapid rate, and results are inadequate or wholly lacking.

Statement B

Generally speaking, the writing of literate Americans is pretty bad. It is muddy, backward, and self-strangled. Almost any college professor . . . will agree that his students' writing stinks to high heaven. It is a rare student who can write what he has to say with simplicity, lucidity, and euphony. Far more graduating [college] seniors are candidates for a remedial clinic than can pass a writing test with honors.

Statement C

The pupils could parse and construe sentences and point out the various parts of speech with great facility, repeating the rules of grammar applicable in each case, yet were utterly unable to put this theoretical knowledge to any practical use, as they showed when called upon to write an ordinary English letter.

When I read these statements at a school board meeting many years ago, I noticed the heads of several members nodding in vigorous agreement: "Yes, kids *today* can't write. It isn't the way it used to be." Then I revealed when the statements were written, and the board members learned that used to be never was.

The C statement obviously comes from a very early date, since it has presumably been a long time since students could parse sentences and repeat grammar rules "with great facility." It was, in fact, written in 1873 by Francis Wayland Parker, to the school board of Quincy, Massachusetts. However, in spite of their great facility in grammar and ability to parse sentences, the students *couldn't write an ordinary letter in English.*

The A statement was made more than a generation later—by a high school English teacher, Edwin Hopkins, in the first issue (1912) of *The English Journal.* His students, too, apparently couldn't write an ordinary letter in English, since Hopkins describes them as "incapable of meeting the simplest practical demand upon their powers of expression."

The middle statement was made by Donald Lloyd, a college English teacher and linguist, in *The American Scholar*, in 1952. The writing of his *college students* stank to "high heaven."

Considering how *few* young people went to school during these earlier periods (even in 1952, only 55.3 percent graduated from *high school*), what can we expect when more than eighty-four percent of Americans age twenty-five or older possess a high school diploma?

The notion that there was a golden age when students wrote much better than our students do today is false. In fact, the Overseers of Harvard College's Standing Committee on Composition during the 1880s and 1890s roundly and regularly condemned the writing of Harvard undergraduates. Sue Carter Simmons says that the students in the required English A composition course "were perceived to be remedial, even 'illiterate'" (1995, p. 328).

Who were these illiterate Harvard students of the 1880s and 1890s? They were the children of a privileged minority of extremely well educated, exceptionally literate parents. The sons of the best and the brightest, they would have attended the premier secondary schools in the nation. We're talking about the professor's son, the minister's son, the governor's son, the senator's son. Graduates of Harvard, then as now, include some of the most illustrious names in America. And *they* were rotten writers?

It seems unlikely that they were truly rotten writers, yet according to Nancy Sommers, Director of Expository Writing at Harvard, who has read the work of Harvard students both from the end of the nineteenth century and at the beginning of the twenty-first, current students are "much better" writers than their predecessors of over a century ago. They have more complex ideas, write more complex arguments, and make more complex use of sources (McCarroll, 2001).

All right, so there wasn't a golden age, but isn't it true that students today could and should write better than they do? Well, what's "better"? Richer content? More logical? Fewer errors? Better organized? Stronger voice?

Merely to ask these questions is to reveal how difficult and diverse are the tasks we set for students and for teachers. "Richer content," for one, depends on what the student knows about a subject and what connections he can make between that and other things he knows. It also depends on whether he is *willing* to use all his mind in making, as James Sledd put it in the quote that opens this chapter. And "more logical"? Have you ever taken a course in logic—or statistics, perhaps—and seen some students get A's without trying and others fall by the wayside regardless of how hard they worked? How much can we fairly ask of English teachers, who are already more heavily burdened than nearly all of their colleagues?

It is no wonder that we so often focus on trivia and retreat to formulas in the teaching of writing. Beyond English A, those beleaguered Harvard writing instructors of a century ago had to grade essays their students did for other courses and were thus "positioned to evaluate writing solely in terms of superficial correctness"

(Simmons, p. 329). Moreover, that is what the Overseers wanted as well; according to James Berlin, they commonly focused on errors in spelling, grammar, usage, and even handwriting (1984, p. 6). And so heavy was what we today call the "paper load" that instructors could not afford to be ill, because if they stopped reading papers for even one day, they would fall too far behind to catch up (Simmons, p. 346).

But bad as the situation was and is, our reliance on formulas and focus on correctness make matters worse rather than better. Our formulas—use topic sentences, never use passives, vary sentence openings—deny students the resources routinely used by good writers, and our concentration on correctness puts the emphasis on the least important aspect of good writing.

The Jonathan Edwards Syndrome

Some years ago, Bill Strong made an NCTE presentation entitled "Sinners in the Hands of an Angry Pedagogue," in which he created a brilliant new term for a familiar disease: *the Jonathan Edwards syndrome*. In a sermon entitled "Sinners in the Hands of an Angry God," the Puritan minister Jonathan Edwards had held his own congregation over the terrifying pit of Hell and portrayed a God of Wrath so vividly that the pews must have shaken. Strong's analogy is between this wrathful Calvinistic god and the typical English composition teacher: As we read and react to student writing, *we* are like that wrathful god, we cannot keep our flaming pens off the papers of our sinning congregation. I know all about it, I'm a victim of the disease myself.

How do you react to student writing? Following are two passages written by fifteen-year-olds. How much editing do they need? Read carefully the introductory remarks before you evaluate the pieces.

Passage A was written by a ninth grader. It is a full paragraph near the end of a six-hundred-word impromptu essay that was written in class within a sixty-minute time limit.

Passage A

Success against the odds; a possibility, but sadly a rarity. People can be what they want to be, but it's an uphill, steep climb, and who's to say you won't lose your grip and fall, no matter how skilled a climber you are. When the very ground you stand on begins to pull you down, with no intention of stopping until you are a corpse, you need a pole to grasp, a foothold. Only by never capitulating can you climb those footholds into the sky towards the elusive pinnacle of success.

The following is a single sentence extracted from a brief discussion of King Henry VIII. It was written at leisure, by a fifteen-year-old student in her own home.

Passage B

It is however but Justice and my Duty to declare that this amiable woman [Anne Boleyn] was entirely innocent of the crimes with which she was accused, of which her beauty, her elegance and her sprightliness were sufficient proofs, not to mention her solemn protestations of innocence and the King's character; all of which add some confirmation, though perhaps but slight ones when in comparison with those before alleged in her favor.

I have distributed Passage A in a workshop and had English teachers rip it to shreds, most of them rating it a D or F. I've tried Passage B only with individuals. Reactions to it vary widely. Many think it is antique and want to change the diction; almost all readers would break it into at least two sentences. It has been called a "dreadfully long run-on." Responders have offered numerous "corrections" of both passages.

The key for me is that both these were written by *fifteen-year-olds*. Moreover, the first of those fifteen-year-olds was working with a severe time limit. Have you ever tried to write a six-hundred-word essay in an hour? When you were fifteen, were you capable of writing a single seventy-word-long sentence that flowed as comparatively smoothly as Passage B does?

If you think these kids were rotten writers and you focused on the errors, your Jonathan Edwards' syndrome index is high. The first paragraph was part of an essay that was declared the *best* ninth-grade essay in the entire Commonwealth of Pennsylvania, in a writing contest that was judged by high school and college English teachers. The second passage was written by Jane Austen.

Actually, I have cheated a little with my test passages. They contain no spelling errors, no fragments or run-on sentences, no serious grammatical errors or nonstandard usage. What would the results have been if they had? Kids who make those kinds of errors are typically *beaten up*. It's not a whole lot different than it was in the eighteenth and nineteenth centuries. Remember the motto of Winchester, where Robert Lowth studied when he was fifteen: "Learn, Leave, or Be Beaten."

Today, in most schools teachers no longer beat kids physically, but too often we return writing assignments looking as if they had been graded on a battlefield. And, of course, most students simply leave them there. (This is also frequently an indication of how little they have *invested* in what they have written.) I'm sure most of us want to be perceived as friendly to students, but that's not the impression conveyed by the bloody paper, however well intentioned our corrections may be.

Some Consequences of the Focus on Writing Errors

One of the major discoveries of Donald Graves and his colleagues was how important *self-confidence* is to the developing writer. How is this self-confidence nourished? What kills it? Following is a paper written by a student for the Pennsylvania System of School Assessment (PSSA) Writing Test. She was writing to a prompt that asked her to narrate an experience that she dreaded but that turned out not nearly as bad as she had expected. The time limit was sixty minutes.

Read the paper first for its overall effectiveness. Then read it a second time, hunting for errors.

> Sweet sixteen. Ahhh . . . driver's license, car, new found freedom and independence. These were the words which came to my mind on my sixteenth birthday. My parents paused my jubilation though when they uttered the words <u>they</u> associated with sixteen years old: get a job. The sheer thought of blindly going out and talking with strangers about my future employment status was absolutely terrifying. Rejection? Let's not even go there.

> My mom helped me compile a resume of my experience (5 years of baby sitting) and my activities and various awards. She had me get dressed up, dropped me off at a strip mall, told me to fill out some applications, and she'd be back in an hour. It was the longest hour of my life.

> The first place I went into was a card shop. I smiled at the woman who gently informed me that they weren't hiring. Okay, I thought, move along. I thanked her and went on to the video store. Yes, they were looking for applicants. So I filled out an application (talk about tedious) and left my resume. I had gotten four more applications done by the time my mom came around again.

> About three days went by without any word, when out of the blue came a call from Loafer's, a family-owned bread company. They wanted to interview me as soon as possible. My stomach was in knots as the questions were fired at me from a lanky guy partially hidden behind a stained white apron. He seemed about as friendly as I was nervous, extremely. He told me he would call the next day.

> It turned out I was exactly what they were looking for and I was to start training next week. Finding a job wasn't nearly as traumatizing as I thought it would be. Everyone experiences rejection at some point in their life. I learned about many things as far as the job-application process is concerned, as well as that it's not always a bad thing to just tackle your fears and go for it. My mother's favorite line is, "With freedom comes responsibility."

For me, for friends who have scored the paper, and for those who originally scored it for the Data Recognition Corporation (DRC), this is a first-rate paper. Moreover, those who read it for content—as we normally read things—notice relatively few errors. But read a second time, *looking for errors*, here is what one Jonathan Edwards' syndrome victim drudged up:

- Three sentence fragments: the first, second, and penultimate "sentences" of the first paragraph
- Two uses of parentheses: in paragraphs two and three
- A missing hyphen: "new found"
- Incorrectly used relative pronoun: "which came to my mind" (should be *that*)
- Misused word: "My parents *paused* my jubilation"
- Redundancy: omit *status*
- Failure to spell out a number: "5 years"
- Missing commas surrounding "though"
- Missing comma, before "and" in first sentence, last paragraph
- Four contractions: *Let's, she'd, weren't, it's*
- Unnecessary word: "She had me get dressed *up*"
- Faulty parallelism: In the penultimate sentence of the second paragraph, "said" should be inserted after "and"
- Sentence beginning with a coordinating conjunction: "So"
- Verb Usage: "had gotten . . . done" should be "had finished"
- Use of the passive: "were fired at me"
- "Weak" word: "*about* as friendly"
- Pronoun agreement: "Everyone experiences . . . in their life" should be in "*her* life"
- Wordiness: "as far as the job-application process is concerned"
- Use of "your": should be "one's"

Counting each instance separately, these amount to twenty-five errors. How many did you discover?

I recently gave this essay to a group of fifteen teachers who were not English teachers whose assignments spread across the grades from K to twelve. They found *fifty-one* separate "errors," and this total included only a handful of the English teacher's errors. Most weren't truly errors in any technical sense. The teachers—a lively, intelligent group—wanted words cut, *and*'s reduced, (unnecessary) commas added, run-ons (that weren't run-ons) corrected, and so on. They would have been surprised to hear it, but they seem to have been infected by the eighteenth-century attitude, "No errors are so trivial, but they deserve to be mended."

Altogether then, nearly seventy distinct errors were identified in this 354-word paper, one of the best eleventh-grade papers in the state of Pennsylvania. That's an error every five words. Is it any wonder that we breed people who are afraid to write? Any wonder that so many people think that "kids can't write"? By the way, according to the study of Connors and Lundsford, error rates of college writers have not changed since at least 1917 (1988, p. 406).

In his seminal essay, "The Phenomenology of Error," Joseph M. Williams (1981) addresses the question: How do we know whether something is an error? Think about it: If you found, say, only three or four errors in this student's essay, should you count the others? In what sense is an unremarked error erroneous? Moreover, some of the presumed errors actually help the writer achieve her voice. Eliminate the fragments, the parentheses, and the contractions, for instance, and you stiffen the tone. Should these, then, be counted as errors?

But to return to my point about student self-confidence: Put yourself in this student's place. If you had written this paper and it was returned to you with all these "errors" noted, what would be the effect on your self-confidence as an author? And how would that, in turn, affect your future attempts at composition?

Recognizing the Difficulty of Writing Well

Human beings are all more or less competent speakers. Why shouldn't we be competent writers, too? To begin, contrast the hours we have spent practicing speech to the hours spent practicing writing.

And writing *must* be practiced. It must be practiced even by those who appear to be gifted writers. It must be practiced much more frequently by those who are not. The "persuasion" that underlies Mina Shaughnessy's book about teaching basic writers (BW) is this:

> BW students write the way they do, not because they are slow or non-verbal, indifferent to or incapable of academic excellence, but because they are beginners and must, like all beginners, learn by making mistakes.

We don't correct the speech of eighteen-month-old children. Well, in terms of the writing experience they have had, many eighteen-*year*-old college students are in the same position.

Complaints by writers themselves about the difficulty of their craft are legion. Hugh Blair, the famous eighteenth-century rhetorician, says in his *Lectures on Rhetoric and Belles Lettres*,

> If . . . his own style shall be thought open to reprehension, all that he can say is, that his book will add one to the many proofs already afforded to the world, of its being much easier to give instruction than to set example. (1853, p. iv)

In chapter 32, the narrator says of *Moby Dick* that the whole book is but the draft of a draft, and adds "Oh, Time, Strength, Cash, and Patience" (p. 140), making it clear that Melville himself is speaking. Dorothy Parker's comment about not being able to write five words without changing seven will strike a chord with nearly every writer who has ever worked at getting his thoughts on the page. Finally, my favorite of all is a comment by John Steinbeck (1990), to his editor, Pascal Covici:

> A book is like a man—clever and dull, brave and cowardly, beautiful and ugly. For every flowering thought there will be a page like a wet and mangy mongrel, and for every looping flight a tap on the wing and a reminder that wax cannot hold the feathers too near the sun. (p. 180)

(If you haven't found any wet and mangy mongrels in these pages, you can thank the editors.)

If writing is this difficult for professionals, why are we so hard on kids? My guess is that it's partly because we English teachers are too familiar with the greatest writers ever to take pen in hand. Judged from that point of view, how could any youngster measure up? We need to recognize that great writers:

- Probably have considerable in-born writing ability
- Have an animus that drives them to write well
- Are able to sit on the seat of their pants for prolonged periods
- Have written millions more words than any student
- Commonly are paid for their writing
- Have had heaps of feedback from sympathetic friends, editors, agents, and fellow writers
- Don't worry about making errors
- Have copyeditors and proofreaders who protect them from the grossest errors

And even with all this, the work of professional writers is far from error-free. In fact, in an article published in *College Communication and Composition*, Gary Sloan (1990) showed that professional writers make nearly as many errors as Freshman English students. (If you subtract the students' spelling errors, the pros made *more errors*.) He reached this conclusion by counting as an error everything so treated in the English handbook he was using in his course. Naturally, the professionals had no spelling, apostrophe, capitalization, or subject-verb agreement errors, but they outscored the students in the verbiage category by nearly two to one, and on triteness by fifteen to one. Interestingly, the professionals had nearly as many comma errors as the students, and they wrote almost three times as many sentence fragments.

However well intentioned our motives, we English teachers must not hold students to the standards of professional writers. I'm tempted to attribute more baleful motives to non-teachers for their condemnations of student work. As I have noted, the Overseers at Harvard were particularly critical of the boys' errors in spelling, grammar, usage, and handwriting. When they looked at essays from Wellesley, behold, they found that the *daughters* of the college professors, the ministers, the political leaders didn't make those kinds of errors. Were the Overseers pleased? Not at all. They criticized the women for being "less robust and less self-assertive" in "thought and form." They asserted that *none* of the women's essays (specifically in 1897) "indicate any especial capacity for observing, or attempt, in pointing out defects and difficulties, anything which might be termed a thoughtful solution for them" (quoted in Crowley, 1998, p. 77). Could there possibly be an anti-youth bias here?

Activity 4–1: Great Student Writing

Goal: To demonstrate that students of today are capable of writing quite well.

Procedure

Good writers, whether intentionally or intuitively, vary sentence length. They are adept at writing very short sentences *and* very long ones. To demonstrate how variety functions, duplicate and discuss this passage, written by the venerable William Strunk, Jr.

> If those who have studied the art of writing are in accord on any one point, it is on this: the surest way to arouse and hold the attention of the reader is by being specific, definite, and concrete. The greatest writers—Homer, Dante, Shakespeare—are effective largely because they deal in particulars and report the details that matter. Their words call up pictures. (2000, p. 21)

A forty-word sentence leads to one half as long, and then the paragraph climaxes in a five-word stroke. Any student can write a five-word sentence: the really mature student writer has to be a master of the *smoothly written* forty-, fifty-, even sixty-and-above-word sentence.

A splendid source of good student writing is *The Concord Review*, published by Will Fitzhugh, who has been editing this anthology of essays on historical topics, quarterly, since 1987. (Substantial prizes are given to the best student work. You will find many examples on his website: tcr.org.)

The following sentences, all but the last two of which were drawn from *The Concord Review*, were written by high school students. Duplicate them, and ask your students to comment on (1) their length and (2) their effectiveness. Keep in mind that the sentences have been taken out of context. (The last two sentences were written by a precocious not-quite-eleven-year-old.)

1. By deciding that the discriminatory draft registration law was necessary for the government's purpose of using the draft to raise troops (the

Court did not address the constitutionality of the policy that only men were allowed to participate in combat), the Court upheld the existing policy and lent credence to the claim that women would lose this one remaining piece of protective legislation if the ERA were passed. (68 words) (Sara A. Newland, *Equal Rights Amendment*, 1999, an Emerson Prize Winner)

2. Though the Altair was modest in its constitution and abilities, a Harvard College student, Bill Gates, saw potential in the computer, and with the help of his friend, Paul Allen, dropped out and set to work creating BASIC software to transform it into a functional device. (46 words) (Priya Bhatia)

3. The damaging effects of the practice of these principles, especially in the field of education, became evident to the second-generation utilitarians, like John Stuart Mill; indeed, Mill considered himself to have been personally victimized by a misguided application of Benthamite educational ideas, which he believed alienated human beings from art and emotion. (53 words) (Patrick Bradley)

4. The school community recognized the war as a huge political event, and were conscious of the delicate balance that resulted from a war of such magnitude, but treated it with the same spirit that they had applied to all of the political events of recent years, perhaps because of the feeling of superiority and isolation that affected the United States at that time. (62 words) (James Engelhofer)

5. Immediately after the war, the Federal government gave a land grant to the Penobscots in gratitude for their role in the war, but the state [of Maine] soon forgot the promise of the young Federal government and they gave the land to unpaid revolutionaries to start families in the 1780s. (48 words) (Amy McNulty)

6. Despite the complexities present in any study to define the extent of the killing in Nanking and the reasons behind it, when taking into account the barbarity manifested by the Japanese soldiers, the historical and ideological framework in which the incident took place, and the consequences of the Second Sino-Japanese War as a whole, the Rape of Nanking corresponds most closely to a partial genocide with some characteristics of a massacre and some attempts to achieve a total genocide. (80 words) (Damaris Yeh)

7. In 1950 Congress refused to expand the public housing programs, despite the increased demand for public housing due to the displacement of low-income families by Urban Renewal programs, and the large migration of blacks to the North. (38 words) (Madeleine Clare Elish)

8. But few people have challenged such regimes with rebellion as far-reaching and as fundamentally radical as Anne Hutchinson, who rejected the entire principle of publicity on which Puritanism had been founded, both by embracing doctrines that exalted privacy and by working in the private sphere to disseminate those doctrines. (50 words) (Jessica Leight)

9. I believe that the link between English and German is stronger than that linking English with Spanish and French, because English and German evolved mainly from Latin, although English does have connections with Latin and other romance languages as well. (40 words) (Nicholas Allred)

10. All of the schools of philosophy over time from the Empiricists, to the Romantics, to the Existentialists, had roots in the famous Greek philosophers: Democritis, Aristotle, Socrates and others, whose thoughts started in motion the flow of ideas about the world. (41 words) (Nicholas Allred)

Note: While there are some minor infelicities in these sentences, I believe you could easily find as many in articles published in any scholarly journal.

Testing Writing Ability

The National Assessment of Educational Progress (NAEP) has been evaluating student writing (in grades four, eight, and twelve) every four years since 1969–1970. If anybody knows how to do it, they should. Yet in April 2000, they removed the long-term trend studies from their website, because of "lack of confidence in the data." (They have not withdrawn their other test results.) I cite this not as a criticism but to illustrate how truly difficult such assessments are.

It's important to observe that NAEP Writing scores are based on timed essays—usually just twenty-five minutes—and that the organization itself maintains that they are a test of "best first-draft" writing. It's an interesting issue as to whether first-draft efforts should even be called tests of *writing*. Clearly, they are not writing tests if we accept Sledd's notion of using "all one's mind in making." How grand and honest it would have been had they spoken of tests of *drafting* from the start.

I know from experience in writing prompts for my home state that we try very, very hard to dream up topics that *all* students can respond to in meaningful ways, but I also know from reading student responses to the prompts, that we often fail. (How can you write about "your favorite possession" if you don't have one? See the next section.) Since Graves and his colleagues demonstrated long ago that the *best* predictor of how well kids write is not their skills, but their emotional invest-ment in and knowledge of their topic, I don't believe that individual scores of a single brief test are reliable.

For a tough but fair and thorough critique of state writing assessments, see George Hillocks, Jr., *The Testing Trap.* For broader criticism Susan Ohanian's *One Size Fits Few* (1999) and Alfie Kohn's *The Case Against Standardized Testing* (2000) are excellent.

The unreliability of brief, single-topic tests was demonstrated dramatically to me several years ago. I call this real-life incident the Anecdote of the Writer and the Fighter. Both the writer and the fighter are real persons, but I have changed a few details to keep them anonymous.

The Anecdote of the Writer and the Fighter

The writer was just that, a professional writer, a person who had published many articles and books over a generation-long career that began when she was still in her early twenties. The fighter was just that, a semi-professional boxer (though he had retired from the ring some years before this incident and was currently a teacher). The boxer had published nothing and had no ambition to do so. He would have happily admitted to anyone that he had no skill as a writer.

Both were at a day-long workshop where they were being instructed in holistic scoring. At one point, the instructor turned the tables on the audience to demon-strate how kids feel during a writing test. She asked the audience to write a piece of their own, using the prompt on which the students had written: "Think of a favorite possession. Describe it and tell how you acquired it. Discuss why it is your favorite."

The writer couldn't think of a favorite possession, but she finally settled on a skirt she had owned as a teenager. It was a particularly "fancy" skirt, and one she had purchased with her own money. The piece sounded doable, but the more she wrote, the less she was able to convince herself that she really cared a great deal about her topic. Yes, the skirt had mattered to her a good deal at the time, but since then, she had had many more articles of clothing that she cared for more. At one point, she decided that she'd have to throw the whole thing out and begin anew with a different possession. However, when she looked at her watch, she realized she did not have time to change topics. Instead, she continued writing more "pop-pycock," as she put it. By the time she had finished, she had written something that, by her own estimate, was "barely worth a C." She was relieved that the instructor did not ask her to read it aloud or share it with anyone else in the room.

After some discussion, stimulated by the leader, of how the group had felt about the experience, the boxer, who was sitting in the back, raised his hand. "Can I read my piece aloud?" he asked. The writer, who knew him slightly, was amazed, but she was even more amazed when she heard what he had written: "I'd give any student who wrote that a straight A," she admitted.

What's wrong with this picture? Nothing. The writer had no investment in her topic; she was merely fulfilling a duty, drudging through an assignment imposed by someone else. Nothing came from inside her. The boxer, in contrast, had written about a gift his father had given him when he was a little boy, a gift that he had with him at that moment, a moment when his father was lying on his deathbed in a local hospital. The piece was packed with details and depth of feeling.

The Importance of the Topic: Some Personal Experiences

Because the topic matters so much, tests that attempt to judge a writer's ability by a single essay on an unfamiliar topic are inherently unfair. And, ironically, such tests are even more unfair to "good" writers than they are to "poor" writers, according to Graves' research (1983), which showed that the variability of good writers is much broader than that of poor writers. Put in quantitative terms, it's easier for an "A" writer to write a "C" paper than it is for a "C" writer to write an "A" paper. The Kincaid study, done at Michigan State University in 1953, came to the same conclusions (see Braddock, Lloyd-Jones, and Shoer, 1963).

Have you ever tried to write on an unfamiliar topic under the conditions we impose on students? I have, on three occasions. On the first one, I managed to get a serendipitous topic and I came close to a four average, the highest possible score, using Pennsylvania's standards—close to, but I didn't quite make it. My judges were myself and a roomful of teachers whom I asked to evaluate my effort.

On the second attempt, I barely made a three average. In not one of the five categories measured by the PSSA Writing Assessment—focus, content, organization, style, and conventions—did I score a four. It was a remarkably pedestrian effort.

Finally, on a third try, I just went on and on and on and produced a shapeless mass that I would have been too embarrassed to submit to anyone for evaluation.

So how good a writer is Ed Schuster, measured by a state test? Well, if you strike an average, I'm about average. If you use my best effort, I'm on the edge between an A and a B. If I were unfortunate enough to have had only one shot and it was my third, I'm a miserably bad writer. The *facts* are that (a) I'm the kind of writer who needs time to do his best work, and (b) even collectively, the tests are measures of my *drafting* ability, not my writing ability.

In reflecting on these three experiences, I made the following additional observations:

1. On all three attempts, I neglected to proofread. (On the second and third, I also had *no desire* to proofread.) Yes, I, who am forever preaching to students that they must proofread; I, who write those words in huge

capital letters on the board of the classroom whenever my students write themes in class; I neglected to do it myself.

2. Revision, global revision, the kind of *re-seeing* that most of us writing teachers say is so important, is not possible, given typical time limits and other conditions. *Consider:* You have before you this mass of material that you've written. (It was in pencil, in two of my cases, and thanks to my poor handwriting, not a pleasure to reread.) It's spread over three or four pages. You don't have a computer. You don't have time. How or where do you even *begin*? Are you supposed to scratch out whole hunks? Draw lines from one piece of the mass to another, to transfer material? Write notes in the margins? It's distasteful even to think about. A few years ago, the NAEP gave some students an extra twenty minutes to work. They discovered that these students did no better than those who didn't have extra time. That's not a surprise to me.

3. When writing in these test situations, conferencing is out of the question. Yet I've never known a writer who failed to solicit feedback.

4. Often, on such tests (including the NAEP), students are not allowed to use dictionaries or other references. I wouldn't think of writing anything more serious than a shopping list without a dictionary at my elbow—not to mention the spell-check and thesaurus on my word processor.

I know that portfolios have their own drawbacks, but if we're interested in measuring *writing*, they are worlds more reliable and valid than these tests of drafting ability.

Authentic Assignments, Real Voices

The best two composition teachers I have ever had had three things in common: (1) They made interesting assignments, (2) they gave choices, and (3) they responded primarily to what I had to say. My teacher in the second half of my senior year in high school always found intellectually engaging topics and gave us enough *choices* within those that I always had plenty to talk about—though often not without some research. In responding to one of my essays, my teacher in the second half of my freshman year in college wrote, "I believe I will see you in print someday." Nothing ever did more to improve my writing, *including* the mastery of some mechanical problems that I had had up to that point. Thereafter, *I* wanted to get things right.

As a teacher, I have always given students choices, and I've also often asked them to address real people in the real world. I've even gone so far as to require that they submit to me an addressed, stamped envelope with their final draft, which I sent to the addressee. I frequently do my assignments myself and have been rewarded on several occasions. To one letter of complaint, I received from General Electric a new motor for a dishwasher that had broken down, even though the machine was out of warranty. (On the telephone, the best I could do was an offer of $50 toward the purchase of a new motor.) On another occasion, I was given a free bottle of wine at my next visit to a New York restaurant.

Students have come up with some marvelous real-world writing ideas of their own, and on a couple of occasions they have had letters published in newspapers. Several times, they have succeeded in getting college officials to make exceptions to regulations. Some really powerful letters have been attempts to persuade friends to stop smoking or taking drugs. One freshman persuaded her father to assume her mother's role for a day, and he did. An adult student I once had made a powerfully persuasive marriage proposal to a man in another state (which he did not accept).

One of the best things that happens when students are given authentic assignments is that they discover that they have voices of their own. What a contrast to the phony voices they have to assume when they write what John Mayher (1990) calls "dummy-runs" and George Hillocks, Jr. (2002) calls "blether," after a Scots word for unfocused, rambling, thoughtless talk. I'll never forget a presentation Tom Romano (1992) made at an NCTE convention some years ago. (You can read it yourself in *Teacher as Writer*, edited by Karin Dahl.) As a high school senior, he wrote a poem to a girl who had rejected him, but knowing only classical English poetry, he wrote it in what amounted to a foreign tongue. I recently read *Writing with Passion* (1995) by this restless seeker of a better way, and recommend it to you.

Here are a few additional suggestions for helping students become better writers:

- Have them *read*, particularly good modern prose. And don't be afraid to assign some reading that is "over their heads."
- Have them *write* often, giving them sympathetic but honest feedback.
- Do everything you can to demonstrate that writing is a skill worth acquiring.
- As often as possible, write with your students.
- In responding to student writing, always put content first *and* second.
- Don't overlook imaginative writing.
- Encourage linguistic experimentation, and don't penalize students if it doesn't work.
- If breaking "rules" leads to better writing, let students break them.

And speaking of breaking rules, that is what the rest of this chapter is about. As in other chapters, I try to base my recommendations on my observations of what real writers actually do.

Allow Free Use of *I* and *You*

In most secondary schools in the United States, we concentrate on the teaching of *transactional* writing. The parties in the transaction are *I* (the author) and *you* (the reader). Isn't it natural to admit as much by allowing student writers to use these pronouns? Yet here is a glimpse into a New York eighth-grade classroom where the kids are preparing for state tests. A student suggests that she might begin answering an essay question by writing, "Using details from the selection, I'm going to . . . ." The teacher's comment: "Stay away from *I*." And here's a statement from Andy Russell, a tenth grader from a good suburban high school in Pennsylvania: "We're not *allowed* to use *I* and *me* in *anything* we write, unless the teacher says it's supposed to be autobiographical." I wish these comments were untypical.

Let's look at the contrast between what professional writers do and the common teacher/textbook advice regarding *I* and *you*.

Do Professional Writers Avoid First-Person Pronouns?

Nearly twenty years ago, when I wanted to discover how frequently writers wrote in their own voice—that is, used *I, me, my, mine*—I grabbed the book of essays on my desk and counted. It was *The Riverside Reader* (1981), and the essays were grouped under the following headings: Narration, Description, Process Analysis, Comparison and Contrast, Division and Classification, Cause and Effect, Persuasion and Argument, Essays for Further Reading, and Essays for Reading and Writing. I mention this table of contents to demonstrate that we're not talking about personal narratives or descriptions. There were fifty essays (or excerpts from them), collected by Joseph Trimmer and Maxine Hairston, all chosen as models of first-rate expository/persuasive prose.

How many of them were written in the first person? Would you believe eighty-two percent?

Even knowing that, I was amazed when I counted the number of essays in *The Best American Essays of 2001* that used first-person singular pronouns. There are twenty-six essays in the collection. *Every one* is written in the first person. Further, in four of them *I* (*my* in one case) is the first *word* of the essay. And altogether, sixteen (61.5 percent) use *I* or *my* in their first *sentence*. One could take this as a sign that we live in an age of egoism. Or in an age of authenticity. The fact is that if you consult any collection of essays written by Americans from the very beginning of our country, you will have some difficulty finding essays that do *not* rely on the first person singular, or occasionally, the first person plural. Franklin, Paine, Jefferson, Irving, Douglas, Emerson, Poe, Thoreau—all wrote in the first person.

For a real ear-opener, read a number of essays from an anthology like *Best American Essays*, then turn immediately to a collection of essays that eschew the first person—such as a pile of student research papers. When I did this, I was amazed at the difference in tone, and the difference in reading pleasure. Even in the *best* student research papers, the voice too often seems to be coming from a nonperson.

Often, we excuse the advice to avoid *I* and *you* by saying that the advice applies to *formal writing*, but does writing get more "formal" than the work of the essayists I have mentioned? What is *formal* writing anyway? I used first-person pronouns in my dissertation, and I've never written anything more formal than that. Thomas Jefferson used the first person in his inaugural addresses. Abraham Lincoln used it in the Emancipation Proclamation. Just what sort of writing are we training our students for?

Avoidance of You

You is a somewhat different matter. *You* may refer to the reader, but it also may refer to some other *you*. Reynolds Price uses it, for example, to refer to his Godchild in his essay, "Dear Harper: A Letter to a Godchild About God." And, of course, *you* may refer to an impersonal someone. (I admit that I find it upsetting if I can't tell *which you* a writer intends.)

Harbrace has been fighting the impersonal *you* for decades, saying that "some writers" prefer not to use it in a "formal situation," and using for many editions, the same illustration of its supposed ill use: "The study of dreams has become a significant and respectable scientific exploration, one that can directly benefit *you*." What should the author (Patricia Garfield) have written? *A person? Someone? One?*

In fact, impersonal *you* was common well before the first Freshman English course was offered. Here it is in Henry David Thoreau's *Civil Disobedience* [italics mine]:

> A common and natural result of an undue respect for law is, that *you* may see a file of soldiers, colonel, captain, corporal, privates, powder-monkeys, and all, marching in admirable order over hill and dale to the wars, against their wills, ay, against their common sense and consciences, which makes it a very steep march indeed. (1849, p. 512)

Even those expert at the work of usage use *you* impersonally. Margaret Nicholson, for example, was Head of the Publishing Department of Oxford University Press and became the editor of *A Dictionary of American-English Usage*, which was based on Fowler's *Modern English Usage*. In the first paragraph of her Preface to that book, she writes [italics mine]:

> Fowler not only teaches *you* how to write, he is a demon on *your* shoulder, teaching *you* how not to write, pointing out and exhibiting, with terrifying clarity, *your* most cherished foibles. (1957, p. v)

Try substituting *one* and *one's* for her second-person pronouns. You won't get very far before throwing up your hands.

Let the Verbs Fall As They May

Students are commonly advised to avoid *be* verbs (because they are static), and to use "strong" or "vivid" verbs instead. I am not opposed to the spirit of this advice, and I confess that I myself have sometimes gone verb-hunting in the hope of enlivening my prose. However, in self-consciously seeking verb substitutes, students often adopt an artificial voice.

Before illustrating this, let's look concretely at what good writers actually do. I examined works by two classic essayists—George Orwell and E. B. White—and added an essay by a modern American female writer whose work I admire, Barbara Kingsolver. Here are their main verbs:

Orwell (first fourteen sentences, "Politics and the English Language")

admit	lies	is	think
assumed	is	becomes	is
is	is	makes	come back
share	become	is	hope
follows	take	is	are

White (last three paragraphs, *The Elements of Style*)

takes	is	sympathize	pattern
remarked	believe	are	recall
is	write	seek	was
have	is	is	be
were	is	plays	say
is	made	start	get
is	been	is	said
knows	is	make	received
determine	be	is	is
			live

Kingsolver (first three paragraphs of "Stone Soup")

rank	includes	dare	attended
turns	is	change	made
leap	am	remain	was
hug	take	are	played
is	thinking	had	think

Here is a summary of their *be* verbs:

Orwell	(8 of 20)	40%
White	(17 of 37)	46%
Kingsolver	(5 of 20)	25%

It does not appear that these authors are going out of their way to avoid *be* verbs. How many of their other verbs are "vivid" or "strong"? *Any?*

Students can also write well without recourse to vivid verbs and without avoiding *be* verbs. If you turn back to "Ah . . . sweet sixteen," (page 94) you will find that the verbs are as natural as the kid who wrote it. Twenty-five percent are variations of *be*.

Even in a successful descriptive narrative, the writer may let verbs fall as they may. Following are all the main verbs in an eighth-grade student's essay, "Fox." The Northwest Regional Education Labs uses it to illustrate excellent concrete writing. The student's essay is packed with good specific details, but what about its verbs?

get along	is	had	had	raced	was
am	looks	shaded	pick	stop	trying
am	live	sit	gets	went	was
walk	was	soak	freeze	went	drowning
are	allowed	soak	got out	went	was
is	was	jumped	was	felt	counts
believe	look	was	chase	pull	owe
is	run	invite	went	grabbed	passed
stands in	were	was	riding	hit	got
do	build	catch	patroling	saw	bought
was	was	blew	was	named	christened
take	lie	was	blew	blew	given
was	passed	be	admired	respected	did
come	moved	visit	be	was	

There are eighty-three main verbs altogether. Twenty-eight percent are parts of *be*. Of the others, perhaps two or three might be described as vivid. Yet this essay is an excellent piece of writing, particularly with respect to style and voice.

Here are two successive sentences from the student's second paragraph, along with a vivid-verb-seeker's revision:

Student: If another person or dog would even look like going near that place, Fox and I would run them off in a frenzy. There was a lot of rocks around, so I could build forts and traps.

Revision: If another person or dog would even *advance* slightly toward that place, Fox and I would *impel* them to leave. Rocks *abounded*, so I could *construct* forts and traps.

It's not a simple matter, because we *do* want students to develop their vocabularies, but experienced teachers know what too often happens when kids try to use words they don't really understand. In this revision, we hear a strained, unnatural, less sincere voice, and one that would be quite out of character with the real voice in the rest of the essay.

Activity 4–2: Effective Verb Choices

Goal: To demonstrate that good writing depends little upon avoiding *be* verbs or choosing vivid/strong verbs to replace them.

Procedure

Ask students to choose poems or brief passages of writing that they admire, and have them underline the main verbs. This may best be done in small groups, so they can help one another identify the verbs. Then count how many of the main verbs are *be* verbs, and discuss how strong or vivid the others may be. As an illustration, I offer one of my favorite poems, by Wallace Stevens:

Debris of Life and Mind

There is so little that is close and warm.
It is as if we were never children.
Sit in the room. It is true in the moonlight
That it is as if we had never been young.
We ought not to be awake. It is from this
That a bright red woman will be rising
And, standing in violent gold, will brush her hair.
She will speak thoughtfully the words of a line.
She will think about them not quite able to sing.
Besides, when the sky is so blue, things sing themselves,
Even for her, already for her. She will listen
And feel that her color is a meditation,
The most gay and yet not so gay as it was.
Stay here. Speak of familiar things a while.

Altogether, more than half (54.5 percent) of the main verbs in the poem are *be* verbs. The others are words my golden retriever would know: *sit, rising, brush, think, sing, listen, feel, stay,* and *speak.* And this poem is not an isolated instance, especially not of Stevens' later poetry.

Forgivable Unforgivable Sins: Fragments and Run-ons

There is no mistaking the fact: the backbone of books published by our most reputable firms, the backbone of the prose in our leading newspapers, the backbone of articles in our most highly reputed magazines is the complete, well-formed English sentence. But make no mistake about this either: Fragments and run-ons are also used in all of these sources, and if we deny students the use of sentence fragments and run-ons—particularly the former—we are denying them a key literary resource. Yet if you consult most handbooks, you will find these structures treated as unforgivable sins. *Harbrace,* for example, discusses them immediately after its opening section, "Sentence Sense," implying that students who write fragments and run-ons lack that sense. This is often not true.

Most of the fragments written by the students I have taught bear little resemblance to those illustrated in handbooks, and students who write run-ons frequently construct perfectly well formed sentences: they just don't punctuate them conventionally. But let's take up these unforgivable sins one at a time.

Sentence Fragments

It is true these days that many textbooks allow for *some* use of sentence fragments, but the attitude of *Harbrace* is typical. Students are expected to look for fragments during the proofreading phase of composition and are cautioned, "Have a good reason for any sentence fragments you allow to stand" (1998, p. 32). What is a "good reason"? Of the four illustrations, three are labeled "informal use."

It doesn't seem to occur to the authors that one might purposely create a fragment during the proofreading phase. Here is part of a letter of complaint that I had written, following one of my own writing assignments:

> The author [of the article] bemoans the fact that she did not dress properly for the elegant, three-star restaurant; she talks about a 10-year-old celebrating her birthday and dressed better than she was; and she notes that the waiters—thankfully, she says—did not sing happy birthday to the little girl. She has nothing to say about the food.

I revised the last sentence to read, "Not a word about the food." To me, this fragment was much more forceful than my first-draft version.

Fragments have been used, and condoned, for a very long time. Even the conservative William Strunk, Jr., says "It is permissible to make an emphatic word or expression serve the purpose of a sentence" (1959, p. 7). He also permits fragments in dialogue. As for E. B. White, he couldn't write without recourse to fragments. Here are a few examples from his Style section in *The Elements of Style* (1959). All of these follow sentences that end in periods.

- But why not? (p. 53)
- A matter of ear, a matter of reading the books that sharpen the ear. (p. 63)
- Why? Because it sounds more violent, more like murder. (p. 64)
- Clarity. Clarity. Clarity. (p. 65) (*Note:* This *opens* a paragraph.)
- Answer: then be one. (p. 70)
- And so must the young writer be. (p. 71)

I don't know for certain whether one would find more fragments in WEAP sources today than yesteryear (probably would), but here is a sampling from the February 17, 2002, *New York Times Magazine* section—forty-three years after the first edition of *The Elements of Style*. I have provided some context for each fragment and have italicized them.

- There's nothing untoward about charging for your labor; you have no obligation to be a volunteer snow patrol. (*Although it would, of course, be wrong to ice down the road to drum up customers.*) (Randy Cohen)
- Judson Welliver . . . elected to use nouns . . . *progress* and *prosperity. No powerful, state-defining adjective.* (William Safire)
- Yet in the district of Abdulgan . . . people were still dying. *Not just a few people, but hundreds, even thousands.* (Michael Finkel)
- . . . his fate in the 21st century is difficult to imagine. . . . *Or possibly not.* (Maria Russo) (*Note:* This fragment opens a paragraph.)
- This time nobody got around to it either. *Except Mark.* (Philip Higgs)
- In pop music, the Beatles were a selection band: you couldn't just replace Paul McCartney. *The Temptations? Pure treatment. . . .* (Bruce Headlam)

Note the range here. We have a subordinate clause, a noun phrase, a negation followed by a noun phrase, a negation introduced by a conjunction, a prepositional phrase, and a Q and A. And *these were no trouble at all to find.* Check out your own favorite magazine.

Activity 4–3: Creating Effective Fragments

Goal: To lead students to discover how fragments may be used effectively.

Procedure

The following are effective uses of fragments by professional writers. In each case, I have supplied, as a "b" version, the full sentence that the writer might have used.

Duplicate the sentences, and have students compare the versions, discussing why the fragment is more effective (unless they don't find it so).

1a. It [a van] wasn't on the road; it was on the shoulder. My shoulder. (Stephen King, *The New Yorker*)

1b. It wasn't on the road; it was on the shoulder. It was on my shoulder.

2a. When I got home, I emptied the envelope onto the floor, amazed at what spilled out. Bits and pieces of strangers' lives, hundreds of markers of personal histories. (Rebecca McClanahan, *The Southern Review*)

2b. . . . at what spilled out. There were bits and pieces of strangers' lives, hundreds of markers of personal histories.

3a. They are people who have no homes. No drawer that holds the spoons. No window to look out upon the world. (Anna Quindlen, *Living Out Loud*)

3b. They are people who have no homes, no drawer that holds the spoons, and no window to look out upon the world.

4a. In midafternoon a curious darkening of the sky, and a lull in everything that had made life tick. (E. B. White, *One Man's Meat*)

4b. In midafternoon there came a curious darkening of the sky, and a lull in everything that made life tick.

5a. Make the newsroom happier. Which I took to mean create harmony and a climate that rewards achievement. (Max Frankel, *The Times of My Life and My Life with The Times*)

5b. Make the newsroom happier, a statement which I took to mean create harmony and a climate that rewards achievement.

6a. Obviously you need to build in some kind of rules, but what kind? Prescriptive rules? (Steven Pinker, *The Language Instinct*)

6b. Obviously you need to build in some kind of rules, but what kind? Should they be prescriptive rules?

7a. Tempura has foot-long bamboo skewers sticking straight up out of it and sits in a gorgonzolo cheese sauce. Sounds weird, tastes great. (James Quinn, *Philadelphia Magazine*)

7b. Tempura has foot-long bamboo skewers sticking straight up out of it and sits in a gorgonzolo cheese sauce. It sounds weird, but it tastes great.

8a. Who can calculate the losses left by Sept. 11? So many wounds to the hearts of families, so many wounds to the souls of New Yorkers, so many wounds to the peace of Americans. (*The New York Times*, first page, 4/11/02)

8b. Who can calculate the losses left by Sept. 11? There were so many wounds to the hearts of families, so many wounds to the souls of New Yorkers, and so many wounds to the peace of Americans.

9a Then when *do* we need them [rules]? When our wires get crossed and we
   fail to understand one another. (Patricia T. O'Conner, *Woe Is I*)

9b. Then when *do* we need them? We need them when our wires get crossed
    and we fail to understand one another.

10a. Why did I write it down? In order to remember, of course, but exactly
    what was it I wanted to remember? (Joan Didion, "On Keeping a
    Notebook")

10b. Why did I write it down? I wrote it down in order to remember, of
    course, but exactly what was it I wanted to remember?

Activity 4–4: Good Fragments, and Bad

Goal: To help students distinguish between effective and ineffective fragments.

Procedure

Following are some examples of fragments written by high school students and college freshmen. Duplicate them, and have students

- Compare them with the effective fragments of the professional writers of
  Activity 4–3.
- Discuss which of these fragments may be rhetorically effective and why
- Discuss why the ineffective fragments are ineffective

1. Sitting at the kitchen table telling my dad about my week at the beach.
    I was interrupted by my boyfriend.
2. After we swept the carpet. The only remnant of our party was the large
    trash bag.
3. It's upsetting to have to sit through AP Chemistry. While the track star's
    coach gets him out of classes.
4. With the Internet, tons of information can be accessed. Such as information for school reports and homework.
5. After a long journey we finally arrived. The fresh air, the beautiful trees,
    the sun glittering on the lake.
6. Ah, sweet sixteen. Ahhh . . . driver's license, car, new found freedom
    and independence.
7. If I would be allowed to make a law I would let skaters skate wherever
    they want. As long as they don't hurt anybody.
8. My mom and me debated it because we had paid $40 for the tickets.
    That we wouldn't be able to use.
9. I don't know very many ways teachers can improve learning in the classroom. I guess just little things.
10. Over the weeks that we have been away from each other. I have realized
    something.

Run-ons, Comma Splices, Rambling Sentences

In their study of three thousand graded college essays (1988), Robert J. Connors and Andrea A. Lunsford found that the *comma splice* ranked as the sixth most common error marked by teachers and the eighth most common error committed by students; the *run-on* or *fused sentence* was listed as the sixteenth most common error to be marked by teachers and the eighteenth most common student error. Since the errors are related, it's obvious that, taken together, they are perceived to constitute a major problem in student writing.

Many issues are involved here, the first of which is a matter of definition: How do teachers define the terms *run-on* or *fused sentence*, and how do they define *comma splice*? It depends on whom you ask.

For nearly twenty years, I participated in interviews of candidates for the position of secondary school English teacher. For twenty years, I asked the question, "What is a run-on sentence?" In twenty years, not a single candidate was able to answer that question with any degree of comfort or confidence.

Before condemning our teacher-training institutions, however, let's confront an interesting irony: There is widespread agreement among English teachers over both the nature of run-on errors and their seriousness. The problem is almost exclusively one of terminology. Consider the following illustrative sentences:

Labels	Illustrative Sentences
Error X:	Error X contains no punctuation between two sentences it is a serious error.
Error Y:	Error Y separates two sentences with only a comma, it is a less serious error.
Error Z:	Error Z is an error of another kind, and it is still less serious, but nevertheless most writing teachers criticize it, and they will mark down students who commit this rhetorical error.

There they are—X, Y, and Z. How would *you* name them? Here are eleven choices, all of which may be found in textbooks. I have put them into three categories, based on what appear to be common characteristics.

Group One	Group Two	Group Three
a. Run-on sentence	d. Comma splice	h. Rambling sentence
b. Run-together sentence	e. Comma fault	i. On and on sentence
c. Fused sentence	f. Comma blunder	j. Psychological run-on
	g. Comma error	k. Stringy sentence

It would be handy if these groups were mutually exclusive, and we could agree to use a single term from each group, but it's not as simple as that.

114

Here are the National Assessment of Educational Progress (NAEP) categories and definitions:

Run-on Sentences:

Fused—A sentence containing two or more independent clauses with no punctuation or conjunction separating them. [Error X]

Comma splice—A sentence containing two or more independent clauses separated by a comma instead of a semicolon or a coordinating conjunction. [Error Y]

On and on—A sentence consisting of four or more independent clauses strung together with conjunctions. [Error Z]

(Quoted from Ballator, Farnum, and Kaplan, 1999, p. 71)

Notice that NAEP uses *run-on* as a *cover* or *umbrella term*, with our X, Y, Z errors each given a separate identity beneath that cover. Neat as it may seem, this approach runs counter to a great deal of practice. In surveys of errors, for example, it is customary to treat run-ons and comma splices independently of each other. (See Hairston, 1981; Connors and Lunsford, 1988; and Kantz and Yates, 1994. These same surveys ignore Error Z.)

In her effort to narrow focus and limit terminology, Constance Weaver separates the comma splice from the "run-on or fused sentence" (1996a, pp. 106, 108). That is, for her, *run-ons and fused sentences are the same thing*. This is also the approach of Rei R. Noguchi (see the fourth chapter in *Grammar and the Teaching of Writing*) and of Mina Shaughnessy, among many, many others.

Here is the crux of the matter, then. We have two choices:

Choice A	Choice B
Run-on sentences	Run-on/fused sentences
Fused sentences	Comma splices
Comma splices	Rambling sentences
Rambling sentences	

(I have adopted the term *rambling sentences* from *Writers INC* and used it instead of NAEP's *on and on*. I have also *added* it to Choice B.)

Which of these choices do grammar textbooks favor? Unfortunately, some of them muddy rather than clarify. The most dominant texts of the last half century were, as we have seen, *Warriner's English Grammar and Composition* (originally *Warriner's Handbook of English*), which began in 1946; and for college, the *Harbrace College Handbook* (originally called the *Harbrace Handbook of English*), first published in 1941.

Warriner did not use the term *comma splice* at all in his Book One, and in most of the later editions that I have seen, it can be found only in the index (which read: *Comma splice* equals *Run-on sentence*). Generally, Warriner discussed *run-on sentences*, using that term to describe *both* Error X and Error Y.

Harbrace seems to have adopted Choice A, treating fused sentences and comma splices as separate entities. In most of the editions I've seen, it does not use the term *run-on*, except in the index. (In the 1998 edition, it says that a *fused sentence* is "also called a *comma fault* or *run-on sentence*," thus distinguishing *comma faults* from *comma splices*, and leaving this English teacher ready to transfer to Math.)

One result of this is that *the same error* may be called a run-on in our secondary schools and a comma splice in our colleges. I have frequently asked my college freshmen what a comma splice is. Almost universally, they do not know.

But not all textbooks are equal. Lynn Quitman Troyka (1999), for example, clearly adopts Choice B, using *run-together sentences* and *comma splices* as her two major categories. She also mentions that *run on* and *fused* are alternative descriptions of *run-together* sentences and that *comma fault* is an alternative to *comma splice*. Perhaps she will lead the way to clarity for other handbook writers. In this book, I have adopted Choice B.

(*Note:* College handbooks tend to ignore *rambling sentences*. They do so, I believe, because this is a different kind of error and because college students are much less likely to write rambling sentences than are younger kids.)

When Do Professional Writers Use Comma Splices?

Run-ons are sometimes found in poetry, where the line itself serves as a sort of punctuation, but in general, professional writers do not use run-ons. Comma splices are another matter. Although they do not use the term, Strunk and White (2000) actually *prefer* comma splices to conventionally punctuated sentences "when the clauses are very short and alike in form, or when the tone of the sentence is easy and conversational" (pp. 6–7). They give several examples, among which are "Man proposes, God disposes," and "The gates swung apart, the bridge fell, the portcullis was drawn up" (p. 7). Quirk et al. also note that commas may be used to separate sentences (coordinate clauses) "especially when the clauses are short, parallel, and (often) three in number" (1985, p. 1616). One of their examples is "Sometimes he would chuckle softly to himself, sometimes he would grunt to some invisible onlooker."

The more progressive college handbooks these days admit that professional writers sometimes intentionally separate independent clauses with a comma. Here, for example, is Lynn Quitman Troyka's statement on the matter (italics mine):

> Professional writers *often* intentionally separate two independent clauses with just a comma. The clauses in these comma splices *never* have internal commas and are normally short, balanced, and closely related in meaning. (Instructor's Edition, 1999, p. 277)

In my looking, I have not found that nonfiction writers intentionally use comma splices "often," though fiction writers may. The statement that the clauses in comma splices "never" have internal commas is not true. (You will find examples below.) The clauses *are* often short, balanced, and closely related in meaning, however.

Are there some guidelines for the effective use of comma splices? I have found two.

Irene Brosnahan (1976), in a *College English* article, summarized the conditions that govern professional writers' use of comma splices as follows:

- The clauses are short, and are usually parallel.
- The meaning cannot be ambiguous.
- Rhetorically, the sentences convey rapid movement or emphasis.
- The usage is General or Informal.

Brosnahan also discusses the semantic relationship between the clauses, finding that it is usually one of paraphrase, amplification, repetition, opposition, or addition.

Simple illustrations would be the usual rendering of Julius Caesar's *veni, vidi, vici:* "I came, I saw, I conquered"; or Charles Dickens' "It was the best of times, it was the worst of times." In these illustrations, heavier punctuation or conjunctions between the elements would retard the desired rapidity of movement. Clearly, there is no ambiguity in either of these.

As an example of where a comma splice should *not* be used because it would create ambiguity, consider this common error:

I spoke with him yesterday, however, he was incommunicative.

The meaning could be either A or B:

A. I spoke to him yesterday, however. He was incommunicative.
B. I spoke to him yesterday. However, he was incommunicative.

In "Unravelling the Comma Splice," Anne L. Klink (1998) lists five "widely accepted" kinds of comma splices (pp. 96–97). (I have used her illustrations.)

1. Between independent clauses of parallel form:

   They were invented as a convenience to the flesh, they have become a chain for the spirit.

2. Between independent clauses in series—often in conjunction with 1:

   She sighed, she cried, she almost died.

3. Between independent clauses in periodic sentences where larger divisions are marked by a semicolon:

> If speech and cinema are akin to music, writing is like architecture; it endures, it has weight.

4. In sentences of the "not only" . . . ("but also") type where the coordinating conjunction is omitted:

> I not only work all day, I work all evening too.

5. Before and after tag questions, tag statements, and comment clauses:

> You can come, can't you?
> You can change it, you know.

Both Brosnahan's and Klink's articles are a good start, but as a glance at the professional examples in Activity 4–5 will reveal, their categories are not exhaustive. Klink's conclusion to her article is notable:

> We should accept that usage is flexible, and allow our students a freedom which more confident writers take for granted. Otherwise we are guilty of multiplying rules for the sake of detecting errors—and so justifying our own status as arbiters of correct English. (p. 98)

In my view, we should be somewhat less eager to promote student uses of comma splices than of fragments. However, I strongly urge that we declassify the comma splice as an unforgivable sin. It might even be better classified as a venial sin.

Activity 4–5: Effective Uses of Comma Splices

Goal: To teach students how comma splices may be used effectively.

Procedure

Duplicate the examples of effective uses of comma splices in the following list, and discuss them with your students. A good additional activity with some classes is to have the students create their own criteria of when comma splices may be used effectively.

1. I hardly knew him, he was so changed. (cited in Strunk and White)
2. The talk rose, it was of Jack. (E. Annie Proulx)
3. Kids grow, musical styles change, people keep inventing things, *Seinfeld* goes off, women get pregnant, men go bald. (John McWhorter)
4. Corky sits heavily in the old, creaking swivel chair at the desk, it's one of those hardwood chairs with the seat shaped to your buttocks. (Joyce Carol Oates)

5. There were still paintings hanging everywhere on the walls, some I recognized, others I did not. (Tracy Chevalier)

6. Dale's nickname is Murph, he's a big grizzly bear of a guy from Bradenton Beach, Florida. (Sebastian Junger)

7. Many of her opinions had doubtless but a slender value, many of her emotions died away in the utterance. (Henry James)

8. I loved to read, that was one of the reasons why I was a writer. (Chitra Divakaruni)

9. If speech and cinema are akin to music, writing is like architecture; it endures, it has weight. (Cited in Sheridan Baker, *Practical Stylist*)

10. A sudden gray rain swept the street, there was a stunning clap of thunder. (Ronan Bennett)

Activity 4–6: Good and Bad Comma Splices

Goal: To compare and contrast student comma splices with those of professional writers.

Procedure

Here are some comma splices written by students in the Pennsylvania System of School Assessment Writing Test. Have your students compare them with the comma splices used by the professionals, and discuss whether the students should have changed their punctuation.

1. That's not fair, other kids would probably pick on us because we're going to school and they are not.

2. I don't think a whole year of school should even be considered, it's bad enough we have only two months off now.

3. Natural dunes are bulldozed, sea oats are trampled, and what was once sand has now become cement.

4. I was scared, I thought the vocals wouldn't come out right, and I was afraid of people's reaction.

5. I am thankful that such a great invention was created, without it I can't even imagine how difficult life would be.

6. When I was about eight years old, I remember one day sister came in and told my mom she was pregnant, I was so mad.

7. I thought I wasn't going to be able to move, I felt stiff.

8. We work hard those ten months of school, we need a break.

9. A lot of students claim that they don't get enough sleep, well this is our chance to sleep late.

10. I feel school will always be somewhat boring, that is like a law written in stone, but I also feel that there are things that can bring life to a class.

Vary Your Sentence Openings—But Just a Little

Most of us like variety; it's the spice of life. But looking at the work of professional writers should convince almost anyone that variety of sentence openings is not the spice of good prose. It is instructive to ask why. But first, let's make the case for teaching students not to vary their sentence openings.

How Much Variety Is There in the Sentence Openings of Professionals?

Harbrace states that writing sounds monotonous when too many sentences begin the same way. It counsels that students should vary their openings by using the following items. (The Warriner clone, *Elements of Language*, has essentially the same list, minus the last two entries, and it warns against using coordinating conjunctions to open sentences.)

Adverbs
Adverbial clauses
Prepositional phrases
Coordinating conjunctions
Conjunctive adverbs (or transitional expressions)
Appositives
Verbal phrases
Absolute phrases
Introductory series of items

To determine how often professional writers use these openings, I first checked this list against a group of essays selected from two textbooks: The sixth edition (1997) of *The Bedford Reader* and volume 2 (1983) of *The Riverside Reader*. The authors of the essays I chose were William Buckley, Jr., Linda Chavez, Joan Didion, Maxine Hong Kingston, H. L. Menkin, George Orwell, Anna Quindlen, John Updike, Margaret Walker, and E. B. White. I purposely chose well-known writers, and an equal number of men and women. I also tried for some range of political views. In each case but one, I counted the first fifty sentences of the essay. (The exception was Kingston's essay, which begins with a long quoted story from her mother. I began where that story ended.)

This gave me five hundred sentences. However, I discounted fifty-four of these (10.8 percent) because they were different sentence *types*. Specifically, I excluded questions, sentence fragments, *there*-patterns, and commands. It seemed reasonable to discount these, since the possibility of varying their beginnings is so limited.

Of the remaining 446 sentences, here is the breakdown. The numbers in parentheses are the number of sentences.

Subjects (305)	68.4%
Prepositional phrases (37)	8.3%
Adverbials (36)	8.1%
Coordinating conjunctions (31)	6.9%
Adverb clauses (23)	5.2%

That makes a total of 96.9 percent of all sentence openings, leaving a pitiful 3.1 percent for all the remaining suggested types of openings. (Actually, it was even less than that because four of the openings had to be classified as miscellaneous—they were not on *Harbrace*'s list.) There were four conjunctive adverbs, three verbal phrases, one appositive, one series of items, and no absolute phrases.

Since I had purposely chosen several "classic" essayists here—writers who are long gone—I next decided to analyze a sample of current writers. I used the first fifty sentences from each of five prize-winning articles from *The American Scholar*. (These were, respectively, Anne Fadiman's "Mail," Francine Du Plessix Gray's "The Work of Mourning," Adam Hochschild's "India's American Imports," David Michaelis' "Provincetown," and Carlo Rotella's "Cut Time." All appeared in *The Best American Essays, 2001*, edited by Kathleen Norris.) Of the 250 sentences, I subtracted twenty-nine because they varied in sentence type. This gave me 221 sentences. Their openings were as follows:

Subjects (134)	60.6%
Prepositional phrases (28)	12.7%
Coordinating conjunctions (19)	8.6%
Adverbials (17)	7.7%
Adverb clauses (9)	4.1%

Completing the total, there were seven miscellaneous, five verbal phrases, and two conjunctive adverbs. I found no appositives, absolute phrases, or series of items.

Adding the two samples together but giving double weight to the first (since it had twice as many sentences), I arrived at the following rough tabulation of sentence openings:

Subjects	66.0%
Prepositional phrases	10.0%
Coordinating conjunctions	8.0%
Adverbials	7.5%
Averbial clauses	5.0%

These account for ninety-six percent of all sentence openings. In the entire 667 counted sentences, their openings included only eight verbal phrases, six conjunctive adverbs, and one each of appositives, absolutes, and items in series. I have analyzed the work of journalists, too, and found them even more conservative. What conclusions can be drawn from these studies?

Conclusions

The advice to vary sentence openings is *very bad advice* indeed. Professional writers open sentences with their subjects approximately two-thirds of the time. When they diverge from this, they choose from a limited number of options. This is not to say that students shouldn't use a wide variety of linguistic options, nor to suggest that they shouldn't occasionally experiment with them. But not in the subject position. In particular, straining to open sentences with structures like appositives, absolute phrases, introductory series, or even verbal phrases is extremely ill advised. Why?

In his discussion of cohesion and coherence, Joseph M. Williams points out that readers feel that a passage is coherent when they can quickly and easily identify the *topics* of individual sentences (1997, p. 110). He goes on to recommend that writers should

- Signal their topics by making them the subjects of sentences
- Locate most of those subjects close to the beginning of sentences, "not obscured by long introductory phrases" (p. 111)

With this advice in mind, consider this *recommended* example of a sentence opening from *Harbrace*:

Light, water, temperature, minerals—these affect the health of plants.

Out of context, one cannot be positive, but presumably the topic of this sentence is "the health of plants." It is not the subject, it is the object. And the reader's desire to know the topic is delayed until the very last words of the sentence.

And here's a recommended example of an appositive phrase being used as subject, taken from *Elements of Language*, Sixth Course (Odell et al., 2001):

An example of positive gravitropism, the downward growth of roots, occurs frequently.

Is there any reader anywhere who would find that sentence coherent?

Both *Harbrace* and *Elements* "publish" exemplary student writing in their texts. Here is my tabulation of the sentence openings of one such essay, "Playing Favorites: It Is All in Our Heads," written by Cody Keller, a student at Van Buren High School in Van Buren, Arkansas. It appears in *Elements* on pages 165–166. It had five uncounted sentences (three questions, a command, and a fragment), and thirty remaining sentences.

Subjects (27)	90.0%
Prepositional phrase (1)	3.3%
Adverbial (1)	3.3%
Conjunctive adverb (1)	3.3%

At least the authors of the handbook recognize good writing when they see it. I studied a few other examples of exemplary writing in these sources. The *least* frequent use of opening with the subject was 58.8 percent; the *most* variation in sentence openings was four.

Activity 4–6: Judging the Effectiveness of Sentence Openings

Goal: To help students see that sentences opening with unusual constructions are, generally, less effective than more straightforward ones.

Procedure
Duplicate the following sentence pairs, and discuss which of the choices is the better of the two. Some of the original sentences were written by students; others, by professionals.

1a. His father said that he could go to the game on Saturday afternoon if he first finished painting the fence.

1b. If he first finished painting the fence, his father said that he could go to the game on Saturday afternoon.

2a. An excellent example of modern architecture, the new city hall is a favorite tourist site.

2b. The new city hall, an excellent example of modern architecture, is a favorite tourist site.

3a. The bell to change classes having been sounded, we ran to our Spanish class.

3b. We ran to our Spanish class after we heard the bell.

4a. Coming to the city from far away and bringing it unusual gifts noticed only by a few sensitive souls, such as hay-fever victims, who sneeze at the pollen from flowers of other lands, the wind brings unusual gifts.

4b. The wind, coming to the city from far away, brings it unusual gifts, noticed by only a few sensitive souls, such as hay-fever victims, who sneeze at the pollen from flowers of other lands.

5a. I followed the curving road through the grounds, past the palace and busy visitors' parking lot, and around the periphery of the Pleasure Gardens.

5b. Through the grounds, past the palace and busy visitors parking lot and around the periphery of the Pleasure Gardens, I followed the curving road.

6a. The body and blood of Jesus, the wafer was then placed on my tongue by the priest.

6b. Then the priest placed on my tongue the wafer, the body and blood of Jesus.

7a. The design of Oak Hill Park was apparently modeled on the town of Greenbelt, Maryland, a model community built by the federal government in 1935.

7b. A model community built by the federal government in 1935, Greenbelt, Maryland, was apparently the model for the design of Oak Hill Park.

Don't Passively Avoid the Passive

Virtually all style advisors counsel writers to avoid the passive. The latest to weigh in is Stephen King (2000), who in *On Writing: A Memoir of the Craft* says, in italics, "*You should avoid the passive tense.*" Strunk and White state flatly, "Use the active voice." In his landmark essay, "Politics and the English Language," George Orwell (1946) gives six succinct rules for writing well; the fourth is "Never use the passive where you can use the active."

Well, first off, one can nearly *always* substitute an active for a passive. In spite of his own advice, Orwell uses passives in over a quarter of the first fifteen sentences of his article. Note that all can be made active. I have italicized his passive verb phrases.

Passives (Orwell)	Active Rewrites
It *is* generally *assumed* that we cannot . . . do anything about it.	People generally assume that we cannot do anything about it.
. . . bad habits . . . *can be avoided* if one is willing to take the necessary trouble.	One can avoid bad habits if one is willing to take the necessary trouble.
Here are five specimens of the English language as it *is* now habitually *written*.	Here are five specimens of the English language as we habitually write it.
These five passages *have not been picked out* because. . . .	I have not picked out these five passages because. . . .

E. B. White is equally "guilty." In the two opening paragraphs of the 1959 Introduction to *The Elements of Style*, he does not consistently use the active voice. In talking about *The Elements*, he writes " . . . as it *was known* on the Cornell campus," "the book *was* privately *printed*," and "it *was copyrighted* in 1918 by the author," all passives. How can one explain why these outstanding writers violate their own rule, and do it so often?

What is a passive in the first place? In a research study of nearly five hundred tenth-grade students at one of the school districts where I was English supervisor, we discovered that the students did not learn how to identify passives, even though this was a major objective of tenth-grade English. Scores on five multiple-choice questions regarding passives averaged 50 percent correct at the beginning of tenth grade and 51.2 percent correct at the end. (Since there were only four choices, a chance score would have been 25 percent correct.) In fact, the end-of-year results would have been negative, were it not for the results on a single question, which increased from 37 to 46 percent correct.

For many, many years I myself "taught" the passive, and then regularly counseled students to use it sparingly, but somehow they didn't seem to follow my advice. When this happened even with college juniors and seniors, it finally dawned on me that one reason might be that the students did not know passives when they saw them. I resolved to try to teach the passive so it would stay taught. Here is the lesson plan.

Activity 4–7: Mastering the Passive

Goal: To teach students how to identify passive sentences.

Procedure

1. Using six sheets of regular white paper or heavier stock, write the following words, one on each piece. I use a different color of pen for the last three.

   Your Name (if you don't mind making a fool of yourself—otherwise, write the name of a student volunteer)

   A (volunteer) Student's Name

   BEAT

   WAS

   BY

   -EN

2. Give the last three sheets to individual students at the start of the lesson. Tell them they will shortly use them to act in a drama.

3. Tell the class that they will watch a race and that at its conclusion, they should write a sentence telling what they saw.

4. Ask a student to volunteer as a runner to compete against you. (If you don't care to run, pick two students; if you do, be sure to wear sneakers.) Choose a starting point and a finish line and select another student to bark, "On your mark, get set, go." (To give the race greater distance, I sometimes start in the hallway.)

5. At the conclusion of the race, ask students what they saw. You should find that nearly all of them have written something like, "Carla beat Ed." (In my experience, no student has ever written, "Ed was beaten by Carla.") Give Carla the sheet with her name on it and take the sheet bearing your name. Select a third student to hold the "beat" sheet. Stand in order at the front of the room so the whole class can see the sentence, and tell the class, "This is an active sentence."

6. Let the students brainstorm a moment about a different way of *saying the same thing*. If they need help, suggest that they start their sentence with "Ed." You should find that nearly all students will come up with "Ed was beaten by Carla." Then explain that you would like to demonstrate in steps how they might have changed their sentences from "Carla beat Ed" to "Ed was beaten by Carla."

7. Standing in the original order, reverse the position of "Carla" and "Ed." If necessary, point out that Ed did *not* beat Carla. This is just a step in the transforming process, not a finished sentence.

8. Call on the students who have been given the cards, "was" and "-en," and ask them to stand in the appropriate places among the three of you—one before, the other after "beat." It's clear that this is still not a finished sentence.

9. Call on the student holding "by" and ask her to stand in the appropriate place—between "beaten" and "Carla," of course. Now we have a complete sentence.

10. Ask the *two students at the end of the sentence*—or ask the class—if they can think of another way of saying the same thing. They should see that the two students can simply disappear. (In some cases, it might be better to coach them in advance that when you ask for an alternative, they should walk out the door or sit down.)

11. Point out that you now have (two versions of) a *passive sentence*. They are quite different from the original active sentence, but they mean the same thing.

12. Finally, ask students to discover what the telltale signs of a passive sentence are. If your "was," "-en," and "by" sheets were in different colors than the others, the students will "see" that these three are *the passive-forming elements*.

LESSON FOOTNOTES

a. Since the *by* phrase can be omitted, it is, strictly speaking, the *be* form and the *-en* form that are the *necessary* signs of the passive. However, a *by* phrase is implied and can be mentally supplied if one wishes.

    b. *Was* is the passive sign in this sentence, but any form of the verb *be* may serve that purpose. One cannot assume that students know the parts of *be*: *am, are, is, was, were, be, being, been.* I know it's old-fashioned, but I often ask students to memorize these eight words, letting them know how helpful that may be for identifying passives.

    c. Technically, the *-en* form is known as the "past participle," and it more often ends in *-ed* than in *-en.* I do not use the technical term, preferring to point out that students need to use the form of the verb that they customarily use after *has/have*: I have *beaten*, she has *defeated*, someone has *bought*.

LESSON EXTENSION

Another illustration will help solidify the concept of the passive.

    A. You will need three additional sheets of paper. On them write DEFEATS, IS, and -ED.

    B. Ask students to write what happened in the race, using *defeats* as the verb, and as if they wished to convey the information in newspaper-headline format. (The answer you should get is "Carla defeats Ed.")

    C. Have the three persons stand in front of the room holding the appropriate sheets of paper. Have "Carla" and "Ed" reverse positions. Then invite your "is" and "-ed" holders to come up. After that, invite the "by" holder, and finally, have the "by Carla" team leave the room, as before.

    D. Discuss why *is* has to be used here, rather than *was* and why *-ed* is used, rather than *-en*. (The reason for the former is that this is present tense, rather than past. The reason for the *-ed* is that it is the ending for the verb *discuss*.)

    You may wish at this point to have your students sum up the rules for the formation of the passive. If they use the sentence about Carla defeating Ed as an example, the rules will look something like this:

Active Sentence: Carla defeats Ed.

Rule	**Example**
Rule 1. Reverse the nouns.	Ed defeats Carla
Rule 2. Add a form of *be* and delete the verb ending.	Ed <u>is</u> defeat_ Carla
Rule 3. Insert the verb ending that follows *has/have*.	Ed is defeat<u>ed</u> Carla
Rule 4. Add *by*.	Ed is defeated <u>by</u> Carla.
Rule 5 (optional). Delete the *by* phrase.	Ed is defeated.

The information about the formation of the typical passive can alternatively be shown in chart form (Figure 4–1).

Emphasize the notion of *optionally*, for it has been estimated that as many as 80 percent of all passives in the written language omit the *by* phrase. (Note that Orwell omitted all his *by* phrases.) However, when they are trying to discover passives, students should be encouraged to attempt to supply the missing *by* phrase, as a nearly sure-fire test of passivity.

The form of *be* that is used always depends on the tense of the verb in the original active sentence. The following chart summarizes the information:

Tense	Active	Passive
present	beats	*is* beaten
past	beat	*was* beaten
modal	must beat	must *be* beaten
perfective	has beaten	has *been* beaten
progressive	is beating	is *being* beaten
modal/perfective	must have beat	must have *been* beaten
with progressive	must have been beating	must have been *being* beaten

The last passive form is sometimes perceived as ungrammatical, but it is not. It's simply the passive version of the active sentence: "The runner must have been beating his opponent."

With all this, can you be sure that all of your students will always be able to identify passives in their own writing? The answer for me was "no," although the lights went on in many students' eyes during the lesson. In addition to these demonstrations, explanations, and the chart, I found that I had to monitor their

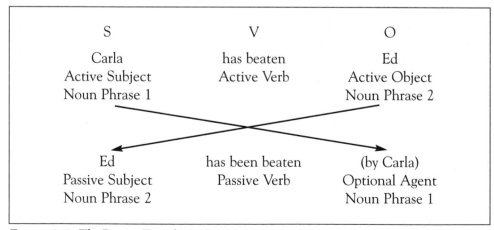

Figure 4–1. *The Passive Transformation*

essays for a time, have them do group activities on the passive, *and* quiz them periodically. All this done, my class scored a 96 percent average on a lengthy final quiz. In a second year, my class scored only 89 percent, because two students still hadn't fully "gotten it."

It is a great deal of work and in many cases perhaps not worth the effort. You must judge that. But let's not claim to be teaching the passive if we are not. Further, as I discovered, there is no point in telling students they should avoid or judiciously use the passive if they do not know what a passive is. This is a major problem with some state standards: Many require students to avoid the passive or use the active, but the standards-bearers show no awareness whatsoever of what such a requirement entails at the classroom level.

Uses (and Abuses) of the Passive in Writing

Returning now to the question of when passives should and should not be used, it is instructive to begin by studying the reasons that textbooks give for avoiding the passive. Perhaps the most frequently given reason for shunning the passive is that it is wordy. *The Bedford Handbook for Writers* (Hacker, 1994) gives this example of wordiness:

> *Passive*: All too often, athletes with marginal academic skills have been recruited by our coaches. (Fourteen words)

> *Active*: All too often, our coaches have recruited athletes with marginal academic skills. (Twelve words) (p. 186)

Net saving: two words, the passive-formers, *been* and *by*. But a different passive would actually save one more word than the active:

> *Passive*: All too often, athletes with marginal academic skills have been recruited. (Eleven words)

The passive is also sometimes said to be "weaker" than the active or "less direct." Presumably, the reporter who screamed on that fateful November day in Dallas, "President Kennedy has been shot," would have used a "stronger," more direct sentence if she had said, "Someone has shot President Kennedy."

I am not defending the dreary prose of bureaucrats or legalists (or even some educators), which frequently is clogged with passives of the kind that students *should* avoid. Occasionally, I've talked one-on-one to students about their use of the passive. (In one case, my final conclusion was that the student had a profoundly passive personality. It was *natural* for her to use passives.) Often, I've found that they use it in the belief that it dresses up their language, makes them sound more formal, more impressive. Clearly, this is not a good reason. Steering a course between language that is too colloquial for the occasion and bureaucratese is not easy for young learners, but we English teachers have to guide them in that direction.

Finally, students sometimes use the passive as a way of avoiding *I*. For instance, instead of "I will next discuss Hawthorne's symbolism," one student put it, "Hawthorne's symbolism will next be discussed." The latter avoids *I* but also might leave us wondering in whose hands we are being placed. If it is important to avoid *I*, perhaps the student could simply use a heading in that section of the paper: *Hawthorne's Symbolism*. We will be better served in all of this if we begin by conceding that the passive has many legitimate uses. Here are a few:

1. *The writer considers the "agent" irrelevant or obvious.* Passives are commonly used in scientific articles and lab reports where who performs the action is assumed or of no consequence. Suppose a student is writing up a chemistry experiment. Which would her science teacher prefer?

   Active: We poured the liquid into a test tube. Then we heated the test tube till the liquid boiled. At that point, we removed the tube from the flames, and we next exposed it to. . . .

   Passive: The liquid was poured into a test tube and heated till it boiled, when it was removed from the flames. Next it was exposed to. . . .

   Here are a few other examples of passives where the agent is irrelevant:

   Students caught smoking will be expelled.

   French is spoken here.

   What is needed now?

2. *The writer does not know the agent(s).* If the writer does not know the agent, he can often use a general noun or an indefinite pronoun in its place, but this is not necessarily better than a passive. Which of the following do you prefer?

   Active: During the riots, people looted dozens of stores.

   Passive: During the riots, dozens of stores were looted.

3. *The writer prefers not to mention the agent(s).* Consider this passive:

   It's time that teachers were paid more money.

   In a given case, the writer may know well who is responsible for the fact that teachers are not being better paid, but it may be impolitic to identify the agent(s).

4. *The writer wishes to emphasize the receiver of the action.* A good example is the passive regarding the shooting of President Kennedy. Even if the writer knew who fired the shot, the passive is much more dramatic:

Effective Passive: President Kennedy has been shot.

Less Effective Active: Oswald has shot President Kennedy.

5. *The writer uses the passive to improve cohesion and emphasis.* Although this use of the passive is not widely recognized, Joseph M. Williams considers it "the main reason the passive exists in the language" (1995, p. 55).

Poor Cohesion: Pete Rose broke the record. Ty Cobb formerly held the record.

Better Flow: Pete Rose broke the record that was formerly held by Ty Cobb.

The second example sentence not only improves the flow, it also puts the stress on the new information—Ty Cobb was the former record holder.

Here is an illustration from Williams' own book. Notice that the (italicized) complete subject of the first sentence is choked with new information, the kind of material that is almost always better placed behind the verb—as in the improved version, which follows.

During the first years of our nation, *a series of brilliant and virtuous presidents committed to a democratic republic yet confident in their own superior worth* conducted its administration.

During the first years of our nation, its administration was conducted by a series of brilliant and virtuous presidents committed to a democratic republic yet confident in their own superior worth. (1990, p. 54)

These days, even second-rate textbooks concede that the passive has its uses. One text, for instance, allows students to use passives, but "only if the performer of the action is unclear, unimportant, or too complicated or obvious to mention" (*Prentice Hall Writer's Companion*, High School, 1995, p. 414). As composition teachers, we should ease up on our opposition to the passive (and on the giving or withholding of "allowances"), and focus more on whether our students have used the language effectively.

Activity 4–8: An Important Use of the Passive

Goal: To teach how the passive can effectively be used to achieve coherence.

Background

This activity is based on a series of facts about Nigeria and on the rhetorical principle that in most sentences old information should be presented in the subject part of the sentence, new information in the predicate. (For a good treatment of this and some other rhetorical principles, see Martha Kolln's *Rhetorical Grammar*, [1998].)

Procedure

1. Arrange students in working groups of four or five and give them the following facts, most of which they are expected to use. Their job is to write a paragraph discussing the question of why Nigeria *did not* choose one of its local languages as its official language and why it *did* choose English.

   a. The country of Nigeria chose English as its official language.

   b. Prior to the adoption of English, people native to the country spoke Hausa, Yoruba, Ibo, Fulani, and other languages.

   c. Yoruba is the most commonly spoken language, but almost as many people speak Hausa.

   d. The combined speakers of the other languages far outweigh the number that speak Yoruba, and they would oppose it.

   e. All speakers whose own language was not chosen would be seriously disadvantaged, both educationally and socially.

   f. Nigeria had been exploited by French, Portuguese, Dutch, and English traders for two centuries.

   g. Nigeria had been an English colony from 1914 till it achieved its independence in 1960.

   Note: Many of these facts are from David Crystal's discussion of the same subject in his book, *The English Language* (1988).

2. Suggest that each group use as its initial sentence, "Why did Nigerians choose English as their official language rather than one of their many local languages?" Part of the assignment is to attempt to use the passive to achieve coherence.

3. When the groups are finished, have them underline the subjects of each of their sentences. (If they are not capable, help them.)

4. Duplicate some paragraphs for discussion, giving special attention to the flow (coherence) of the paragraphs. Note whether passives help in achieving good flow.

5. Make an overhead of the following model paragraph and have students discuss its coherence. *Note:* The subjects have been italicized.

Model Paragraph

Why did *Nigerians* choose English as their official language rather than one of their many local languages? Obviously, *they* could have selected only one of the several languages that the natives spoke. *They* might have chosen Yoruba, which is the most widely spoken language. However, almost as many *Nigerians* speak Hausa. In addition, even if a language had a clear majority, *its selection* would have been opposed by the combined weight of

132

the other languages, whose speakers would have been disadvantaged both educationally and socially. Why did *they* choose English, rather than French, Portuguese, or Dutch? *That choice* was determined by the historical dominance of Nigeria by England for almost 50 years.

6. In the course of the discussion, bring out the fact that all subjects but two refer to Nigerians, illustrating the fact that the subject of the sentence typically contains known or old information.

7. Isolate the two sentences that do not have *Nigerians* as their subject, and lead the students to see that their subjects, too, contain old/known, rather than new, information. Help them to see, as well, that both of these sentences are passives.

> Known   Passive Verb Phrase   New Information
>
> *Its selection* **would have been opposed** by the combined weight of the other languages, whose speakers would have been disadvantaged both educationally and socially.

> Known   Passive Verb Phrase   New Information
>
> *That choice* **was determined** by the historical dominance of Nigeria by England for almost 50 years.

8. It is instructive to compare these passives with their active versions, noting how much new information appears in the subject slot of the actives, thereby retarding the flow of the paragraph:

> New Information
>
> **The combined weight of the other languages, whose speakers would have been disadvantaged both educationally and socially,** would have opposed its selection.

> New Information
>
> **The historical dominance of Nigeria by England for almost 50 years** determined that choice.

Reinforcement Activity

The following partial paragraph may be analyzed by students as a further example of how the passive may be used to achieve coherence (in its third full sentence). The excerpt comes from the beginning of chapter 14 of Jane Austen's *Pride and Prejudice*. Subjects have been made bold.

. . . from Lady Catherine. **She** had been graciously pleased to approve of both the discourses which he had already had the honour of preaching before her. **She** had also asked him twice to dine at Rosings, and had sent for him only the Saturday before, to make up her pool of quadrille in the evening. **Lady Catherine** was reckoned proud by many people he knew [passive], but *he* had never seen anything but affability in her. **She** had always spoken to him as she would to any other gentleman; she made not the smallest objection. . . . . **She** had even condescended to advise him to marry. . . .

For Linguistically Curious Students: Outknowing the Grammar Checker

Although Activity 4–7 covers the most common way of forming passive sentences, it does not cover all. In addition, there are at least these three:

- *Be* deletion passives: Smoking not permitted here.
- Existential *there* passives: There is nothing to be gained.
- *Get* passives: I hope you won't get caught.

A way to discover that these are passives is to try to insert a *by* phrase naming the agent:

- Smoking is not permitted [by the fire department] here.
- There is nothing to be gained [by you].
- I hope you won't get caught [by your parents].

To change the sentences into actives, all one has to do is put the agent in the subject slot:

- *The fire department* does not permit smoking here.
- *You* cannot gain anything.
- I hope that *your parents* won't catch you.

Be deletions are common in notices and headlines. At a college gym where I used to work out, a notice read: "Alcoholic beverages strictly prohibited in this facility." (In fact the notice went on to include two additional passives: "Anyone caught using them will be banned from the gym.") An interesting fact is that my computer doesn't identify this as a passive. It is too mindless to know that *prohibited* is a past participle here, not a past-tense form.

Existential sentences beginning with unstressed *there* also go unrecognized by my computer. To see if your students can do better, ask them to compare these two sentences. The agent (who will do the leaving) is unspecified in both.

A. Nothing will be left for me.
B. There will be nothing left for me.

Since they are synonymous and A clearly is passive, then B is passive, too, yet my computer recognizes only A as a passive.

Finally, for the *get* passive, ask students to consider the following pairs of sentences. The A sentence in each pair is obviously passive. Is the B?

A. If we are beaten by our rivals, it won't be the coach's fault.
B. If we get beaten by our rivals, it won't be the coach's fault.
A. Many of our possessions were left behind in the storm.
B. Many of our possessions got left behind in the storm.

Again, since both pairs are synonymous, they are both passives, but that fact is not known by my computer's grammar check, which apparently does not recognize *get* as a *be*-verb substitute.

Topic Sentences, Thesis Statements, and Clinchers: Helps or Hindrances?

Let's begin with the clincher sentence, since it's easier to dispose of. Incidentally, I have *not* found reference to clinchers in college handbooks, but they are commonly discussed in secondary school texts; even *Writers INC* mentions them.

Here is John Warriner's treatment of clinchers, in his first edition, Book One (1948):

> It is a good plan, in descriptive and explanatory writing especially, to add a concluding sentence to a paragraph. This sentence sometimes repeats the idea expressed in the topic sentence. Its purpose is to sum up, to "clinch" the central thought. Teachers of composition call it the "clincher" sentence. (p. 220)

Thirty years later, Warriner (1977) was a bit more cautious about clincher sentences:

> Sometimes a writer may wish to reemphasize the main point of a paragraph by restating it in a concluding sentence. This kind of restatement is sometimes called a *clincher sentence*. It is used to very good effect by skillful writers. A paragraph concluding with a clincher sentence has two statements of its topic: one in the topic sentence and one in the clincher. Use clincher sentences sparingly. A clincher is unnecessary in a very short paragraph. (p. 250)

Finally, although the clincher is listed as one of the three parts of the "main idea" paragraph in the 2001 Warriner clone, *Elements of Language* (Odell et al.), there is a specific "Style Tip" that states:

> Not every paragraph needs a clincher sentence. Use one for a strong or dramatic touch or for renewing a main idea in a lengthy or complicated paragraph. (p. 465)

Perhaps even conservative teachers are becoming more realistic about the value of clincher sentences. At any rate, the clincher about clinchers is that if writers actually used them, they would cease to have readers. About the *only* place where clincher sentences have value is in the single-paragraph theme, and the only place where the single-paragraph theme is written is in school.

The Tyranny of the Topic Sentence/Thesis Statement

The topic sentence for the paragraph, the thesis statement (or controlling idea) for the composition or research paper—both are linguistic straightjackets for student writers interested in writing anything beyond dummy-runs or blether. I'm not claiming that topic sentences aren't useful for *some* paragraphs or that thesis statements are totally useless, but far more often than not, each is not the best approach to real-world writing.

If you look for thesis statements in collections of essays, you will regularly be disappointed. Merely reading the titles of most of the works in *The Best American Essays* should be enough to convince anyone of that: "How to Pray: Reverence, Stories, and the Rebbe's Dream"; "Travels with R.L.S."; "Mail"; "The Work of Mourning" are a few examples. Indeed, even if a paper has a thesis, it is usually something the writer winds up with, not something she begins with. The best student research paper I have ever read addressed the question, "Is There Such a Thing as Extrasensory Perception?" The writer concluded that the evidence was uncertain; he couldn't make up his mind one way or the other. If he had started with that thesis, I doubt that I would have relished reading his paper.

Even the model research papers in the handbooks rarely set out with a thesis to be proved. In the 1998 *Harbrace*, for example, the first of the two sample student research papers is on using cinematic techniques to emphasize time in Shakespeare's *Richard III*. What it "proves" is that differing cinematic techniques can be used to good effect. Don't we already know that? The other paper "proves" that young adults move back home "for a myriad of financial considerations." Imagine that! Both of these are good papers, but they are good not because they prove a thesis but because, as Mies Van der Rohe once put it, "God is in the details."

As for topic sentences, to get an idea of just how complex and frightfully difficult a task it is even to find them in good writing, I recommend Richard Braddock's 1974 essay, "The Frequency and Placement of Topic Sentences in Expository Prose." Braddock examined twenty-five complete essays, five each from *The Atlantic, Harper's, The New Yorker, The Reporter,* and *The Saturday Review.* He quickly gave up on the idea that he could simply underline topic sentences. Indeed, he decided that he had to do his own *sentence outlines* of the major points of each essay before he could even hope to arrive at any meaningful conclusions. Braddock's article is really a mind-opener (more about his conclusions in a moment), but if you can't find it, the next best thing is to try the game yourself. Ideally, attempt to find topic sentences in the work of one of your own favorite authors. Or try it with one of my favorites.

Here is Anna Quindlen's essay, "Homeless" (1998), one of my favorite essays by one of my favorite essayists. (She once autographed a program for me: "To Ed, who does the work of the angels [i.e., teaching]".) Read "Homeless," then try to locate its topic sentences.

Homeless

Her name was Ann, and we met in the Port Authority Bus Terminal several Januarys ago. I was doing a story on homeless people. She said I was wasting my time talking to her; she was just passing through, although she'd been passing through for more than two weeks. To prove to me that this was true, she rummaged through a tote bag and a manila envelope and finally unfolded a sheet of typing paper and brought out her photographs.

They were not pictures of family, or friends, or even a dog or cat, its eyes brown-red in the flashbulb's light. They were pictures of a house. It was like a thousand houses in a hundred towns, not suburb, not city, but somewhere in between, with aluminum siding and a chain-link fence, a narrow driveway running up to a one-car garage and a patch of backyard. The house was yellow. I looked on the back for a date or a name, but neither was there. There was no need for discussion. I knew what she was trying to tell me, for it was something I had often felt. She was not adrift, alone, anonymous, although her bags and her raincoat with the grime shadowing its creases had made me believe she was. She had a house, or at least once upon a time had had one. Inside were curtains, a couch, a stove, pot holders. You are where you live. She was somebody.

I've never been very good at looking at the big picture, taking the global view, and I've always been a person with an overactive sense of place, the legacy of an Irish grandfather. So it is natural that the thing that seems most wrong with the world to me right now is that there are so many people with no homes. I'm not simply talking about shelter from the elements, or three square meals a day or a mailing address to which the welfare people can send the check—although I know that all these are important for survival. I'm talking about a home, about precisely those kinds of feelings that have wound up in cross-stitch and French knots on samplers over the years.

Home is where the heart is. There's no place like it. I love my home with a ferocity totally out of proportion to its appearance or location. I love dumb things about it: the hot-water heater, the plastic rack you drain dishes in, the roof over my head, which occasionally leaks. And yet it is precisely those dumb things that make it what it is—a place of certainty, stability, predictability, privacy, for me and for my family. It is where I live. What more can you say about a place than that? That is everything.

Yet it is something that we have been edging away from gradually during my lifetime and the lifetimes of my parents and grandparents. There was a time when where you lived often was where you worked and where you grew the food you ate and even where you were buried. When that era passed, where you lived at least was where your parents had lived and where you would live with your children when you became enfeebled. Then, suddenly, where you lived was where you lived for three years, until you could move on to something else and something else again.

And so we have come to something else again, to children who do not understand what it means to go to their rooms because they have never had a room, to men and women whose fantasy is a wall they can paint a color of their own choosing, to old people reduced to sitting on molded plastic chairs, their skin blue-white in the lights of a bus station, who pull pictures of houses out of their bags. Homes have stopped being homes. Now they are real estate.

People find it curious that those without homes would rather sleep sitting up on benches or huddled in doorways than go to shelters. Certainly some prefer to do so because they are emotionally ill, because they have been locked in before and they are damned if they will be locked in again. Others are afraid of the violence and trouble they may find there. But some seem to want something that is not available in shelters, and they will not compromise, not for a cot, or oatmeal, or a shower with a special soap that kills the bugs. "One room," a woman with a baby who was sleeping on her sister's floor, once told me, "painted blue." That was the crux of it; not size or location but pride of ownership. Painted blue.

This is a difficult problem, and some wise and compassionate people are working hard at it. But in the main I think we work around it, just as we walk around it when it is lying on the sidewalk or sitting in the bus terminal—the problem, that is. It has been customary to take people's pain and lessen our own participation in it by turning it into an issue, not a collection of human beings. We turn an adjective into a noun: the poor, not poor people; the homeless, not Ann or the man who lives in the box or the woman who sleeps on the subway grate.

Sometimes I think we would be better off if we forgot about the broad strokes and concentrated on the details. Here is a woman without a bureau. There is a man with no mirror, no wall to hang it on. They are the homeless. They are people who have no homes. No drawer that holds the spoons. No window to look out upon the world. My God. That is everything.

What did you discover about topic sentences? Here is my analysis.

An Analysis of Topic Sentences in Quindlen's "Homeless"

Paragraph 1 describes a meeting between Anna and Ann, a homeless person, in the Port Authority Bus Terminal. It is a brief narrative. It has no topic sentence.

Paragraph 2 continues and concludes the narrative. It ends with a point: that Ann through her actions is trying to prove that she is somebody, that she is not truly homeless. Even if we accept this as a single topic for the paragraph, what *sentence* would be considered the topic sentence?

Paragraph 3 contains a number of major assertions:

1. Anna isn't good at taking a global view.
2. This is due to her overactive sense of place.
3. Anna thinks what's most wrong with the world right now is that there are too many people without a home.
4. Certain fundamental things are important for survival.
5. Anna begins to define *home*, the topic of the *next* paragraph.

If there is a single topic sentence here, I can't find it. The boldest assertion is the third (the second sentence of the paragraph), and the sentences that precede and follow are related to it, but they don't precisely support it. Moreover, the first sentence of this paragraph anticipates the *ending* of the essay, and the fourth anticipates the next paragraph. Overall, the paragraph comes perilously close to something we urge our students *never* to do: write a series of unsupported topic sentences.

Paragraph 4 essentially defines *home*, but no one sentence serves as its topic.

Paragraph 5 finally gives us something resembling what many teachers ask students to do all the time. Its first sentence *does* state a topic—we've been moving away from Quindlen's conception of home gradually. The other sentences support this by giving a brief "history."

The last two sentences of Paragraph 6 certainly have the feel of a topic sentence (or rather a topic split into two sentences), but the rest of the paragraph doesn't support the opinion expressed in the last two sentences, but rather describes it, by offering details of what homelessness feels like.

Paragraph 7 gives three reasons why people prefer not to go to shelters. It's a prime candidate for a topic sentence, such as "There are three reasons why. . . ." But no such sentence is used (thankfully). We have the support without the topic. One could say that this paragraph has an *implied* topic sentence. From a pedagogical point of view, however, this raises a tricky issue: When is it legitimate to imply a topic and when does one need to actually supply a topic sentence?

Paragraph 8 asserts that "in the main" we "work around" the problem of homelessness by turning it into an issue to lessen our own participation. Although the cumulative effect of what Quindlen has said up to this point may convince us that she is right, she doesn't support this assertion *in this paragraph*. We have a topic without interparagraph support.

Paragraph 9 presents the "thesis" of the essay; namely, we'd make a better beginning toward solving the problem of homelessness if we "forgot about the broad strokes and concentrated on the details." In an indirect way, Quindlen supports this topic sentence within the paragraph by glints of homelessness. It is a brilliant stroke, but far from a classic instance of support by examples.

If it's difficult to summarize what I have just described, you can imagine what Braddock faced with his twenty-five essays and 889 total paragraphs. But at the risk of some oversimplification, one can say that handbook-recommended topic sentences appeared in *far fewer than half* of all his paragraphs.

Based on work much more recent than Braddock's, Joseph M. Williams says that it is misleading to talk about topic sentences in the first place, since in the real world, writers *just as often* use two, three, or even more sentences to introduce new topics (1990, p. 101).

Yet Mid-continent Research for Education and Learning (McREL) recommends that students should use topic sentences and should learn to recognize a paragraph as a group of sentences about one main idea, beginning in grades three through five. (McREL is the outfit that Achieve—that group of business leaders and governors that is trying to tell educators how to run our schools—is so high on.) And such "standards" are indeed embedded in the documents of many states across the country. Moreover, state writing tests frequently expect that essays will be built around thesis statements or controlling ideas and that paragraphs will be developed around a topic. In doing so, they are encouraging the notion that writing is a mechanical rather than a creative act.

Paragraphs: Breaks for Readers

It has always seemed to me that one of the most mythical of all myths is the notion that there is such an entity as *the* paragraph. Yet that is exactly how the concept is typically introduced in handbooks and traditional school grammars. True, things are opening up some recently, but here is the second paragraph at the beginning of Chapter 13, "The Paragraph," of the tenth-grade book of *Warriner's English Grammar and Composition* series. (I have numbered the sentences.)

> (1) The indentation, or spacing, that marks the beginning of a paragraph signals a change in the direction of the writer's thought—a new idea, a change in place, time, or situation, a slightly different point of view. (2) One paragraph is different from another in length, content, and organization, but it is possible to form an idea of the kind of average paragraph that is likely to appear in a student composition. (3) It is likely to be from 100 to 150 words in length, to consist of a general statement supported by specific statements, and to have a single unifying idea. (4) It is not always easy to organize what you have to say into good paragraphs with these characteristics. (5) This chapter provides you with instructions, examples, and practice to help you master the writing of effective paragraphs. (1977, p. 247)

Immediately after this is a statement that defines the paragraph as "a series of sentences developing a single topic." Tell me what "single topic" the authors' own paragraph develops.

Apart from the trivial point that the authors refer to paragraphing in every sentence, there is *no single topic and no development.* The first sentence talks about the theoretical function of indentation. The second shifts ground completely, talking about how different paragraphs are from one another and winding up with the notion of an "average paragraph." The third sentence does develop this notion of the average paragraph, but in the fourth there is again a total shift of topic, having to do with the ease of making paragraphs. Finally, the last sentence is again almost totally unrelated to the sentence that precedes it, telling the reader how the textbook will help her. In essence, we have four topics instead of one and virtually no "development."

A vintage *Harbrace College Handbook* (Hodges and Whitten, 1982) is no better; indeed, it may be worse. Here are the first two paragraphs of the chapter entitled "The Paragraph." Again, I have numbered the sentences.

(1) The paragraph is the essential unit of thought in writing. (2) Although it may consist of a single sentence, it is usually a group of sentences that develop one main point or controlling idea. (3) The form of a paragraph is distinctive: the first line is indented, about one inch in handwriting and five spaces in typewritten copy.

(4) Certain conventions or rules govern the construction of a paragraph. (5) The reader expects a paragraph to be *coherent* (with its organization following a definite plan), *developed* (with its sentences adequately explaining or qualifying the main point), and *unified* (with all its sentences relevant to the main point). (6) In general, most paragraphs are between 100 and 250 words long and usually consist of five to ten sentences (p. 346).

There is no support whatsoever for the main idea in the first sentence of the first paragraph. *Why* are they calling the paragraph "the essential unit of thought"? *What* makes it so? The second sentence mainly talks about length, though it also provides a kind of definition—that a paragraph develops a main point. The third sentence shifts ground to a dull, superficial observation about paragraph format.

The second paragraph appears to have a topic sentence, its first, and Sentences 5 and 6 appear to develop that topic: that there are conventions or rules governing the construction of paragraphs—though I would not call coherence, development, and unity "conventions or rules," would you? But it does violence to the stated criteria. It has three sentences and sixty-six words, even though it proclaims "in general" "most" paragraphs "usually" contain five to ten sentences and "100 to 250 words." (Have you ever seen more hedging in a single sentence?) It's also not very coherent, shifting subjects in every sentence, from "conventions or rules" to "the reader" to "most paragraphs."

In fact, the opening *two pages* of this chapter contain six paragraphs. Here is how they break down:

	Words	Sentences
Paragraph 1	56	3
Paragraph 2	66	3
Paragraph 3	38	2
Paragraph 4	31	1
Paragraph 5	52	2
Paragraph 6	51	2

Average word length here is forty-nine, and average sentence length is 2.2. Yet the average "should" be 175 words and 7.5 sentences. How can the authors justify being so far off the mark?

One can only assume that handbook paragraphs do not follow the same "rules" that students are expected to follow. Perhaps we ought to seek the ideal instead in the exemplary student research paper that the authors provide later in the book? It is twenty paragraphs long, five of which contain very long quotations from the student's sources. I calculated the word and sentence lengths of the remaining fifteen paragraphs. Here is how those paragraphs compare with the "ideal":

	Ideal Paragraph Length	Student Paragraph Length
Words/paragraph: average number	175	88
Words/paragraph: range	100–250	27–154
Sentences/paragraph: average number	7.5	4.8
Sentences/paragraph: range	5–10	2–7

Textbook authors go to great pains to find exemplary student writing, yet this exemplary research paper fails miserably to come up to expectations regarding paragraphing. In fact, the *longest* student paragraph falls twenty-one words short of the ideal *average*. And the *average* number of student sentences per paragraph falls two-tenths below the *minimum* number of the ideal. How can one account for such discrepancies?

Paragraphing Is an Art, Not a Science, and Wider Than Our Views of It

Many years ago in a workshop at a national convention in San Antonio, Texas, I handed out an unparagraphed United States Supreme Court order, and asked the audience to divide it into paragraphs. There were thirty-eight sentences in all, and every one of them was deemed a proper place to paragraph by at least a handful of the members of the audience. True, there were maybe two sentences that were chosen markedly less often than the others; but in general, it was remarkable how much diversity there was.

In my own effort to reparagraph the piece, I did not agree precisely with the divisions made by the Supreme Court; neither, as I recall, did anyone in the large audience. But that's not all. A few months later, I used the same activity for a statewide workshop in the Pocono Mountain region of Pennsylvania—with the same result from the group. Since I had lost my own divisions, I reparagraphed the Court Order so my audience could tell how I would have paragraphed it.

Sometime after I returned, I found my San Antonio paragraph division and discovered that I *disagreed with myself*. I paragraphed the Order differently in the Poconos than I had in San Antonio.

Now, one can draw various conclusions from these experiences. One might be that I am a dunderhead where paragraphing is concerned. Another might be that whoever wrote the Supreme Court Order wasn't a particularly good paragrapher herself. The variety of paragraphing decisions in my audiences might be accounted for by their lack of paragraphing skill—though they were all professional adults.

But consider a few things that I discovered through this research. First, one's initial paragraphing decision affects one's second, one's second affects one's third, and so on. Suppose, for example, that Participant A decided to make a paragraph break after the first sentence of a given text, and Participant B decided to make his first paragraph break at the end of Sentence 3. Now, the end of Sentence 3 might be a very good place for a paragraph break, but Participant A, having already paragraphed at the end of Sentence 1, would be reluctant to make another break so soon, especially if a break at the end of Sentence 5, say, also seemed a good place for a break. Participant B, on the other hand, could decide that the end of Sentence 5 would be too soon. And on and on.

Second, consider this. That Supreme Court order said what it said and said it cohesively or incohesively, logically or illogically, *regardless* of whether it contained three, six, ten, or even no paragraphs. Since emphasis would be affected, it's likely that a five-paragraph version would be easier to read and would be preferred by most readers, but apart from emphases, it would be *the same piece of work*.

Looking at writing globally, the chief fact about paragraphing is that it is a convenience for the reader. Strunk and White say as much in *The Elements of Style*:

> The paragraph is a convenient unit; it serves all forms of literary work. As long as it holds together, a paragraph may be of any length—a single, short sentence or a passage of great duration. (2000, pp. 15–16)

There was, after all, a time when paragraphing did not exist. People managed to read texts regardless.

The reality is that there is no such thing as *the* paragraph. There are memo paragraphs and business-letter paragraphs, there are report paragraphs and, apparently, handbook paragraphs, there are paragraphs in fiction and paragraphs (stanzas) in poetry, there are news-article paragraphs and feature-article paragraphs, though the differences between them are narrower than they used to be. There are paragraphs in *People* magazine and paragraphs in *The Atlantic* magazine and paragraphs in *The New Yorker* magazine.

In Pauline Kael's film reviews in the old *New Yorker*, the three-hundred- to four-hundred-word paragraphs would flow one after another the length of the Mississippi, but I never knew any readers who canceled their subscriptions over the fact. And her paragraphs were not always especially coherent either. In a review of Alan Alda's *Sweet Victory* (June 2, 1986), for example, she begins a paragraph talking about the performance of Bob Hoskins, shifts without so much as a blink to the performance of Saul Rubinek, discusses how this role functions in the structure of the film, suddenly shifts to what director Alda might have had in mind, talks next about the viewer's view of the Rubinek character, and climaxes the whole thing with a single forty-four-word *parenthetical* sentence regretting the fact that "we" don't get to see Rubinek's rushes of some scenes.

Kael's sentences and paragraphs went on and on and on like thirsty nomads in a desert, yet I never minded, because *what she said* (and often *how* she said it) was nearly always so absorbing, so well informed, so colorful, so insightful. Sometimes, I would be downright angry over her reviews, but after reflection, I would often change my mind completely about the quality of a film I had just seen. That's *writing*, and to hell with paragraph length.

Recently, I looked at some articles in *The New York Times* Sunday Magazine section. The average number of words per paragraph was only 97.2, and the average number of sentences per paragraph was just 6.2. If you think these figures are meager, consider Safire's column "On Language," in the same magazine. It contained just 57.4 words per paragraph and 2.4 sentences. The paragraphs in Safire's "Language" columns rarely exceed four sentences, and not uncommonly, they include just one. However, his average sentence length is a very respectable 23.6 words.

Activity 4–9: The First Paragrapher's Paragraphing

Goal: To let students themselves discover something of the inconsistencies in paragraphing advice.

Procedure

Duplicate the following, which is the first discussion of paragraphing that I know of in a grammar book. It appeared in Lindley Murray's *English Grammar* (1795).

Ask students to analyze it, and determine whether Murray follows his own advice. Does he seem to follow the advice of *today's* experts on paragraph writing?

> It may not be improper to insert, in this place, a few general directions respecting the division of a composition into paragraphs.
>
> Different subjects, unless they are very short, or very numerous in small compass, should be separated into paragraphs.
>
> When one subject is continued to a considerable length, the larger divisions of it should be put into paragraphs. And it will have a good effect to form the breaks, when it can properly be done, at sentiments of the most weight, or that call for peculiar attention.
>
> The facts, premises, and conclusions, of a subject, sometimes naturally point out the separations into paragraphs: and each of these, when of great length, will again require subdivisions at their most distinctive parts.
>
> In cases which require a connected subject to be formed into several paragraphs, a suitable turn of expression, exhibiting the connexion of the broken parts, will give beauty and force to the division. (pp. 247–248)

EXTENSION SUGGESTION

An example of paragraphing by Lindley Murray's predecessor, Robert Lowth, is on page 153–154. You might ask students to compare the two.

The Five-Paragraph Theme

Everything I have said about *the* paragraph is not to be interpreted as meaning that I stand against *development* and *coherence*. I could not be more *for* them. In fact, in all the Freshman English courses I have taught throughout my life, these may be the two things in student work that were most often missing and most sorely missed.

The well-known "five-paragraph theme" encourages both development and coherence, and in that way, it *could* be a good thing. It can be a good exercise, just as writing certain types of paragraphs can be a good exercise. But the five-paragraph theme has severe limitations as well, and it seems to be a form that exists only in the English classroom. Indeed, in all the books I've ever used in Freshman English classes to illustrate good writing, *I have never seen a five-paragraph theme*. If the form is so worthy, why don't writers use it? Even essays defending the use of this format do not employ it.

As for student writing and the five-paragraph theme, consider these facts:

• Students who score high in writing assessment tests in the state of Pennsylvania (and some other states that I have examined) almost never use it.

- Student winners of state-wide writing contests—in my home state, at least—do not often win with five-paragraph themes.
- I don't recall ever reading a five-paragraph essay in a student literary magazine—and I was the NCTE Literary Magazine Award State leader for Pennsylvania for many years.

Since the form has been widely taught—at least throughout my lifetime—it's remarkable how little used it is in published writing.

Its proponents ought to do a study to determine whether students who are taught the form subsequently write more fully developed and more coherent compositions than students who are not. It would be an easy study to design, and if it yielded positive results, I, for one, would be willing to change my estimate of its worth.

Activity 4–10: Paragraphing Does Matter

Goal: To help students understand that paragraphing does matter and that both anorectic and obese paragraphs need to be revised. (An obese paragraph is one that needs reduction; an anorectic paragraph needs building up.)

Note: The following pieces of writing—both of which were originally paragraphed by their authors—earned the highest score possible in the Pennsylvania state-mandated writing test for ninth graders.

For the paragraph that I have made obese, the student was addressing a prompt that asked him or her to persuade people in the community to build or not to build a recycling plant in the only place in the community where it could be located—the community park and recreation area. I have removed all of the paragraph breaks from the first sample and numbered its sentences. Here is the obese essay:

(1) Have you ever been to a landfill? (2) If you have, you know that they are ugly, demeaning scars on the surface of our beautiful planet. (3) Pungent odors constantly emanate from them, and stray chemicals always seem to end up in our water. (4) The only feasible plan that we are aware of to cut down on landfill use is to recycle everything that we possibly can. (5) Only after we do this, can we look for the ultimate solution. (6) Recycling will buy us a great deal of time. (7) I understand that the facility to carry out the valuable process will replace our recreation area. (8) What good will it be in a decade anyway? (9) The water in the lake will be cloudy and polluted from the use of a new landfill that will be necessary for us to build. (10) The meager destruction of our park is only a slight inconvenience when considering the potential that the plant will bring. (11) In fact, it might not even eliminate our community park; it might only be a temporary closing for relocation and repair. (12) If the recycling plant is as successful as expected, the landfill's burden will ease a considerable amount. (13) In that case, the plans for

another landfill could be altered. (14) Much of the money and land could be used to create a new community getaway. (15) We would have enough money to make significant improvements to the quality of our current park. (16) Even a man-made lake filled with clean sparkling water is not beyond reality. (17) The possibilities and benefits of this joint plan are limitless. (18) I ask you to realize the magic that this projection holds. (19) It has no major downfalls haunting the area between the lines. (20) Any of the slightest difficulties are tremendously outweighed by this attainable vision of the future. (21) It is your choice, an overabundance of horrendous landfill space and one sorry-looking polluted park, or a reduction in landfill space, a curve in air and water pollution, and a beautiful, clean park where people, as well as animals, of the community would be happy to go. (22) The solution to our problem is perfectly clear, so unless your family is keen on swimming in antifreeze, and you like seeing poor, defenseless animals die because of our recyclable trash, you know what this town needs as well as I do. (23) We have already experienced the consequences that are suffered as a result of our hesitation to care for our own planet. (24) Please do not allow us to continue making the same mistakes.

In the following essay, which I have made anorectic, the writer was addressing a prompt that required her or him to write to a teacher, suggesting activities that would improve learning. This time, I have made a paragraph division after every sentence. I've also numbered each sentence. Here is the anorectic piece:

(1) Teaching is obviously an extremely demanding job.

(2) Rarely am I able to come across an imaginative teacher who brings new, fresh, and creative instructive activities to the classroom.

(3) As each school year progresses the work assigned to me grows more tedious and boring.

(4) I could definitely lend my teachers a few good suggestions which would help keep learning fun.

(5) Group work is a way students could become interested in their studies.

(6) I am personally not an advocate of out-of-school group meetings, which cause scheduling problems and arguments between workers.

(7) Supervision by the teacher who assigned the group project is needed to prevent confusion and provide control and organization.

(8) Therefore, group work should mainly be done **in the classroom**.

(9) This way, students could interact and encourage one another by sharing a work load and explaining new research topics to their peers.

(10) Sometimes it is necessary and entertaining for kids just to work in a small study group without adult instruction.

(11) When a teacher doesn't allow this, learning seems monotonous and dull because the class is always forced to listen to the same person speak.

(12) Students, no matter what their age, are often easily amused by childlike activities.

(13) Instructors should take time in class to view films and sing songs.

(14) I'm totally serious when I say that hearing a catchy tune which goes along with a new vocabulary definition helps plant the word permanently into memory.

(15) Singing grabs the students' attention and is a fun idea that involves more kids in class.

(16) Chances are that teachers will wake up even the laziest students and even hear them chanting the jingles down the hall.

(17) As for the movies viewed in class, allow kids to bring in popcorn if they wish.

(18) They'll be less fidgety and more attentive if they have something to munch on.

(19) Also, it is helpful either to inform students of the story they will be watching or have them read the book as a class before the film is shown.

(20) They will be aware of what goes on during the story and view the film more closely, looking for key occurrences.

(21) Lastly, trips outside in nice weather could be helpful.

(22) Students enjoy a sunny atmosphere and can read, write, or have discussions while sitting comfortably in the grass.

(23) A change of surroundings is important every once in a while.

(24) These outdoor visits would keep the students from getting bored.

(25) I would be surprised and appreciative if some of my ideas were ever considered by school faculty members.

(26) Sadly, it is rare that teachers use their students' suggestions to improve situations in the classroom, especially in high school.

(27) Teachers don't yet seem to realize that some kids know better than they do what works when it comes to effective and enjoyable learning.

Procedure

1. Distribute copies of the obese and anorectic selections to your students—individually, in pairs, or in larger groups—and ask them to evaluate them. (The samples were holistically rated six on a scale of one to six, but you might find a different scale convenient.) Your students should keep in mind the grade level of the writer (ninth) and the conditions under which she or he was writing; two forty-minute sessions, a day apart.

2. Discuss the reasons for the ratings your students suggest. Someone is sure to comment that the first piece needs paragraph breaks and the second needs sentences combined into paragraphs. Discuss how much paragraphing should count in a final evaluation. An interesting issue is whether students have a preference between the obese paragraph and the anorectic ones.

3. Ask students to paragraph the selections, and compare results throughout the class. One way to do this is to ask students to write the number of the sentences where they would start a new paragraph. Then you write the numbers from 2 to 24/27 on the chalkboard, and as the students read aloud the numbers of the sentences where they would paragraph, simply put a mark next to each.

If your results are similar to mine, you will find that there is much more agreement on where the "Teaching" piece should be paragraphed than the one on the "Landfill." Discuss whether this is because "Teaching" is a better organized essay.

An Alternative Suggestion

If you think the students may be distracted by the fact that these are two separate essays, try typing the same essay both as obese and anorectic.

A Final Word

This is the longest chapter, by far, because teaching writing is the hardest thing we English teachers are asked to do. In view of that difficulty, it is not surprising that we seek formulas, simple lists of what to do and what to avoid. But if James Sledd (1996) is right—"Learning to write is learning to use all one's mind in making"— then there can be no shortcuts or formulas. Indeed, they will only stand in the way of the expression and articulation of ideas. If we forbid students to use passives, if they must have topic sentences, if they can't use the first-person pronoun, then we limit them, we circumscribe the growth of their minds.

Perhaps in no other area of the curriculum do we need so much patience. Yes, there may be growth spurts in a given student's writing, and certainly, the chemistry between an individual teacher and an individual student may accelerate such growth, but all in all, it is best to recognize that "Writing is a skill that improves with glacial slowness." I read this anonymous statement many years ago, when I myself was a high school English teacher. I hope it gives you as much comfort now as it gave me then.

5

Punctuation Today

Punctuation is and always has been a personal matter.

—M. B. PARKES

In the earliest Western texts, punctuation was not used; in later texts, it was not always welcomed. Cicero, for example, scorned readers who relied on it, and some early monks considered the "marking" (i.e., punctuating) of Biblical passages a kind of cheating, believing that the reader should have to discover the meaning of passages on his own. In the earliest Bibles, words weren't even separated from one another, a practice known as *scriptio continua* (now coming back in vogue in Internet addresses?). Try reading the following paragraph—and try it with your students.

> The basic purpose of punctuation is to make writing clearer or easier to read but as you can see from this paragraph it is not absolutely necessary in fact there was a time when punctuation did not exist indeed when words were not even separated from one another yet people managed to read texts in spite of the fact that they did not contain periods colons semicolons commas or any other mark of punctuation just as you were able to read this.

Punctuation conventions are always in flux. In the first six sentences (231 words) of his discussion of punctuation in *A Short Introduction to English Grammar* (1762) (see Activity 5–2), Robert Lowth used twenty-one commas, five semicolons, and one colon. In repunctuating the same passage, I used only eight commas and one semicolon, and even some of my commas are optional. In Lowth's time, writers typically used about three times more punctuation than we do today.

They employed a hierarchy that ran from period to colon to semicolon to comma. The period represented a pause double the length of the colon, the colon was double that of the semicolon, and the latter, double that of the comma. Lowth had very little to say of other marks and didn't even acknowledge the dash (though a generation later, Lindley Murray did).

Much has changed since. The colon is no longer a part of this hierarchy, and the semicolon is much less used than it once was. Dashes are common in contemporary prose. But the biggest change is simply that we do not use as much punctuation as writers did formerly. Some speculate that this is because readers today need less help than they did in the past.

By secondary school, most students have developed some feel for the different effects of the various punctuation marks, even if their knowledge of how to use them is shaky. To determine how much feel for the several marks your students may have, try this activity.

Activity 5–1: How Did Walt Kelley Punctuate His Slogan?

Goal: To demonstrate to students that they have an intuitive feel for the effects of various marks of punctuation.

Procedure

Walt Kelley, author of the "Pogo" comic strip, created the Earth Day slogan by playing off the famous Oliver Hazard Perry quotation, "We have met the enemy, and they are ours." Duplicate the following six versions of the slogan and ask your students to discuss the different effects. (You might also discuss their "correctness.")

1. We have met the enemy. And he is us.
2. We have met the enemy—and he is us.
3. We have met the enemy: and he is us.
4. We have met the enemy; and he is us.
5. We have met the enemy, and he is us.
6. We have met the enemy and he is us.

The first version creates the strongest separation and the second, almost as much. Both put heavy emphasis on the second element. The colon and the semicolon make for less of a pause between the two parts and produce more of a sense of balance. The semicolon has a heavier, more formal feel; the colon raises anticipation yet also creates a smoother transition. There is minimal separation between the parts in version 5, and of course, none at all in version 6.

Traditional grammar handbooks say that the fifth is the "correct" version, though they usually do not disallow the sixth, especially when the clauses are short. (Kelley used the sixth.) If we judge, however, by the standards of Well-Edited American Prose (WEAP), *all* are correct; that is, one could find any one of them in well-edited texts. More important from a pedagogical point of view, students need to be able to use all of these marks in order to write most effectively.

Activity 5–2: Contrasting Punctuation Styles

Goal: To demonstrate how much less punctuation is used today than was employed formerly.

Procedure

Following are two passages of roughly the same number of words and sentences (245 words/7 sentences vs. 231 words/6 sentences). The first is from *The Handbook of Research on Teaching the English Language Arts* (Flood et al., 1991); the second is the beginning of Lowth's discussion of punctuation in his *Short Introduction* (1762). Compare and discuss their differences in internal punctuation. (It is also interesting to contrast their paragraphing styles.)

The Handbook of Research

A recently reported study (Clarke, 1988), for example, in which first-grade children who were encouraged to use invented spelling in creative writing were compared with other first graders who were prompted to use correct spellings reveals that more of the inventive spellers were able to write independently early in the school year. Significant differences favoring the inventive spellers were also found with respect to text length and variety of words used. Moreover, the children using invented spelling scored higher on subsequent posttests of spelling and word recognition, even though their written productions showed no increase in the percentage of correct spelling over the term of the study. Clearly, these young writers were expanding their understandings of the nature and functions of spelling, even in the absence of direct instruction.

Herein lies a basic issue concerning the treatment of spelling and other writing conventions in the English language arts curriculum in the years ahead; namely, whether students' control over the conventions of writing is most effectively achieved by teacher-directed instruction using texts and other prepared materials or whether such control grows incidentally out of students' uses of these conventions in natural writing. The issue is not a trivial one. For at its heart lie basically different views about the nature and purposes of the English language arts curriculum (and curriculum in general), views that provide fuel to a general ongoing debate concerning the merits of "student-centered" versus "teacher-centered" approaches to curriculum development.

A Short Introduction to English Grammar

Punctuation is the art of marking in writing the several pauses, or rests, between sentences, and the parts of sentences, according to their proper quantity or proportion, as they are expressed in a just and accurate pronunciation.

As the several articulate sounds, the syllables and words, of which sentences consist, are marked by Letters; so the rests and pauses between sentences and their parts are marked by Points.

But, though the several articulate sounds are pretty fully and exactly marked by Letters of known and determinate power; yet the several pauses, which are used in a just pronunciation of discourse, are very imperfectly expressed by Points.

For the different degrees of connection between the several parts of sentences, and the different pauses in a just pronunciation, which express those degrees of connection according to their proper value, admit of great variety; but the whole number of Points, which we have to express this variety, amounts to only Four.

Hence it is, that we are under a necessity of expressing pauses of the same quantity, on different occasions, by different points; and more frequently, of expressing pauses of different quantity by the same points.

So that the doctrine of Punctuation must needs be very imperfect: few precise rules can be given, which will hold without exception in all cases; but much must be left to the judgment and taste of the writer.

The article excerpt from the *Handbook* employs twelve marks of punctuation to Lowth's twenty-seven. The largest percentage difference is in the semicolon, a ratio of five to one. The comma's ratio is twenty-one to nine, but notice that many of the Handbook's commas are of extremely minor consequence, little graphic tics, like the commas after *moreover, clearly, namely*, and the one between *Clarke* and the year. Eliminate these, and the comma ratio becomes about four to one. Some might argue that Lowth used more punctuation because he wrote longer sentences, but in fact there is little difference in sentence length in these two passages—38.5 words per sentence for Lowth to 35.0 for the *Handbook* article.

In addition to demonstrating how much less punctuation contemporary writers use, these activities also underscore the truth of M. B. Parkes' statement that punctuation has always been a personal matter. (Parkes, of Keble College, Oxford, is author of the authoritative *Pause and Effect: An Introduction to the History of Punctuation in the West* [1993].) But it's one thing to admit that fact and to acknowledge that punctuation isn't absolutely necessary, and quite another to try to help students learn to punctuate more effectively. And anyone who thinks that punctuation skills do not matter—particularly to secondary school English teachers—should consider the following little experiment.

In a workshop in a very good suburban school district, I passed out two versions of a spectacularly good essay written by a ninth-grade student describing her favorite place: an empty church. One copy was exactly what the student had written; the other was the same, *word for word*, except that I had corrected the student's punctuation. Half the teachers were asked to evaluate the original student essay, the other to evaluate the corrected version. No teacher gave the *corrected* essay anything less than an A−, and several rated it an A+. Of those who read the original essay, no one gave it more than a C+, and several rated it an F. Certainly, punctuation should not matter this much, but in many teachers' actual scoring practices, it does.

Can one be a good writer, even a great writer, without knowing much about punctuation? Certainly. Jean Jacques Rousseau, William Wordsworth, Alexandre Dumas, and Charlotte Bronte are all examples. But they were geniuses and had editors. We teachers mine a far more modest vein, and whatever we can do to help students express themselves more effectively should be done. That's what punctuation is after all—a tool for expression of the self.

A Fresh Look at the Comma

Randolph Quirk in *A Grammar of Contemporary English* says the comma "is the most flexible of all punctuation marks in the range of its use and it has eluded grammarians' attempts to categorize its uses satisfactorily" (1972, p. 1058). The following fresh look at the comma no doubt also fails to categorize its uses satisfactorily, but most of my students have found it more helpful than the twenty-seven independent items after the *comma* heading in the index of the *Harbrace College Handbook*. It avoids most technical jargon and radically reduces the number of "rules," grouping comma uses under five broad types.

The Clarifying Comma

A comma may be used between any two words to prevent a misreading of the writer's intended meaning. One might argue that all commas are clarifying, but I am using this term for commas that are necessary to prevent misreadings. Here are three examples. I have marked the places where clarifying commas are required.

> By noon / time had run out.
> Because prisoners had tried to escape / a fence was constructed.
> While he was hunting a white gazelle that cast no shadow/ the wings of his red hunting falcon blinded the animal.

Readers might understand these sentences without their respective commas, but only after rereading. It is the writer's responsibility to make her meaning clear on the *first* try.

The clarifying comma may also be useful to distinguish certain kinds of sentence starters from others:

> Now, I'm not sure of that. (*Now* is purely prefatory, a sort of verbal throat clearing.)
> Now I'm not sure of that. (i.e., at this time)
> Again, he felt hesitant. (i.e., it should be added that)
> Again he felt hesitant. (i.e., once more)

However, did you solve the problem? (*However* is conjunctive.)
However did you solve the problem? (*However* is intensive of *how*.)

The Courtesy Comma

A principle similar to the one involved with the clarifying comma is involved here, but the courtesy comma is usually less of a necessity. The two main uses of courtesy commas are

- to separate introductory material from main patterns, and
- to separate main patterns joined by conjunctions from one another.

It is a *courtesy* to let readers know where the introductory matter of a sentence ends by marking that spot with a comma:

Introductory matter   *Main pattern*
If a woman doesn't use a ritual apology, she may seem hard-edged. (Deborah Tannen)

Sometimes, teachers, students, and even editors fret over how long the introductory matter has to be before a comma becomes necessary. Some years ago, for example, while a colleague and I were working on a language arts textbook series, our editor insisted that we needed a *length rule* telling teachers and students when a comma should be used to set off introductory matter. We finally settled on "four or more words," but in reality there is no length requirement. Good writers or editors sometimes do not set off even relatively long introductory material. Nor does the structure of the material matter. In the following commaless examples, we find, respectively, an introductory adverb clause, a participial phrase, a prepositional phrase, and a pair of prepositional phrases. Note that all are relatively lengthy.

But whenever he closed his lids some glimpse of the last hours scorched them. (John Updike)
Given my black face and upbringing it was easy for me to flee into the anonymity of blackness. (James McBride)
In its original old blue-and-white Spode compartments there sparkle olives, celery, hard-boiled eggs, radishes. (E. B. White)
In the safe harbor of each other's company they could afford to abandon the ways of other people. (Toni Morrison)

Secondly, a courtesy comma is often inserted before connectives like *and*, *but*, and *so* when that connective comes between two main patterns:

Pattern 1   Pattern 2

I found that I missed being with schoolchildren, and I felt a longing to spend time in public schools again. (Jonathan Kozol)

The comma in this example notifies readers that the first full pattern is over, and that the second is about to begin. It's a courtesy. It isn't necessary. In fact, writers often omit it, especially when both patterns are short:

Teachers talk and students listen. (Martin Nystrand)
India emerged as the world's third largest publisher of books in English and forty-one percent of titles produced there were in English. (Randolph Quirk)

This use of the courtesy comma is supposedly limited to cases where a full sentence precedes *and* follows the connective. The reality is otherwise. With *but* especially, a comma is often used, even when the second pattern is less than a full sentence:

The fault may lie not in the approach, but in a failure to apply the approach in the appropriate writing situations. (Rei R. Noguchi)

With *and*, too, a comma may be used even when the second pattern is without a stated subject:

He could hear the ducks passing in the darkness, and feel the restless lurching of the dog. (Ernest Hemingway)

The Contrary (or Contrast) Comma

For the sake of simplicity you might want to consider this comma under the courtesy heading, but I prefer to treat it separately. It is widely used in WEAP and easily taught, easily identified. It reinforces the fact that the words it introduces are in contrast to the preceding statement. It is commonly found before a *not*, as in these examples:

No one paid any attention to me, not even to get me a glass of water. (Tracy Chevalier)
It's important to recognize that the word *optional* refers only to grammaticality, not to the importance of the adverbial information to the sentence. (Martha Kolln)

Students may need to develop an awareness of other words that trigger contrary commas, words like *instead, rather,* and *though/although.*

Furthermore, the teacher facilitates learning and collaborates with the learners, instead of dispensing information and testing students on it. (Constance Weaver)

Art is not difficult because it wishes to be, rather because it wishes to be art. (Donald Barthelme)

The contrary comma accounts for the fact that we so frequently find commas before the word *but*, even when it is not linking two full sentences. Note this example from James Thurber:

This was not because facts about the hero as a man were too meager, but because they were too complete. (James Thurber)

The Parenthetical Comma Pair

I stress the similarity of this type of comma to parentheses. The first comma indicates the beginning of the parenthetical material, the second marks the end:

Grant, the son of a tanner on the Western frontier, was everything Lee was not. (Bruce Catton)

Notice that Catton might just as readily have used parentheses:

Grant (the son of a tanner on the Western frontier) was everything Lee was not.

Catton also could have used a different grammatical structure:

Grant, *who was* the son of a tanner on the Western frontier, was everything Lee was not.

The point—and it seems difficult for some students—is to see that such commas come in *pairs* or *sets*. A single comma might even cause a misreading:

Misleading: Grant, the son of a tanner on the Western frontier was everything Lee was not. (Is the writer addressing someone named Grant, telling him something about a tanner's son?)

Misleading: Grant the son of a tanner on the Western frontier, was everything Lee was not. (Is *Grant* being used as a verb, with *son* as its object?)

Of course, no one would entertain the second misreading for more than an instant, but again, the careful punctuator makes sure the reader gets the correct impression the first time.

A *Testing Alert*: Because they lend themselves so well to a four-part answer key, questions on the parenthetical comma pair are commonly used on objective tests.

The parenthetical comma pair may also surround an individual word or a brief phrase:

Suffering a bout of insomnia, however, I was stalking sleep. (Brent Staples)
The purpose of all imitation is, of course, to enrich the grammatical options for original creation. (Harry Noden)

Of course, the need for the second comma in a parenthetical comma pair is obviated when the sentence ends where the second comma would have occurred:

This was the case with middle school teacher-researcher Rita Johnson, who was teaching a new subject in her science classroom. (Marion MacLean and Marian Mohr)

The Throwback Comma

Here's a great example of the need for what I'm calling the "throwback comma":

He tried in vain to find her, in his underclothes. (Quirk, 1972)

This type of comma throws the concluding phrase of a sentence back to the word or words that it modifies. Without it, the reader might assume that the phrase referred to the word or words immediately preceding. The comma is often needed when the concluding phrase is an *-ing* form:

He tried in vain to find her, wandering around in his underclothes.

Note: There is a discussion of the use of commas in a series in Chapter 2, pages 32–33.

Once students have a reasonably good grasp of the basic uses of commas, a superb rule for them to follow is: *When in doubt, leave the comma out.*

Three Useful Punctuation Marks: Colons, Dashes, and Parentheses

Although commas and periods account for more than eighty percent of all punctuation marks, students who want to learn to write must know how to use internal punctuation marks other than commas. To discover how useful colons, dashes, parentheses, and semicolons are in contemporary American prose, I studied their use in a WEAP standard—*The New York Times.*

I first examined an issue of the Sunday Magazine section (April 22, 2001), using four of the regular columns and one randomly chosen long article. Next, I studied six Sunday book reviews from the same issue. Finally, I analyzed seven articles that began on the front page of a daily issue (April 20, 2001). Table 5–1 shows the results.

Table 5–1. *Summary of Research on Four Internal Marks of Punctuation in* The New York Times

	Dash*	Colon	Parentheses	Semicolon
Four Sunday Magazine columns	13	11	13	9
One long Sunday article	25	32	11	11
Six Sunday book reviews	23	22	16	19
Seven front-page news articles	16	8	5	4
Totals	77	73	45	43

*A pair of dashes is counted as a single instance of a dash. Naturally, a pair of parentheses is also counted as one item.

Although the dash and colon are far more popular than the other two marks, there is considerable variation from writer to writer. For example, of the nineteen semicolons in the book-review data in Table 5–1, nine are from the same article. Similarly, of the twenty-three dashes, ten are from one review, and of the twenty-two colons, eleven are from a single review. The range is interesting, too. One book reviewer used a total of just five of these internal punctuation marks; another used twenty-three—in articles roughly similar in length.

To obtain what I thought would be an even more representative sample, I next analyzed articles from the "Writers on Writing" series, published in *The New York Times*. In this series, writers comment on a wide range of issues related to writing. Many of the authors are mainly fiction writers, but, of course, these essays are nonfiction. I began with the column that appeared on the day the idea occurred to me—April 23, 2001—and went back ten columns to December 18, 2000. Table 5–2 provides a summary of that research. Here, the utility of colons, dashes, and parentheses stands out even more. The semicolon finishes a distant fourth.

Again, individual variation is the rule. Amy Tan and Donald Westlake use very few of these internal punctuation marks, whereas David Shields and Susan Sontag use a great many. (The highest average use is actually by Divakaruni and Shields, as you can see from the last column of Table 5–2.) Susan Sontag is a heavy user of dashes; Shields, of colons. Over a third of all the semicolons are used by one writer, Rosellen Brown.

To develop modern punctuation skills in our students, we must teach colons, dashes, and parentheses. All appear to be used notably more frequently than semicolons. Indeed, in this survey, dashes and colons are used nearly twice as often.

Table 5–2. *Summary of Research on Four Internal Marks of Punctuation in* The New York Times' *"Writers on Writing"*

Author	Date	Words	Dash	Colon	Parentheses	Semicolon	Avg*
Susan Sontag	12/18/00	1,746	13	1	8	3	0.014
Rosellen Brown	1/1/01	1,982	7	7	3	9	0.013
Gail Goodwin	1/15/01	1,804	2	9	8	4	0.013
Donald Westlake	1/29/01	1,068	1	0	3	0	0.004
Chitra Divakaruni	2/12/01	1,285	4	6	7	3	0.016
Amy Tan	2/26/01	2,060	0	6	0	1	0.003
Allegra Goodman	3/12/01	1,513	2	8	0	1	0.007
Richard Stern	3/26/01	1,293	4	5	2	1	0.009
David Shields	4/ 9/01	1,418	4	10	3	4	0.015
Brad Leithauser	4/23/01	1,368	9	3	4	0	0.012
Totals		15,537	46	55	37	26	0.01
Average words		1,553					

*The total number of these marks used in the article divided by its total words.

The Colon

As a mark of punctuation, the colon is one of the oldest, going back to the Greeks. At one time, the colon was the main medial mark between the comma and the period. When the semicolon came into use, the sequence ran from comma, through semicolon, to colon, and period, as noted earlier.

Gradually, the colon was set aside for special uses, and the semicolon took over as the main medial pause. In more recent times, however, uses of the colon have multiplied. In spite of this, the typical handbook spends far more time on the semicolon than the colon. In the 1998 *Harbrace College Handbook*, for example, the colon is given about six lines (apart from trivia, such as its uses in salutations of letters or indications of time), whereas the semicolon merits about four *pages*.

Uses of the Colon

I first teach that the colon calls attention to what follows. It means or implies: *as follows, the following,* or *namely/that* or *which is.* (When a writer actually uses these terms, the colon is also called for.) Here are some examples:

Bring me the following: your tired, your hungry, and your sick. ["the following" is stated]

Bring me: your tired, your hungry, and your sick. ["the following" is implied]

I have three requests, namely: your silence, attention, and patience. ["namely" is stated]

I have three requests: your silence, attention, and patience. ["namely" is implied]

Activity 5–3: Colon Basics

Goal: To introduce the most general use of the colon as an announcer of what follows.

Possible Procedure

   A. Duplicate the following real-life uses of the colon. (Where brackets appear, the author used a colon. You may prefer simply to leave an extra space.)

      1. There were five slices [ ] red cabbage, onions, leeks, carrots, and turnips. (Tracy Chevalier)

      2. But this figure did not take into account what is currently happening in the country where data about anything has traditionally been notoriously difficult to come by [ ] China. (David Crystal)

      3. We must recognize first that the term "summary" is used to cover at least four different types of writing [ ] the synopsis, the abstract, the precis, and the paraphrase. (Mina Shaughnessy)

      4. The men on the Corner were honorable drinking men, with their own code of ethics [ ] A man's word was his bond, you never insulted anyone's woman, ... (James McBride)

      5. Inside [the British Museum] you'll find some of the greatest relics of humankind: the Elgin Marbles, the Rosetta Stone [ ] everything, it seems, but the Ark of the Covenant. (*Fodor's 2001: Great Britain*)

      6. Yammering about standards, of course, has a political purpose [ ] It shifts responsibility and perpetrates a fraud. (Susan Ohanian)

      7. But perfection has one grave defect [ ] it is apt to be dull. (Somerset Maugham)

      8. If I have learned from my times, I know something of the future [ ] It will rain again, on the world and on *The Times*. (Max Frankel)

      9. It was impossible to decide otherwise than he had done [ ] he must see Madame Olenska himself rather than let her secrets be bared to other eyes. (Edith Wharton)

    10. And she said [ ] "Do not ask, I beg you." (A. S. Byatt)

   B. Ask the students whether they can insert *as follows, the following, namely,* or *that* or *which is/are/was/were* where the brackets appear, suggesting that if they can, the best punctuation is a colon. Here are possible answers:

1. . . . *the following* five slices . . . .
2. . . . to come by *namely* . . . .
3. . . . at least *the following* four . . . .
4. . . . code of ethics, *namely* . . . .
5. . . . humankind, *as follows* . . . .
6. . . . has *the following* political purpose . . . .
7. . . . one grave defect, *namely* . . . .
8. . . . something of the future, *which is* . . . .
9. . . . than he had done, *namely* . . . .
10. . . . she said *the following* . . . .

Problems with the Traditional List of Colon Uses

Apart from conventional situations—such as to separate hour from minute, chapter from verse, title from subtitle, and after a salutation in business letters—textbooks typically list the following uses of the colon:

1. Before a list of items
2. Before a long, formal statement or quotation
3. Between independent clauses when the second explains or restates the idea of the first

Colons indeed *may* be employed in these situations, but they are not necessarily the only marks used. A list may be introduced by a dash rather than a colon, and Quirk et al. maintained three decades ago that "one will find the colon replaced by a comma at many points where a list is clearly to follow" (1972, p. 1067).

The second use is so commonly taught for student research papers that it is almost unthinkable—to students and some teachers—that any other mark could be correct. In the sample student research papers in the 1998 *Harbrace*, for example, it is the mark used in six of the seven possible places, and I believe the seventh case is a proofreading error (no punctuation at all is used).

In good contemporary writing, however, long, formal statements or quotations are introduced in all sorts of ways. In a "Centerpiece" article in the *Atlantic Monthly*, for example, Simon Winchester introduces his three lengthy, indented quotes twice by a comma and once by a period. In an article in *The English Journal*, three successive indented series of bulleted items are introduced by a colon, no punctuation at all, and a period, respectively (Rebecca Bowers Sipe, May 2001, pp. 36–37). Usage is changing.

The third "rule"—the notion that the colon is used "between independent clauses when the second explains or restates the idea of the first"—is an extremely limited view of what modern practice actually is. First of all, there is no need at all for both of the clauses to be "independent." It is quite common to find uses like these:

To sum up: the classical words adopted since the Renaissance have enriched the English language very greatly and have especially increased its number of synonyms. (Otto Jespersen)

One possible drawback: When you do die, the beneficiary gets the money immediately. (Jane Bryant Quinn)

Woodrow hovered, feeling threatened, which was how he felt whenever he entered her house: a country boy come to town. (John le Carré)

Well-known fact: In neither K–12 nor college English are systematic SWE [Standard Written English] grammar and usage much taught anymore.
(David Foster Wallace)

Note: Usage varies regarding whether to capitalize the first word after colons, as can be seen in these examples. A good guide for students is to capitalize when the material following the colon is lengthy. However, individual publishers do not necessarily follow this practice.

In addition, the part of a sentence after a colon may do many more things besides explaining or restating the idea of the first part. Here is a list of colon uses taken from *The Concise Oxford Companion to the English Language* (1996, p. 215), with its own examples:

- To introduce an antithesis/highlight a contrast.
    He died young: but he died rich.
    They spoke bitterly: and yet they were forgiving.
- To produce a staccato effect or in a progression or sequence.
    I called: you did not answer.
    He arrived: he knocked at the door: we waited: he went away
- To point from one clause to the next, in the following ways:
    a. Introduction to theme
        I want to say this: we are deeply grateful to all of you.
    b. Statement to example
        It was not easy: to begin with, I had to find the right house.
    c. Cause to effect
        The weather was bad: so we stayed at home.
    d. Premise to conclusion
        There are hundreds of wasps in the garden: there must be a nest there.

e. Statement to explanation

    I gave up: I had tried everything without success.

FOR LINGUISTICALLY CURIOUS STUDENTS

Students needn't memorize rules for the use of the colon: what is important is that they experiment and begin to appreciate what a fine tool in their punctuation kit it can be. It's liberating. To help students appreciate this, let them do colon searches on their own, bring examples to class, and discuss them.

Here are a few offbeat examples that I have discovered. How might you—or your students—characterize these uses? (Use the preceding *Concise Oxford Companion* list as a base, if you wish.)

1. . . . but he couldn't complain either: the wound had healed beautifully. (T. Coraghessan Boyle)
2. . . . he buttonholed me to talk about the guided Everest expedition he was planning: I should come along, he cajoled, and write an article about the climb for *Outside*. (Jon Krakauer)
3. "What if I am a pioneer, or even a genius?" Answer: then be one. (E. B. White)
4. If there's justice in the world, he'll rattle some cages. I know: big if. (David Gates)
5. Woodrow meanwhile was again visibly consulting his memory: bringing his eyebrows together in an amused and rueful frown. (John le Carré)
6. Notice that, by this definition, there is no fun in literacy: reading a novel, a magazine, or a poem doesn't count. (Gerald W. Bracey)
7. The fonts in all the churches are dry. I run my fingers through the dusty scallops of marble: not a drop for my hot forehead. (Frances Mayes)
8. So, indeed, Peter Mark Roget, physician, chess genius, expert on bees, phrenology, and the kaleidoscope: for all your noble ideals and Aristotelian logic, your book [Roget's *Thesaurus*] offers comfort only to the few. . . . (Simon Winchester)
9. Strawberry fields, milkmaids, a water conduit to supply London's needs, roadside inns: these were the Sunday afternoon joys of a walk in Islington for more than two centuries. (Gillian Tindall)
10. It was, of course, a miserable childhood: the happy childhood is hardly worth your while. (Frank McCourt)

As you can see from many of these sentences, the colon is *a tool of compression*, often replacing a connective or preposition, such as *by* or *because*. Indeed, it may often replace a good deal more, as in the fourth example above ("I know *that that is a* big if").

A Postscript

We English teachers have long taught that no punctuation should be used before a list or quote when the list or quote itself is a complement of the verb. But this practice is not always followed:

> The *Oxford English Dictionary* says that religion is: *Belief in, reverence for, and desire to please, a divine ruling power.* (Reynolds Price)
>
> For example, if the numbers read aloud were: 1, 2, 3, and 4, the answers would be 3, 5, and 7. (*Education Week*)
>
> . . . it is exciting to reread . . . of this noble theme. It goes: "Vigorous writing is concise. . . ." (E. B. White)
>
> You know what charm is: a way of getting the answer yes without having asked any clear question. (Albert Camus)

The Dash

The dash has always been suspect among traditionalists, who perhaps fear that once students meet it, they will use it everywhere. The 1998 *Harbrace College Handbook* employs a special icon and the word *caution* printed in color and capital letters, warning students: "Use dashes sparingly." (Emily Dickinson apparently never read that advice.) But if students are denied dashes, they will have to punctuate differently than real-world writers.

In fact, *even in top-flight literary magazines, dashes are used much more frequently than any other internal mark of punctuation, except for the comma.* (E. B. White used five *more* dashes in his 1979 Introduction to *The Elements of Style* than he did in the 1959 edition. The pieces are similar in length.)

Let's examine why the dash *is* an effective weapon. To begin, we accept the principle that clarity is promoted when subjects are close to their verbs and verbs are close to their complements. However, when a writer wishes to include more than one proposition within a given sentence, it has to be placed somewhere. Consider these two propositions.

The batter hit a home run.
She had two strikes on her.

How would you express these within the same sentence? Standard composition advice suggests that students should make a dependent clause out of the second sentence and place it either before or after the main clause:

A. Although she had two strikes on her, the batter hit a home run.
B. The batter hit a home run, although she had two strikes on her.

The advantage of both of these is that the key words *batter, hit,* and *home run* remain close to one another. But are there disadvantages as well? The A version holds up readers a long time before they reach the main action—or even know who *she* is. The B version suggests that the fact that the batter had two strikes on her is an afterthought. (I'm assuming that my readers know that it's much more difficult to hit a home run when one is batting with two strikes.)

On the other hand, I suspect that most readers would prefer either the A or the B version to these:

C.   The batter, although she had two strikes on her, hit a home run.
D.   The batter hit, although she had two strikes on her, a home run.

The problem with these is obvious—they do not follow the principle of keeping the subject close to its verb and the verb to its complement. In C, the reader, focused on *the batter,* has to read seven words before he finds out what the batter did. D needs no commentary: it's hard to imagine anyone actually writing it.

However, look what a writer can do with word deletion and a pair of dashes:

E.   The batter—with two strikes on her—hit a home run.
F.   The batter hit—with two strikes on her—a home run.

Yes, there is still a holdup between subject and verb, or verb and complement, but the dashes (plus word deletion) make the meaning easier to grasp visually. Furthermore, unlike A and B, E and F put proper emphasis on the critical clause that the batter accomplished her feat with two strikes.

Nothing is new here. Writers have been using dashes effectively for a very long time. Here are two century-plus-old examples. The first is Henry James. See how his dash pair creates a less intrusive break between subject and verb than some other structures might have:

> Very few Americans—indeed I think none—had ever seen this lady,
> about whom there were some singular stories.

And here is Stephen Crane, using a dash to emphasize a series of modifiers:

> Perhaps there was to him a divinity expressed in the voice of the other—stern,
> hard, with no reflection of fear in it.

Activity 5–4: Uses of the Dash

Goal: To help students appreciate the various placements and effects that can be achieved by the use of dashes.

Procedure

A. Duplicate the following effective uses of the dash in well-wrought sentences and discuss them with your students.

1. All the basic skills of composition—outlining, organizing ideas, using the library—are fully presented. (John E. Warriner)

2. "O God!" I screamed, and "O God!" again and again; for there before my eyes—pale and shaken, and half fainting, and groping before him with his hands, like a man restored from death—there stood Henry Jekyll! (Robert Louis Stevenson)

3. Above all—we were wet. (Frank McCourt)

4. And to retake control we need a new perspective—here called *uncommon sense*—on the nature of the problems we face. . . . (John S. Mayher)

5. I hope that *Portrait of America* remains as balanced as ever, for it offers samplings of virtually every kind of history—men's and women's, black and white, social and cultural, political and military, urban and economic, national and local—so that students can appreciate the rich diversity of the American experience. (Stephen B. Oates)

6. Suddenly machine-gun bullets hit a whitewashed building in front of me—and a long line of holes instantly appeared, just like stitches when the thread is yanked out fast. (Amy Tan)

7. Vouchers vanished, and school choice was limited to public schools—cold comfort for many children trapped in urban school systems. Even Mr. Bush's signature education proposal—to test every child from third to eighth grade—may be at risk. (William Bennett and Chester Finn, Jr.)

8. Thus, a brief description, a brief book review, a brief account of a single incident, a narrative merely outlining an action, the setting forth of a single idea—any one of these is best written in a single paragraph. (William Strunk, Jr., and E. B. White)

9. She came in with a smile—smiled all the time of her visit, except when she laughed, and smiled when she went away. (Jane Austen)

10. Keith was fifteen years old and this was one of the easiest of the Dr. Seuss books—not near the level of sophistication of, say, *Cat in the Hat*. (Susan Ohanian)

B. Of particular interest in the preceding sentences is *where* the dashes occur and *what alternatives* they replace. Here are some observations on these:

1. Break between complete subject ("all the basic skills of composition") and the predicate.
2. Break between an adverb ("there") and the sentence of which it is part ("there stood Henry Jekyll"). Note that Stevenson repeats the adverb, for clarity and emphasis.
3. Used between a sentence fragment and a full sentence.
4. Break between a complement ("perspective") and a prepositional phrase ("on the nature") modifying it.
5. Break between a sentence and an adverbial clause modifying it.
6. Used instead of a comma before the conjunction *and*.
7. Break between subject and predicate—in the second sentence.
8. Used to mark the end of a series of appositives (of "these") and the beginning of a sentence.
9. Used instead of a comma, in a compound predicate.
10. Used instead of a comma before a negation.

Parentheses

Most textbooks say that parentheses are used for "material of minor importance" or "nonessential matter." *Harbrace* warns, "Use parentheses sparingly" (1998, p. 228). But who is to say whether a bit of information is essential or not? Essential to whom? For what reason? In a grammatical sense, all appositives and all adjective clauses that have been set off by commas (nonrestrictive) are nonessential. Should we use *them* "sparingly"?

Reasons for Using Parentheses

The reality is that there are many good uses for parentheses, considerably more than I have space to catalogue. Here are a few:

1. Especially in technical material, a common use of parentheses is to clarify, define, or illustrate a term. Here are some examples from the book, *The Yard*, by Michael S. Sanders, which discusses building a destroyer at the Bath (Maine) Iron Works:

   . . . not yet even put out a request for proposals (RFP)

   various drawings that describe the ship deck by deck (the *scantling* plan)

   MAPP (Methyl Acetylene Propadiene) gas flows through the torch head

   . . . overall descriptions of . . . every hull plate, their thickness and where they are attached to each other (called a shell expansion)

These run through a thrust bearing (which absorbs the thrust of the turning screws) to the seventeen-foot-tall propellers.

This use of parentheses is often found in research papers.

2. Parentheses may simply be an *alternative* to some other way of expressing oneself. Here, for instance, is part of a recipe from *Under the Tuscan Sun* (Mayes, 1997):

> Meanwhile, in another pot, heat 5-1/2 cups of seasoned stock (chicken, veal, or vegetable) and 1/2 cup of white wine to a boil. . . . (p. 131)

The author might have written:

Meanwhile, in another pot, heat 5-1/2 cups of chicken, veal, or vegetable stock and 1/2 cup of white wine to a boil.

Does it really matter which of the two the writer chooses?

3. Oftentimes, it may indeed be "unnecessary" for a writer to include a detail that she has placed in parentheses, yet it may nevertheless have a *gracious* function:

> . . . its [the Council of Trent's] decrees became Church doctrine through a series of Papal bulls (so named for the *bulla*, or round lead seal, affixed to pronouncements from the pope himself). (Dava Sobel)

Frankly, I've heard and known the meaning of the expression "Papal bull" most of my life. I've also wondered about the origin of the term. Now I know, and am grateful to Dava Sobel for telling me.

4. Parentheses may be effectively used when one parenthetical remark is embedded within another:

> . . . if you happen to enter the same word in the thesaurus that comes with Microsoft Word (but which is made under contract by a firm with the name—somewhat less than encouraging for lexicographers—Soft-Art Inc.), you will be obligingly informed that. . . . (Simon Winchester)

5. Still another use is illustrated in the following quote, from James McBride's *The Color of Water:*

> I had dropped off my ex-girlfriend, Karen, a black model who renamed herself Karone ("My agent told me to do it") at her grandmother's house in Petersburg.

Here the parentheses seem more effective than a pair of dashes. Of course, it's not essential that the reader know why Karen renamed herself, but wouldn't you agree that it adds a bit of *texture*?

6. Finally, parentheses may be used to inject *humor*, as in the following:

> Appendix A at the back of the book lists usage problems and solutions that most writers and readers regard as valid. (In other words, usage problems and solutions that seem valid to me.) (Joe Glaser)

The material in parentheses is certainly not essential, but for a reader who finds books on style dull, it may be a welcome relief.

Here's an example, from *The New York Times* columnist Maureen Dowd:

> He [a TV character, Micky] is also fantasizing about cheating with his comely new assistant, who flatters Micky by saying, "I've read quite a few of your columns and I think you are very, very talented." (That line always works on me.) (July 25, 2001, p. A17)

Naturally, any given writer—whether professional or student—is free to use parentheses or not, but it is a mistake to assume that they should necessarily be used "sparingly." In her article "Mail," Anne Fadiman used twelve parentheses (and only five semicolons). The article was printed in *The American Scholar*, which Ms. Fadiman edits, and was republished in *The Best American Essays of 2001*.

Activity 5–5: Effective Uses of Parentheses

Goal: To help students see that parentheses can be used effectively, in numerous ways.

Procedure

Duplicate the following sentences, each of which contains an expression in parentheses. Let students discuss their purpose and effectiveness. A particularly good question to ask is whether the information is minor or nonessential. Share findings.

1. With the crowds waiting in line, it was almost like a holiday, and I would sell three times as many of my boiled peanuts as usual. (Selling peanuts was my summer job.) (Jimmy Carter)
2. . . . if they paid their way with 1,000 smuggled English pounds (about $5,000) each. (Max Frankel)
3. Even in the twentieth century, they [runes] can be found in tales of mystery and imagination (such as the work of J. R. R. Tolkein). (David Crystal)
4. Here he sat . . . timing his exploration by the library clock and the faint constriction of his belly. (Coffee is not to be had in the London Library.) (A. S. Byatt)
5. The recently deceased Penelope Fitzgerald is much cited by Byatt, as the author of a rare kind of historical fiction (short, diffident, but rich in

resonance), and before her there was Anthony Burgess. . . . (John Updike)

6. We are more familiar with essays resembling trains that huff and puff a lot but never seem to get out of the station. (At this moment, for instance, I am worrying about whether my own engine has enough power to make it up the gentle slope we are presently climbing.) (Robert Scholes)

7. In 1877 Samuel Clemens (Mark Twain) delivered a humorous speech telling an imaginary story of three great contemporary poets. . . . (Jean Malmstrom)

8. . . . to wait patiently for their eventual rescue in the form of graduation (if applicable), college (ditto), a job (in Empire Falls?), marriage (implausible) or death (finally). (Richard Russo)

9. [The stunned silence] was soon broken by a great cheer. . . . *Lo lop es mort!* (The wolf is dead!) (Stephen O'Shea)

10. The masons simply moved around the perimeter of the cupola on *ponti* (narrow platforms made from willow withes and supported on wooden rods inserted into the masonry). (Ross King)

Let Sleeping Semicolons Sleep

The semicolon is a relatively young mark of punctuation. In George Puttenham's *Arte of English Poesie*, published in 1589, which included advice on punctuation, the semicolon is not even mentioned. The mid-mark between a comma and a period at the time was the colon. However, not long after authors and printers distinguished the colon from the semicolon, the latter became much employed. In the two-thousand-word Preface to his 1762 *Grammar*, for example, Robert Lowth used nineteen semicolons (and only thirteen colons). In contrast, how many semicolons would you imagine E. B. White used in his roughly 1,600-word Introduction to *The Elements of Style*? One.

There isn't much question that many editors today shun semicolons. A friend of mine who wrote a book on Shakespeare for a popular audience (Robert Thomas Fallon, *A Theatergoer's Guide to Shakespeare*, [2001]) was told by his editor to remove all semicolons from his manuscript. He got rid of most of them—or his editor did.

Many modern writers and editors eschew the mark. Kurt Vonnegut, for example, is on record as saying that people enjoy reading him because he writes in simple sentences and never uses semicolons. The great poet W. S. Merwin, whose prose works are equally as beautifully written as his poems, uses a single semicolon in the 159 pages of his most recent book of nonfiction, *The Mays of Ventadorn*

(2002). And try to find a semicolon in the work of some of our better contemporary writers: in E. Annie Proulx's multiple prize–winning, *The Shipping News*, for example, or Charles Frazier's 1997 National Book Award winner, *Cold Mountain*. It isn't simply a matter of tastes or styles having become less complex, either. I semicolon-searched for ten minutes in one of the most complex novels I've read recently—Don DeLillo's *Underworld*—and found none.

It would be premature, however, to declare the semicolon dead. Reynolds Price used twenty of them in his essay, "Dear Harper: A Letter to a Godchild," which was included among the best American essays of 2001. (He also used twenty-eight parentheses and forty-seven dashes.)

It is hard to imagine a beautiful novel like Pulitzer Prize–winning, *The Hours*, by Michael Cunningham, without plentiful semicolons. (I opened the book randomly and found five on a single page—51.) They were a favorite mark of Cunningham's admired Virginia Woolf as well. And the tour de force short short story "Girl," by Jamaica Kincaid, which covered only a single page in the *New Yorker*, employed fifty semicolons—and no periods (it ends with a question mark). There is no doubt that the semicolon *can* be used to good effect.

But do *students* need it? In the two exemplary student research papers reprinted in the *Harbrace Handbook* (1998) (which total over sixteen pages, not counting indented quoted material), there is *not one semicolon* in either paper.

Students also do not need it to score well—or badly—in state writing examinations. Table 5–3 summarizes the use of semicolons in the 2001 Pennsylvania *Writing Assessment Handbook Supplements*. (*Note:* Pennsylvania requires that the semicolon be taught beginning in grade eight.)

Are these results unusual? Not a bit. In California and Texas, the semicolon is supposedly taught beginning in grade six, yet in the eight sample high school exit examinations in California, not one paper uses a semicolon; in Texas, there is one semicolon in sixteen sample exit tests.

In a study of state standards, I found the introduction of the semicolon ranged from grade five to grade nine, with the mean and median being grade seven.

Table 5–3. *Semicolons Used in Student Papers: Pennsylvania*

	Grade 6	Grade 9	Grade 11
Correctly used	0	0	2
Incorrectly used	2	0	2
Total semicolons	2	0	4
Total number of papers	27	40	38

Check your own state's semicolon standards. Then observe how frequently the mark is correctly used by students, even in exit exams.

This is madness. It's hard enough to teach the semicolon to college freshmen. Why attempt it with middle school kids? Probably, "Standardistas" like to give the illusion of completeness—and tough standards—to their list of punctuation marks. It's also a handy item in multiple-choice tests: (*Answer Key:* a. comma b. semicolon c. period d. no mark). At a college where I once taught, we used to give our freshmen a "Minimum Essentials Test." The semicolon was a *choice* in the answer key for all eleven punctuation questions. It was the *correct choice for not one item.*

My advice to my own college students is this: If you think you might one day become a writer, see me and I'll do what I can to teach you a little about the semicolon. (See Activity 5–6.) But if you don't, forget it. You can definitely write well without using the mark.

Why Is It Difficult to Teach the Uses of Semicolons?

To begin with, there are today two basic uses of the semicolon: as a *light period* (period with a shorter pause than a regular period) and as a *heavy comma* (comma with a longer pause than a regular comma). Since the former is far more common, let's discuss it first.

The two main uses of the light-period semicolon, according to handbooks, are:

1. Between closely related thoughts in compound sentences with no conjunction
2. In compound sentences before conjunctive adverbs or transitional expressions (*however, in addition*, etc.)

The semicolon is used—to quote *Harbrace*—to link "closely related independent clauses." Forget the fact that the average student doesn't know an independent clause from a minefield: How does he determine whether the clauses are "closely related"?

With a few words omitted for simplification, here are the opening independent clauses of one of *Harbrace*'s own student research papers:

> Jim and Carole Williams appear to be a comfortable couple in their fifties. The Williams own a home, drive nice cars, and were able to pay for a college education for their children.

Are these sentences "closely related"? They are both about the Williams couple, and both deal with their economic status. Must a student therefore use a semicolon between them? In fact, think about it: Especially within paragraphs, *every sentence is likely to be closely related* to the sentence that precedes it. That's what coherence is about.

The basic writing expert Mina Shaughnessy (1977) observed, "Explanations of when to use the semicolon instead of the period tend to be elusive (p. 34)." You bet they do, as anyone who has ever tried to teach the semicolon will testify. They will probably also agree with Shaughnessy's observation that after the semicolon is introduced, it tends to "take over"; that is, students tend to use it where they should not, as for example, after introductory and before concluding clauses:

> Although I expect to go to college someday; I'm not going right after high school.
>
> We always put our car in the garage; because we want to keep it looking good as new.

Shaughnessy also warned that teaching the semicolon as a way to avoid comma splices is ill advised (p. 23), yet that is exactly why it is found in so many state standards.

If you have a class full of budding professional writers who are interested in learning to use semicolons properly, the following lesson is a suggested approach.

Activity 5–6: Venturing to Teach the Semicolon

Goal: To teach the use of the semicolon as a light period to writers who are seriously interested in learning about it.

Background: As noted, a major problem concerning the semicolon is the determination of when it may be used effectively. The key problem with the rule is the phrase "closely related in meaning." How is a student to decide whether clauses are closely related in meaning?

Possible Procedure

A. Duplicate the sentences in section B, all of which were punctuated with semicolons by the professional writers who used them—or find examples of your own.

B. Ask the students to answer three questions for each sentence:
   - Are the sentences closely related in meaning?
   - Can you describe the relationship—for example, is it an *and* relationship, or a *but* relationship?
   - What difference would it have made if the writer had used a period instead?
     1. She will exist in archives, in books; her recorded voice will be stored away among other precious and venerated objects. (Michael Cunningham)
     2. Wash the white clothes on Monday and put them on the stone heap; wash the color clothes on Tuesday and put them on the clothesline to dry. (Jamaica Kincaid)

3. In good years the quota might be met in September; in bad years it might not be met at all. (Sebastian Junger)
4. Genetic evolution itself has taken millions of years; cultural evolution is a child of no more than twenty or thirty thousand years. (Ruth Nanda Anshen)
5. This person was neither Ralph nor his mother; it was a lady whom Isabel immediately saw to be a stranger to herself. (Henry James)
6. One construction is considered to be a sign of educated speech or writing, and is recommended for use; the other is considered uneducated, and banned. (David Crystal)
7. He tries to show it to her; the candlelight is too weak. (Saul Bellow)
8. Those are the basics; now we can discuss how to apply them. But that's only half the story; the other half has to do with verbs. (Joseph M. Williams)
9. The *notaio* is nothing like a notary; she's the legal person who conducts real-estate transactions in Italy. (Frances Mayes)
10. Norma Jean has never complained about his traveling; she has never made hurt remarks, like calling his truck a "widow-maker." (Bobbie Ann Mason)

C. The following are key observations we would like students to make. Writers may use semicolons when:
1. The logical relationship between the two sentences is unmistakable; no additional word is needed to tell the reader what it is.
2. The writers want their readers to give equal weight to the two sentences.
3. The effect of the period would be to make the relationship between the sentences less close.

Semicolons Before Conjunctive Adverbs: Do As I Say, Not As I Do

The second rule for use of the light-period semicolon is pure myth. Many years ago, while I was writing a ninth-grade textbook, I myself issued the injunction to use a semicolon before conjunctive adverbs. Then, I tried to find ten examples of the rule in print—just ten. Though my large desk was piled eyebrow-high with collections of essays and stories, it took me a good part of a day to find those illustrations. The reason became obvious early on: Good writers do *not* use semicolons before conjunctive adverbs and other transitional expressions. They use periods.

To prove that point, I studied a wide range of textbooks (see the following list), including some for which I have great respect. In each case, I have quoted the *mythrule* from the text verbatim. I have then quoted (after the *Reality* heading) the first use of a conjunctive adverb or transitional expression *in the author's own book*. (I have underlined the author's conjunctive adverb or transitional expression.) I began with the first page of text, in all cases but one. The reason for the exception will be mentioned.

Remarkably, in all of the texts, I found *not a single instance* of a semicolon being used before a conjunctive adverb or transitional expression in these first-instance uses. Not one. Here's the proof. Only look, and connect.

Examples

1. John E. Warriner. *English Composition and Grammar*. Benchmark Edition. Fourth Course [Tenth Grade]. Harcourt Brace Jovanovich, 1988.

   Mythrule: Use a semicolon between independent clauses joined by such words as *for example, for instance, that is, besides, accordingly, moreover, nevertheless, furthermore, otherwise, therefore, however, consequently, instead,* and *hence.*

   Reality: If your purpose is to inform, you will include specific details. . . . <u>However</u>, if you are telling a story you will use less formal language and choose amusing details or events. (pp. 5–6)

2. Sheridan Blau, Peter Elbow, and Don Killgallon. *The Writer's Craft.* [Grade 11]. McDougal Littell, 1998.

   Mythrule: Use a semicolon before a conjunctive adverb or a transitional expression that joins the clauses of a compound sentence.

   Reality: . . . many of these wild imaginings . . . turn out to be remarkably prophetic. <u>For example</u>, . . . , you have probably seen the seemingly preposterous ideas of science-fiction writers . . . routinely become reality. (p. 3)

3. Dave Kemper, Patrick Sebranek, and Verne Meyer. *Writer INC.* [High School]. Great Source Education Group, 2001.

   Mythrule: A semicolon is used *before* a conjunctive adverb (and a comma after it) when the word connects two independent clauses in a compound sentence.

   Reality: Barb could have tried another shaping activity like free writing. <u>However</u>, after her initial gathering, she felt more than ready to write her first draft. (012)

4. John V. Thill and Courtland L. Bovée. *Excellence in Business Communication*. Third Edition [College]. McGraw-Hill, 1996.

Mythrule: Finally, a semicolon should be used to separate independent clauses when the second one begins with a word such as *however, therefore,* or *nevertheless* or a phrase such as *for example* or *in that case.*
Reality: So by the time a message makes its way all the way up or down the chain, it may bear little resemblance to the original idea. <u>As a consequence</u>, people at lower levels may have only a vague idea of what top management expects of them. . . . (p. 4)

5. Diana Hacker. *The Bedford Handbook for Writers.* Fourth Edition [College]. Bedford Books of St. Martin's Press, 1994.

    Mythrule: Use a semicolon between independent clauses linked with a conjunctive adverb or transitional phrase.
    Reality: It is unlikely that you will make final decisions about all of these matters until later in the writing process. . . . <u>Nevertheless</u>, you can save yourself time by thinking about as many of them as possible in advance. (p. 3)

6. Susanna Rich. *The Flexible Writer: A Basic Guide.* Third Edition [College]. Allyn & Bacon, 1998.

    Mythrule: When a comma is insufficient to mark off part of a sentence, use a semicolon as follows: To make a transition into an afterthought, such as *nevertheless, furthermore, hence.*
    Reality: Students have many insights into language that the teacher may not have. <u>In addition</u>, students know things that their writing teachers may not but would like to learn. (p. 7)

7. John C. Hodges et al. *Harbrace College Handbook* (Revised 13th Edition) [College]. Harcourt Brace, 1998.

    Mythrule: A semicolon precedes conjunctive adverbs only when they come between independent clauses.
    Reality: Three versions of a new student essay illustrate these chapters, and we have expanded our discussion of invention and revision. <u>Similarly</u>, we divided what had been a one-hundred-page chapter on the research paper into two. . . . (p. vii)

    (I have gone to the Preface of this text because in the first thirty pages of the text itself there are no conjunctive adverbs between sentences. In fact, there are virtually no conjunctive adverbs and no semicolons in these thirty pages.)

8. Lynn Quitman Troyka. *Simon & Schuster Handbook for Writers.* Fifth Edition [College]. Prentice Hall, 1999.

    Mythrule: Conjunctive adverbs and other transitional expressions link ideas between sentences. When these words fall between sentences, a period or semicolon must immediately precede them.

Reality: Doing so prepares you for today's highly technological work-place, in which jobs demand reading with understanding and writing with skill. . . . <u>Also</u>, the ability to write well identifies you as an edu-cated person. . . . (p. 3)

At last. With the Troyka text, we find an author who acknowledges that peri-ods may be used before conjunctive adverbs and other transitional expressions. I applaud her. Still, it is noteworthy that in her first chapter, Ms. Troyka herself *never* uses a semicolon before a conjunctive adverb or transitional expression, though she uses a large number of such expressions. Moreover, there are only three semi-colons in her entire first chapter. (I have not counted boxed material, lists, or the exercises.) Perhaps, in a subsequent edition, Ms. Troyka will be the first to note that the period is the *customary* mark before conjunctive adverbs and other tran-sitional expressions.

One final observation: Mina P. Shaughnessy says that logical connectives appear most commonly "at the beginning of the sentence when the preceding sen-tence is terminated by a semicolon and at varying points after the subject when the preceding sentence is terminated by a period (p. 36)." But in her own book—though she uses notably more semicolons than the average writer—she does not use them before conjunctive adverbs *at all* in her first two chapters. In Chapter 1 she uses eight conjunctive adverbs at the beginning of a second sentence, and in Chapter 2 she uses twenty. That's forty-three pages without a single illustration of the "rule."

The Semicolon As a Heavy Comma

Textbooks typically allow use of the semicolon as a "heavy comma" in just two instances:

1. Before a simple conjunction joining sentences that already contain commas
2. Between items in a series if the items contain commas

Basically, these rules help to keep sentence parts distinct. They are not unreason-able rules, but only occasionally does one encounter either situation in profes-sional writing, much less in the writing of students. Check out your grammar book: The examples of these two rules are almost always made up by the editors, not drawn from real-world writing.

As usually stated, the first rule is oversimplified: It is not mainly a question of *how many* commas are contained in the existing clauses. Here, for example, are two sentences from Jonathan Kozol's *Savage Inequalities.* The sentences are roughly equal in length. Notice that Kozol uses no semicolon in the sentence that contains five additional commas, while a semicolon *is* used in the sentence with only two. (Italics are mine.)

> Even in the suburbs, nonetheless, it has been noted that a differential system still exists, *and* it may not be surprising to discover that the differences are once again determined by the social class, parental wealth, and sometimes race, of the school children. (pp. 119–20)
>
> It is unlikely that the parents or the kids in Rye or Riverdale know much about realities like these; *and,* if they do, they may well tell themselves that Mississippi is a distant place and that they have work enough to do to face inequities in New York City. (p. 132)

The second heavy-comma rule applies to items in a series. It is rarely used, partly because writers write in contexts, not in vacuums. Consider the two following examples, where heavy commas *might* have been used but were *not:*

> Galileo paid out dowry installments to his newly married sister Virginia's fractious husband, Benedetto Landucci, supported his mother and sixteen-year-old brother, Michelangelo, and maintained his sister Livia at the convent of San Giuliano until he could arrange for her to be wed. (Dava Sobel)
>
> . . . will point the finger at the kangaroo court of unelected aides including press secretary, Alastair Campbell, Lord Irvine, the lord chancellor, and chief of staff, Jonathan Powell. (*The Guardian, Europe*, March 10, 2001)

In each case, the writer is assuming that the reader has certain information and therefore does not need the help of heavy-comma semicolons. Dava Sobel assumes her readers are attentive enough to know, for one thing, that the *artist* Michelangelo is not a character in her book. The journalist who wrote the second item assumes that his readers know who the named governmental officials are.

Frankly, I taught the heavy-comma use of the semicolon to high school and college classes for decades: it seemed so intellectually interesting. Yet in the thousands of student essays that I read through those years, I can't recall a single instance in which a student *needed* this type of semicolon in a list.

FOR LINGUISTICALLY CURIOUS STUDENTS

There are numerous heavy-comma uses of the semicolon that are *not* mentioned in the handbooks, as illustrated by the following sentences. Give your students these examples, and see if they can determine what the underlying "rules" are—if any. Keep in mind that these are idiosyncratic, hard-to-find uses of the semicolon (believe me, they are—but not as difficult to find as semicolons before conjunctive adverbs).

1. . . . they parted; a wonderful instance of advice being given on such a point, without being resented. (Jane Austen)
2. Tears sprang into my eyes; Susan's too. (Tom Romano)
3. Sula's because he was dead; Nel's because he wasn't. (Toni Morrison)
4. Commercial fishing simply wouldn't be possible without ice. Without diesel engines, maybe; without loran, weather faxes, or hydraulic winches; but not without ice. (Sebastian Junger)
5. Lucy did not have lots of children after all; just two. (Anne Tyler)
6. It has been vouchsafed, for example, to very few Christian believers to have had a sensible vision of their Saviour; though enough appearances of this sort are on record, by way of miraculous exception, to merit our attention later. (William James)
7. He [Michelangelo] worshipped beauty in others; and had so little himself. (Irving Stone)
8. Isaac Wister quickly clarified the purpose of the museum . . . as "for the use and study of investigators; rather than a mere gaping public." (Joan P. Capuzzi Giresi)
9. French, for example, is the official language of Chad; Portuguese in Angola. (David Crystal)
10. For British troops, Vera Lynn, "the forces' sweetheart", was a favourite pin-up; for Americans, Betty Grable. (Robert McCrum)

A Postscript

We have all along taken the position expressed by M. B. Parkes that the use of punctuation is and has always been a personal matter. Thus, it should come as no surprise that others punctuate sentences differently than we might. Here are some examples involving the marks we have been discussing. After each one, I have made a comment (in brackets) telling what I think the more conventional punctuation might have been. Discuss these with interested students. And viva diversity!

1. Behind Benito's back he makes a strange gesture; he nods toward Benito, then pulls down his eyelids. (Frances Mayle)
    [Colon rather than a semicolon.]
2. Such codes are designed to protect students from sexual harassment, always a risk when there is a power imbalance in a couple—for example, when one gives grades to the other. (Randy Cohen)
    [Semicolon rather than the dash.]

3. He looked at his watch; five-forty already. (David Guterson)
    [Colon rather than a semicolon.]

4. Hence their insistence that the spoken language must defer to the writ-
    ten and that custom must sometimes defer to criticism—for in that era
    "custom" was simply another name for the practices of the privileged.
    (Geoffrey Nunberg)
    [A comma rather than a dash is the customary mark.]

5. Here is the great difference between reading and writing. Reading is a
    vocation, a skill, at which, with practice, you are bound to become more
    expert. (Susan Sontag)
    [A colon, rather than a period, would be used by most writers.]

6. Only two facts about his youth stand out. He married. . . . (Richard
    Brookhiser)
    [Many would use a colon rather than a period, though the length of the
    statement after *out* would be a factor in the choice.]

7. At the heart of Bakhtin's social logic is a reciprocity of roles: that is, the
    roles of teacher and learner . . . each respectively and mutually entail
    those of the other. . . . (Nystrand et al.)
    [The typical punctuation before *that is* is supposed to be a semicolon,
    not a colon.]

8. Looking through the front window, he had seen no people: none of the
    busy afternoon crew of Street Cleaners, Landscape Workers, and Food
    Delivery people who usually populated the community at that time of
    day. (Lois Lowry)
    [Many writers and editors would prefer a dash.]

9. But here's the thing. I am certain that if you tracked down the competi-
    tors to see what has become of them since, you would find that every
    one of the Americans was pulling down $850,000 a year . . . while the
    British were studying the tonal qualities of sixteenth-century choral
    music in Lower Silesia and wearing sweat. (Bill Bryson)
    [Many writers would ordinarily use a colon—though the excessive
    length of the second sentence lends some justification to the period.]

10. His curious eyes rested long upon her face and on her hair: and, as he
    thought of what she must have been then, in that time of her first girl-
    ish beauty, a strange, friendly pity for her entered his soul. (James Joyce)
    [Surely, most writers would use a semicolon, yet James Joyce is as expert
    and self-conscious a punctuator as we have ever had.]

The Possessive "Apoxtrophe"

The history of punctuation in the West is littered with "marks" that have come and gone, like the *simplex ductus* (a 7-shaped stroke that indicated pauses), the *hedera* (a kind of ivy leaf on its side, which had several uses, historically), and the *punctus elevatus* (a mark like the semicolon, but with the period placed below the comma and the comma on its side with its head facing left). It's all the more curious, therefore, that one of the oldest punctuation marks to retain its original form and function, the apostrophe, gives English writers so much trouble. Actually, most of the difficulty does not arise from the apostrophe in its original Greek usage, as a symbol to indicate elision of a vowel. It stems, rather, from a usage that did not exist until the late 1500s, when the apostrophe was first employed to indicate possessive case, a function that had been performed in Old and Middle English by endings and that is currently performed in user-friendly languages like French, Italian, and Spanish exclusively by prepositions. This is the mark I am calling the possessive *apoxtrophe*.

How did English get into this unique difficulty? And what are some ways we can help our students out of it?

Some Sources of the Problem

First of all, while possessive case is typically said to "indicate ownership," the reality is that if we take *ownership* literally, it *often* does not. Even if ownership is understood in a more general sense, nouns ending in 's frequently do not indicate ownership. Compare these phrases:

the child's toy
the child's foot
the child's brother
the child's arrival
the child's kidnapper

The child may literally own her toy, but certainly does not own her foot in the same sense, and she clearly does not own her brother (just ask him). In the last two examples, there is no ownership of any kind; indeed, in the last example, it's the kidnapper who possesses the child, not the other way around. Yet all are correctly punctuated with an apostrophe plus *s,* by the standards of contemporary usage.

Linguist Charles Carpenter Fries' study of letters written by American citizens to the United States Government (reported in *American English Grammar* [1940]) revealed that only 40 percent of the inflected genitives (i.e., possessives indicated by 's) indicated possession, and Fries noted that he arrived at that high a figure only by a "liberally interpreted" notion of "possessive" (p. 75).

Secondly, writers and editors themselves have never been in full agreement regarding the "rules" for use of the apostrophe, and the rules have changed over time. Indeed, even grammarians have differed among themselves. The editors of *The Concise Oxford Companion to the English Language* point out: "It appears from the evidence that there was never a golden age in which the rules for the use of the possessive apostrophe in English were clear-cut and known, understood, and followed by most educated people" (p. 76). To illustrate, which of the following do you think is "correct"?

A. the teachers credit union
B. the teacher's credit union
C. the teachers' credit union

Every English teacher I have asked has answered that the correct version is C, and with good reason, since the teachers (plural) do own the credit union. Very well, but when I emailed a very cooperative Karen Ketterer in Harrisburg, she told me that with only two exceptions, every Pennsylvania credit union owned by teachers or employees spelled its name without any apostrophe. Not very long ago, many more did. Usage has simply changed.

What about place names, like Pikes Peak and Devils Island? If you consult a dictionary or atlas, you will discover that the former has no apostrophe but the latter does. Incidentally, the U.S. Board of Geographic Names recommended an end to possessive forms in place names in 1891—apparently to little effect, since the American Cartographic Association made the same recommendation in the early 1950s. (Most geographical place names in the United States today seem to omit the apostrophe.)

Brand names are yet another problem. Within a block of each other on my way to the college where I taught for several years, there are two signs that read, respectively:

Starbucks Coffee
Breugger's Bagels

Clearly, the relationship between Starbuck and coffee and Breugger and bagels is identical. Do the Starbuck advertisers then not know "good grammar"? Don't tell me that the people who named their coffee after George Starbuck, Captain Ahab's first mate aboard Melville's *Pequod*, are illiterate. I suspect they found the apostrophe aesthetically unpleasant, particularly for their famous circular logo.

Ask your students to do their own sign search the next time they're traveling, or in their own neighborhood, for that matter. They are sure to discover many "missing" apostrophes (and some that ought to be missing), regardless of the literacy level of the perpetrator.

Third, English is the only language that assigns double duty to the apostrophe. In other languages, it is used mainly for contractions. (*Note:* Modern German uses an apostrophe plus *s*—with names only—if the name ends in an *s* sound: Gunther Grass's novels, Leibnitz's philosophy.)

The fourth root of the problem is historical. Old English had noun case endings, including one for the genitive (possessive). Our *stone's,* for example (as in "a stone's throw"), was *stanes* in Old English. In Middle English the *-es* ending was frequently written and pronounced *-is*. By the time of Bishop Robert Lowth (1710–1787), phrases like "Godis grace" had been contracted—"very improperly," Lowth says—to "God's grace." Thus the possessive inflection simply became a contraction.

An alternative possessive, the *his* genitive (sometimes used by Shakespeare: "Nor Mars *his* sword, nor war's quick fire shall burn" [Sonnet 55]), began in Old English times and was widespread in the seventeenth century. The *her* form was also common.

Although apostrophes were not used in England to mark possessives until the *late* 1500s, once the practice was instituted, it spread rapidly. For instance, in the First Folio (1623) of Shakespeare's plays only 4 percent of possessives were marked with an apostrophe, and most of these were loanwords. However, by the Fourth Folio (1685), there is a "fairly consistent use of the apostrophe for possessives in the singular" (Little, 1986, p. 15).

Finally, we can put a good share of the blame on textbooks. Every one that I know (mis)defines possessive nouns as nouns used to show "possession or ownership." Some qualify this with "usually," and especially at the college level, there is sometimes a further qualification, as in *The Bedford Handbook for Writers,* which admits that ownership is sometimes only "loosely implied" (Hacker, 1994, p. 385). (One of the two examples of this loosely implied ownership is "a day's work." You decide in what loose sense *day* possesses *work.*) The *Simon & Schuster Handbook for Writers* says the possessive apostrophe may mark ownership or "close relationship" (Troyka, 1999, p. 439). But "close relationship" is a vague phrase at best: How "close" is the relationship between a person and his or her ex-spouse, for example? Of course, it's easier to criticize than to correct. These two are among the best handbooks in print.

At elementary and secondary levels, the notion of "possession" or "ownership" is virtually universal in textbooks, and school children grow up having internalized this false idea. Why do textbook writers do this? Do they themselves not know any better? Not necessarily, I suspect. As a person with a lifetime of experience in writing English textbooks, I can testify that there is an enormous pressure to *keep things simple*. If one were to confront a textbook editor with a manuscript that paid a great deal of detail to possessives, he or she would likely respond, "No one cares about that. Just keep it simple." There is in fact an unwritten law in the school divisions of major publishing houses: "What's simple is what sells." Alas, this proposition is strongly supported by the entire history of textbook publishing.

A Suggested Solution

The most essential part of any solution is to disabuse people of the notion that the possessive apostrophe denotes ownership. As indicated in Fries' research, writers who act on that misinformation are going to get it wrong—more than half of the time.

The most helpful thing for students is to alert them to look for two nouns in succession: a *possessing* noun and a *possessed* noun. "You can't have one," goes the song ("Love and Marriage"), "without the other." While this strategy has some pitfalls of its own—for instance, one has to remember the point about possession not being literal—it has the great virtue of preventing students from making the most egregious of all apostrophe errors: putting apostrophes on verbs and nouns that end in *s*: "This store take's credit cards" or "We feature cake's and pie's" are two examples that I have seen. Better for students never to use apostrophes on possessive nouns than to make these kinds of errors.

Activity 5–7: Prevailing over the Possessive

Goal: To lead students to the discovery that in most cases of noun, plus an *s* sound, plus another noun, they will need an apostrophe before or after the *s*.

Procedure

1. You may begin in either of two ways: Give the students a series of phrases like those below, or let them find their own examples of N#1+*s* sound+N#2. (I have purposely chosen examples in which there is clearly no literal possession.) Ideally, the labels at the top of the columns should be supplied after the discussion.

Determiner	N#1	+s	N#2
	Friday	+s	child
one	train	+s	departure
a	moment	+s	hesitation
the	children	+s	kidnapper
two	week	+s	salary
several	neighbor	+s	concerns

2. Ask students what they find significant about the types of words in the second and fourth columns (both are nouns).

3. Next ask students whether they would use an apostrophe before or after the *s* sound. In all cases, they should, even though no items involve ownership.

4. Ask next *where* the apostrophe should be placed. Students should be able to see that if the *s* sound is not part of the first (possessing) noun, the apostrophe is placed between the noun and the *s*. On the other hand, if the *s* sound is part of the first noun—*weeks, neighbors*—one must first attach it to them, then add the apostrophe: *weeks', neighbors'*. This has the virtue of forcing students to look first at the meaning of the first of the two successive nouns.

   Note: We cannot break a phrase like "my mathematics teacher" into the components my+mathematic+s+teacher. Thus, there is no possessive apostrophe.

5. A final check is widely and wisely recommended in many textbooks: Transpose the two nouns and put an *of* or *for* between them:

child	of	Friday
departure	of	one train
hesitation	for/of	a moment
kidnapper	of	the children
salary	for/of	two weeks
concerns	of	several neighbors

   Occasionally, this test may not work. Indeed, some may consider "child of Friday" awkward, and—bringing in another example—many might feel that a "ladies' man" is not a man *for* the ladies. But the check is very much worth using nonetheless and can be particularly useful in differentiating between possessive singular and possessive plural in many instances. For example, in speech, "the witness(es) testimony" doesn't tell how many witnesses were involved. But an *of*-phrase check would:

testimony	of	the witness	——	the witness's testimony
testimony	of	the witnesses	——	the witnesses' testimony

Student writers simply need to ask themselves which meaning they intend.

Here are a few caveats regarding this noun+s+noun approach:

1. Traditional grammarians tend to call *all* words that modify nouns "adjectives." We need to disabuse students of this notion.

2. Modifiers of the possessed noun may be found between it and the possessing noun. In the writing of professionals, this may occur as much as thirty percent of the time, as exemplified by the italicized words in the following phrases:

the students' *daily* homework

the house's *true* value

a teacher's *most delicate and essential* task

The words that are modifiers rather than possessed nouns can usually be dropped without affecting the meaning:

Wrong: the students' daily (*daily* is not a head noun)

Right: the students' homework (*homework* is a head noun)

3. The noun that is being possessed is sometimes understood. In my research on the writing of professionals, this occurred only 5.5 percent of the time. In a study of five carefully edited student research reports, it occurred in only one case of forty-eight correctly punctuated possessives (two percent of all cases): "The tell-tale heart was the narrator's [heart]." In teaching the possessive to Freshman English students, therefore, I make only passing mention of this possibility. You may wish to ignore it entirely.

Activity 5–8: Nonpossessing Possessives

Goal: To furnish some sense of the range of relationships signaled by "possessives."

Procedure

Intellectually curious people—and certainly any student who may wish to become an English teacher—might be made familiar with at least some of the various relationships that actually exist between the "possessing" and the "possessed" nouns. Here are some of these relationships. (*Note:* An alternative to giving these to students is to provide an example or two of each type and ask the kids to discuss the nature of the relationship between possessing and possessed noun.)

1. *Subjective genitive:* The possessing noun is the *subject* of the possessed noun (which is actually a verb in disguise; that is, a nominalized verb):

   his mother's request (mother requests)

   the train's arrival (train arrives)

   the dictionary's discussion (dictionary discusses)

   our doctor's advice (doctor advises)

2. *Objective genitive:* The possessing noun is the *object* of the possessed noun—which is, again, a nominalized verb form:

   the convict's release (someone released the convict)

   the policy's critics (persons criticized the policy)

   the stagecoach's pursuers (people pursued the stagecoach)

3. *Genitive of origin:* The possessing noun states the *origin* of the possessed noun. This is like the subjective genitive but may be distinguished from the latter when attention centers on the result rather than the activity:

the child's story	(the child originated the story)
Webster's dictionary	(Webster made the dictionary)
the inventor's ideas	(she originated them)

Out of context, one cannot tell whether a phrase like "the writer's books" indicates literal possession (the books owned by the writer) or is a genitive of origin (the books written by the writer).

4. *Genitive of measure:* The possessing noun *measures* the possessed noun—in time, space, or value:

a moment's hesitation	(hesitation lasted a moment)
an acre's crops	(crops covering an acre of space)
a dime's worth	(the value of a dime)

5. *Descriptive genitive:* The possessing noun *describes* the possessed noun:

a boy's school	(what kind of school)
a ladies' man	(what kind of man)
Chaucer's time	(which time period)

With reference to this whole matter, I'm reminded of the lexicographer who once said, "He who worries about hyphens will surely go mad." The same fate may befall those who worry about the possessive apostrophe. To escape it, I propose giving the mark a distinct name: the a*pox*trophe. (I first coined this term in an article published in *Education Week*.) Ultimately, we might decide to declare a pox on all apoxtrophes, and use apostrophes only for contractions. It would save embarrassment for those trying to sell cake's and pie's and relieve anxiety for many others. And who but a thimbleful of schoolmasters and -marms would mourn the loss?

In his *Grammatical Institutes*, originally published in 1760, the conservative grammarian/lexicographer John Ash (1785) indicated that he had little use for the apostrophe as an indicator of possession, and he predicted that it would disappear (p. 31). One could take this as an indication of what cloudy crystal balls grammarians own—or mark Ash as a man who was two and a half centuries before his time.

Contractions Are Not Linguistic Lice

Some years ago an editor friend of mine told me the story of an author who insisted, when he saw her editing job of his manuscript, that she change all contracted forms to the uncontracted forms that he had used initially. I wondered how that contributor conceived the idea that contractions were some form of linguistic lice, and I tried to discover what the root of that notion might be.

I didn't have far to look. The copy of the *Harbrace College Handbook* (1982) that some of my own students were using had this to say:

189

Contractions are common in informal English, especially in dialogue: see the examples on page 162. But contracted forms (like *won't* or *there's*) are usually written out (*will not, there is*) in a formal composition—which is not as casual or spontaneous as conversational English is. (p. 220)

What Is a "Formal Composition"? And Who Writes Them?

The *Harbrace* advice is seconded by the most recent Warriner revival: "Contractions are rare in formal writing." But what is this "formal" writing, and who are the formal writers? All right, I confess: I'm one of them myself. I recently checked my Ph.D. dissertation, and sure enough, no contractions. But how many of our students will ever do this kind of writing?

I also checked the articles in *The Best American Essays, 2001* (Norris, 2001). A contracted form is used within the first three pages of twenty of the twenty-six essays. Some examples: *you wouldn't, it'll, it's, there's,* and *I've.* Doesn't it make sense to train our students to write for magazines like *The New Yorker, Harper's,* and *The American Scholar,* rather than for doctoral dissertations?

Try the following quiz, which I made up a few years ago (for "Let's Get Off the Mythmobile," *The English Journal,* October 1985). Can you guess where these sentences might have appeared? Are they largely from "informal" sources?

1. . . . most economists expect *they'll* be worse.
2. Even if it should be a fiction *it's* produced under pressure, *there's* a lot at stake.
3. If I had it to write over, *I'd* choose "relative."
4. We *don't* know who the speakers are . . . and we *can't* ask them for clarification.
5. . . . by an American resident of Paris I happened to know—Matthew Pillsbury, *who's* ten.
6. *I'm* sorry we asked . . . we starve ourselves and pray till *we're* blue.
7. Like many humanists, I hate to talk about money in connection with my profession. *It's* demeaning.
8. Frankly, we *don't* know, since the collected data does not address these questions.
9. . . . others *aren't,* and *that's* that.
10. *You'll* never confuse a reader with sprawl, wordiness, or muddy abstraction.

And here are two more, for a reason that will be revealed in a moment:

11. *That's* all there is.

12. *It's* not much of an improvement, but it does sound less cadaverous, and it made Will quite happy.

Before continuing, notice the comparatively wide range of the contractions used here. Perpetuators of the linguistic-lice myth sometimes maintain that some contractions are more defensible than others—*n't*, for example—but in fact it was no trouble at all to gather this range of examples.

The first three come from *The New York Times*: an editorial, a book review, and a Safire "On Language" column in the Sunday edition. The fourth and fifth are from distinguished magazines, *The Atlantic* and *The New Yorker*, respectively. Item six is from Annie Dillard's *Teaching a Stone to Talk*. The seventh and eighth are from professional magazines: *College English* and *Research in the Teaching of English*, both publications of the National Council of Teachers of English. The ninth is from Linda Flower's textbook, *Problem-Solving Strategies for Writing*, and the tenth is from Joseph M. Williams' *Style: Toward Clarity and Grace*.

For those who think of Williams as a radical, I have added two examples from a widely admired other book on style. The *Will* in sentence twelve is William Strunk, and both sentences come from E. B. White's 1959 Introduction to *The Elements of Style*.

I do not maintain that avoidance of contractions is characteristic of doctoral dissertations only, and it is true that one finds them less often in some types of books than in others, but contractions are bread and butter items not only in speech, but also in writing in very respectable quarters. They are nearly as pervasive in the world of publishing as they are in the world of speaking, so much so that we generally do not even notice them. (Have I used contractions in this book?) Unless we are training our students to write on some planet other than Earth, we ought to worry about more important things than whether they use contractions.

A Final Note

The thesis of this book is that traditional school grammar has left a heritage of definitions that do not define and rules that do not rule (in usage, writing, and punctuation). These inadequate definitions and mythrules hamper students rather than help them in their development as speakers and writers.

As a classroom teacher, I tell my students never to believe something merely because I say it is true; I urge them always to look at the evidence, and to believe or disbelieve based on that. I hope I have provided enough evidence in this book to persuade you that much of our school grammar tradition is counterproductive, that even those students who seem to learn from traditional school grammar learn in spite of it, not because of it. I hope I have also persuaded you that there are better ways, and in particular that breaking rules is often more liberating than following them.

I haven't the slightest doubt that many readers of this book have already found better ways of teaching grammar, usage, writing, and punctuation. Probably some of your ways are better than mine, and I would appreciate your telling me about them. (I can be reached at Edhs2@aol.com.) In the meantime, I wish you all well as you "do the work of the angels." Grace.

Appendix: An Updated Treatment of the Parts of Speech

The purpose of this appendix is to assist teachers to help students learn parts of speech, in cases where such knowledge is required by state or local mandate.

The parts of speech may be divided into two broad groups:

Form (Lexical) Classes	Structure Classes
Nouns	Pronouns
Verbs	Prepositions
Adjectives	Conjunctions
Adverbs	Determiners/numbers
	Auxiliary verbs
	Intensifiers

Form-class words (also called *lexical*, because they have distinct dictionary meanings) are often referred to as "open classes." That is, they have open membership; new words may be added to the class. Structure classes, in contrast, are "closed classes." Rarely are new words added to these classes. Structure words have meaning of a sort, but the most important thing about them is their function.

Form and structure words are often compared with the bricks and mortar in construction work. Though structure words, the mortar, are relatively few in total number, they are used with great frequency to "cement" form-class words together. A glance at any word-frequency list will show that all of the most commonly used words are from the structure classes.

In addition to the structure words in the preceding list, some others are so unique as to form a class by themselves. Infinitive marker *to*, for example, is not the same as the preposition that is spelled the same way. Similarly, the *there* used to start sentences ("There are no freedoms in dictatorships") is not the same as the adverb *there*, and it does not fit into any of the other categories. (Traditional grammars call it an "expletive.") Finally, the negative (*not*) is different enough from adverbs that it probably should be considered a separate part of speech.

Form-Class Words: Nouns, Verbs, Adjectives, Adverbs

Form refers to the shape of words: mainly their spelling, particularly the endings they have or may take. Thus, we know that *agreement* is a noun because of its -*ment* ending. Also, we may make it plural, *agreements*, or possessive, "the *agreement's* purpose," which further reinforces the word's noun status. *Agreeable*, in contrast, has the form (shape) of an adjective; and *agreeably*, of an adverb. The plain word *agree* has no ending, but we can put *to* before it, and we can add endings -*s*, -*ed*, and -*ing*. These indicate that *agree* is a verb. Here are some other examples:

Noun	Verb	Adjective	Adverb
action	act	active	actively
argument	argue	arguable	arguably
beauty	beautify	beautiful	beautifully
critic	criticize	critical	critically
difference	differ	different	differently

In defining the form-class words, form is only one criterion. Second, these words also have *function*. Nouns, for example, typically function as *subjects and complements of verbs and prepositions* and as *appositives*. Verbs function as main words in *predicates of sentences*. The function of adjectives and adverbs is to *modify*; they are often distinguished from one another either by (1) the types of words they modify or by (2) the kinds of questions they answer, such as *what kind of?* or *how?*

Third, we sometimes define words according to their *meaning*. We may say that nouns are *naming* words and verbs *express action or being*. We may say that adjectives *express the quality of a noun* and that adverbs *express a quality of an action*. Andrew Radford suggests that this third criterion is easily the least reliable (1988, p. 57). I believe most linguists would agree.

To sum up, there are (1) formal, (2) functional, and (3) semantic (meaning-based) criteria for defining the four major parts of speech. A problem with definitions of the parts of speech is that these criteria sometimes conflict with one another. For grammarians or linguists, such conflicts may not be troubling; indeed, they may fascinate and challenge. But students, although they are good intuitive grammarians, are not sophisticated grammarians; they have knowledge *of* but not knowledge *about* such things as parts of speech.

Nouns

Students who can identify nouns use a variety of clues, rather than the traditional definition. If you deem it important that your students identify nouns, try making the clues conscious. I've found these most useful:

Noun Clues

- Is the word working with a preceding determiner? A, *an*, and *the* are the most commonly used. (See page 212 for a list of determiners.)
- Can the word be made plural (or singular, if it is plural)?
- Does the word contain a noun-marking derivational ending? (-*er/or*, meaning "one who," -*ist*, -*ism*, -*ation/-tion*, -*ance/-ence*, -*ary/-cry*, -*ment*, -*ness*, -*ship*)
- Does the word fit in a test frame: "(The) _____ was/were good"? (*Note:* This test tells whether a word *can* be used as a noun, not whether it is being so used. *The* is in parentheses because it may be omitted.)

More important than the identification of nouns is the identification of *noun phrases* (NPs). Noun phrases typically function as subjects or complements in sentences. An NP is simply a headword noun plus its modifiers. The *headword* of an NP is usually a noun form; it is that part of the phrase that cannot be omitted, the part that the other words in the phrase modify. Here are a few examples:

Noun Phrases

The first rule of politics	is to do no harm.
That new girl from Ohio	just talked to me.
A few good men	are wanted by the Marines.

The respective headwords—*rule, girl,* and *men*—are all nouns. Another test of an NP is that a pronoun may substitute for it.

It	is to do no harm.
She	just talked to me.
They	are wanted by the Marines.

Note: A single noun or pronoun may also be called an NP.

In sentences, NPs are commonly found in the subject slot, the complement slot, and as objects of prepositions. Here is an example:

Subject NP   Complement NP   Object of Prep NP

My *mother* will be *the next mayor* of *our wonderful town.*

The complement NP is all the words from *the* to *town*. *Our wonderful town* is an NP within this. It serves as object of the preposition *of*.

Activity A–1: Basic Noun Phrase Lesson

Goal: To introduce the concept of the noun phrase and the various slots within sentences that they may occupy.

Procedure

Duplicate the following sentences, and let students attempt to discover the noun phrases in each. They should also isolate the headword of each phrase and try to tell how they know the headwords are nouns, by using the clues. (The noun phrases are italicized for your convenience and the headwords are in boldface italic.)

Note: Prepositional phrases—such as *of his cloth* and *in the pub*—are part of their preceding noun phrases, but they also contain their own NP objects.

1. *The shoeshine **boy*** gave *a final **snap** of his **cloth***. (Peter Mayle)
2. *The **men** in the **pub*** are talking about *the terrible **state** of the **world***. (Frank McCourt)
3. *Little orange **flags*** have sprouted along *the **sidewalks** in **Bethesda***. (*National Geographic*)
4. *A surprising **number** of **headlines** from that **week*** could as easily appear today. (Bill Bryson)
5. *The human **consciousnes****s* is not *a perfectly clear **mirror***. (George Santayana)
6. ***Visitors** to my **house*** are often served ***food*** in *a large blue stoneware **bowl***. (Alice Walker)

Activity A–2: Compound Nouns

Goal: To introduce students to the range of compound nouns, and their spellings.

Procedure

Many nouns are made up of two words. These may be spelled as two words, as one word, or they may be hyphenated. A list follows. Challenge students to discover how the two words are related. For example, *lifeboat* is composed of two nouns, the first of which limits or narrows the second.

back talk	campground	middle class	outlaw
bench-press	downfall	lamppost	team-teach
bluebird	high school	off-season	

Note: It is good to consult an up-to-date dictionary to determine how these compound nouns are spelled, because this type of usage changes more readily than most.

Verbs

As we saw in Chapter 2, the attempt to define *verb* semantically is bound to fail; there simply are too many different kinds of semantical meanings that verbs convey other than "action" or "being." Once again, students who need to know how to identify verbs should rely on clues that students who can identify them use unconsciously. Here are the main ones.

Verb Clues

- Is the word working with a preceding auxiliary? Modal auxiliaries and the parts of *be*, *have*, and *do* are the most common. *Please* and *let's* also commonly signal verbs.
- Does the word contain or can it take the inflectional endings *-s, -ed,* and *-ing*? (The last may be added to all base verb forms.)
- Does the word contain the derivational endings *-ify, -ize,* or *-ate,* or the prefixes *en-/em-* or *be-*?
- Does the word fit in a test frame: "Please _____ (it)"?
  Notes: (1) The *it* must be omitted for intransitive verbs; for example, *dine*. (2) The verb must be tested in its base/infinitive form. (3) The test reveals that a word may be used as a verb, not whether it is a verb.

As with nouns, we may talk about *verb phrases* (VPs). A VP is any group of words whose headword is a verb. We often find that the predicate of sentences is not a single verb but a VP. Here are some examples:

Verb Phrase

The runner *should have scored.*

Verb Phrase

Someone *must have been watching.*

The headwords of these VPs are *scored* and *watching,* respectively. They are the main verbs, those that convey the meaning.

These examples contain only verbs and auxiliaries, but VPs also include other kinds of modifiers and, not uncommonly, noun phrases.

Verb Phrase

The runner *never should have scored from second base.*

Verb Phrase

Someone *must have been watching the woman who escaped.*

FOR LINGUISTICALLY CURIOUS STUDENTS

Quirk et al. (1985) distinguish between *dynamic* and *stative* verb meanings. They indicate that some of the same verbs may be used both ways. For example, *have* can mean "to possess": "I have a new car." This is plainly stative (it describes a state). In contrast, "I had a good time at the party" is the dynamic use of *have*.

The difference between the two can be seen in the fact that the former can be progressive—for example, "I *am having* a good time"—and the latter cannot: "I am having a new car" is not possible.

When Is a Verb Not a Verb? Verbals

It's a paradox: Most students—even those who graduate high in their class and go on to do a significant amount of writing in their lives—are mystified by *verbals* (rhymes with *gerbils*, and might as well be); yet all of us use verbals all the time, both in speech and in writing.

The traditional grammar verbal is a word (or headword of a phrase) that is a verb in form but that is used in a function *other than* the main verb of a predicate. Verbals may occur as subjects of sentences, objects of sentences and prepositions, and as modifiers of many types. Traditionally, there are three subgroups of verbals:

1. *Participles.* The present or past participial form of a verb used to modify. The present participle ending is *-ing*; the past participle ending is usually *-ed* or *-en.*
   Examples
   The *sleeping* cat was rudely awakened.
   I suddenly remembered the *forgotten* melody.
2. *Gerunds.* The *-ing* form of a verb used as a subject or as an object of a verb or preposition.
   Examples
   Winning is always delightful.
   She enjoys *playing* golf.
   I'm weak from *laughing.*
3. *Infinitives.* The base form of a verb introduced by the infinitive marker *to.* Infinitives may be used as subjects and objects of sentences and prepositions, or as modifiers.
   Examples
   To win is always delightful.
   Our team is ready *to win.*

Here are a handful of verbals chosen at random from essays written by *sixth* graders in the Pennsylvania System of School Assessment. (Most of these come from low-scoring essays, proving that even below-average writers can readily use verbals.)

I heard a *threatening* growl. [present participle]
Throughout the world, *disappointed* viewers have been hoping for one more season. [past participle]
My dad told us *to run and hide*. [infinitive used as noun]
There are several points *to be made* about this show. [infinitive used as adjective]
Thank you for *reading* this. [gerund]

Here's a great example of the same verb form used first as a participle and then as a gerund in the same sentence:

A sheltered life can be a *daring* [participle] life as well, for all serious *daring* [gerund] starts from within. (Eudora Welty)

Activity A–3: Willie Nelson: "Crazy" for Gerunds

Goal: To give students a handy way of remembering what a gerund is.

Procedure

You may have heard the story of the New York City students who hung around Madison Avenue asking passersby what a gerund was. The fact that no one knew is no surprise, but it might surprise some that two of the intercepted pedestrians were editors of an internationally famous news magazine.

And yet, why should they have known and what difference would it have made? The knowledge would not have affected in any way either their ability to use gerunds themselves or their skill in editing those of others.

The reality is that every speaker of English uses gerunds every day and easily interprets the gerunds of others. They are simply verbs ending in *-ing*, which are used in noun slots: subjects, for example, or objects of verbs and prepositions.

A particularly good illustration of the everydayness of gerund usage is the lovely classic "Crazy," written for Patsy Cline by Willie Nelson. In each case, the gerunds follow the phrase "crazy for" and are objects of *for*. It is easy to shift them to subject position. Here I have italicized the entire gerund phrases:

Feeling lonely is crazy.
Feeling blue is crazy.
Thinking that my love could hold you is crazy.
Trying is crazy.
Crying is crazy.
Loving you is crazy.

Nelson has another song, whose title uses gerunds as subjects: "*Forgiving* You Was Easy, but *Forgetting* Seems to Take the Longest Time."

If you can play one of the many recordings of "Crazy" and point out its use of gerunds, perhaps your students will remember what they are, should anyone ever stop them on the street and ask.

Activity A–4: Great Uses of Infinitives

Goal: To demonstrate effective uses of infinitives and encourage students to use them.

Procedure

An infinitive is a verbal composed of *to* plus a verb in its base form. (Sometimes, the *to* may be omitted.) Ordinarily, these are easily recognized, but students should also see how infinitive phrases can vivify prose. In particular, the pattern of infinitive plus linking verb plus infinitive or some other complement is capable of producing very effective sentences. Consider, for example, the popular song, "To Know Him Is to Love Him"; Hamlet's "To be or not to be, that is the question"; or the famous philosophical statement of Bishop Berkeley, "To be is to be perceived." Here are other examples. (The infinitives themselves are in italic.)

1. *To breathe* is *to judge*. (attributed to Albert Camus)
2. *To approach* Carcassonne for the first time is *to dream* with your eyes open. (Stephen O'Shea, *The Perfect Heresy*)
3. *To love* oneself is the beginning of a lifelong romance. (Oscar Wilde)
4. *To be* great is *to be* misunderstood. (Ralph Waldo Emerson)
5. *To deny* our own impulses is *to deny* the very thing that makes us human. (Film: *The Matrix*)
6. *To fear* love is *to fear* life. (Bertrand Russell)
7. *To love* another person is *to see* the face of God. (Victor Hugo)
8. *To read* a book for the first time is *to make* an acquaintance with a new friend; *to read* it for a second time is *to meet* an old one. (Anonymous Chinese saying)
9. *To fall* in love is *to create* a religion that has a fallible god. (Jorge Luis Borges)
10. *To be* interested in the changing seasons is, especially in this middling zone, a happier state of mind than *to be* hopelessly in love with spring. (George Santayana)

After discussing these, ask students to imitate them by making up their own sentences. Celebrate language, rather than dissect it.

Activity A–5: Be Careful, the Word You Condemn May Be in the Dictionary

Goal: To demonstrate and practice the notion that many words are both nouns *and* verbs.

Procedure

When I was doing my doctoral thesis, a member of my committee objected when I said, "I will research that." *Research*, she insisted, could not be used as a transitive verb. Well, as a matter of fact, there was a time when this usage was not recognized in dictionaries—if I may trust my old 1948 *Webster's Collegiate*. But at an even earlier time, the usage was acceptable. (The *Oxford English Dictionary* cites examples going back to the late 1500s.) Moreover, *research* is recognized as a transitive verb in the 1968 *Webster's Unabridged*, and my third edition *American Heritage Dictionary* claims "the usage . . . is common in reputable writing." What goes around comes around, as they say. Steven Pinker estimates that twenty percent of our verbs are converts from the noun category (1999, p. 228).

Have students think of nouns in common usage, then make sentences in which they are used as verbs. Example—*tree:* "Let's tree it." Students might then discuss the effectiveness and originality of their sentences, and check to see if their words are listed as that part of speech in the dictionary.

Adjectives

Traditionally, any word that modifies a noun is called an adjective. As we saw in Chapter 2, this position has the disadvantage of obscuring some important distinctions among the various modifiers of nouns. Nothing dreadful will happen if you continue to call all modifiers of nouns adjectives, but if you prefer to distinguish true adjectives from other types of modifiers of nouns, here are some clues for the former:

Adjective Clues

- Does the word pattern with the intensive *very?* Most adjectives will fit comfortably after this word; in fact, this test often helps distinguish adjectives from verbs.
- Does the word take the inflectional endings *-er/-est*, or can it be premodified by *more/most?* (These are called the comparative and superlative degrees of adjectives.)
- Does the word contain an adjective-forming derivational ending? Among the most commonly used are *-al, -able/-ible, -less, -ful, -ive, -ish, -ic*, and *-ous*.
- Does the word fit in both slots in the test frame, "The ___ (girl) seemed very ___"? Note: *girl* can be replaced by some other noun.

Here is a demonstration of how these tests would differentiate *wonderful* from *career* in the phrase, "a wonderful career choice," which is referred to in Chapter 2:

Clues	Word: *wonderful*	Word: *career*
Very test:	*very* wonderful	**very* career
Comparative/superlative	*more* wonderful	**more* career
	most wonderful	**most* career
Derivational endings:	*-ful*	none
Test frame:	passes	fails

Obviously, *wonderful*, which passes all the tests, is an adjective. *Career*, on the other hand *fails* all the tests. It is indeed a modifier of the noun *choice*, but it is *not* an adjective by *any* other criterion. Furthermore, the *word order* in our phrase must be *wonderful career* choice; it cannot be **career wonderful* choice. This also suggests that there is a difference in kind between the two words.

As suggested, a wide range of parts of speech can be used to modify nouns. So true is this that we are probably better off using a broad term like *noun modifier* or *adjectival* for modifiers of nouns in general, and saving the term *adjective* to describe only those words that pass the tests.

Suffix Knowledge

No doubt many students are not be able to make such statements as, "*-ous* is an adjective-making suffix." But that does not mean they do not *know* that such statements are true. In fact, native speakers have an enormous amount of intuitive knowledge of suffixes, both inflectional and derivational.

Take the words *teacher* and *brighter,* for example. Both are formed by adding a suffix *-er* to a word, and a Martian might imagine that the *-er* meant the same thing and marked the same part of speech. In fact, we speakers of English here on earth *understand* instantly that the first *-er* is a noun-marking ending; the second, an adjectival inflectional ending. We *know* that *teach/teacher/teachest* is not a paradigm, whereas *bright/brighter/brightest* is. Nor would we ever think that a *brighter* is one who brights, though we know that a *teacher* is one who teaches.

As another illustration, consider the commonly used adverbial ending, *-ly*. We know that—attached to adjectives—it indicates *manner:* "The animal moved swiftly." But the same ending attached to a noun doesn't tell about manner but about *kind:* "She gave us some friendly advice." In short, we *know* that when we attach *-ly* to adjectives we make adverbs; when we attach it to nouns, we make adjectives.

Extension of Activity 2–7 (See page 32.)

1. Write on the chalkboard or an overhead, the sentence:
   She wore a _____ suit.

2. Give students the words *white*, *new*, and *beautiful*, and ask them to place them in order in the blank space. After they have done so, ask whether there is any alternative order. You should find that most students will select "She wore a beautiful new white suit." (If the speaker/writer had reason to emphasize the newness of the suit, he might place *new* before *beautiful* and put heavy stress on *new*.)

3. Once again, discuss punctuation and its rationale. Here, unlike the adjectives in Activity 2–7, we do not use commas within the series. The reason seems to be that adjectives denoting age and color are perceived as being separate subcategories of the adjective class, and they, in turn, are both different from the group of adjectives of which *beautiful* is a member.

Activity A–6: How Vital Are Adjectives and Other Modifiers of Nouns in Nonfiction Writing?

Goal: To help students determine the varying extent to which professional non-fiction writers employ modifiers before nouns and to provoke a discussion of what makes the professionals' writing effective.

Assuming that students can identify true adjectives and other modifiers of nouns, how frequently should they *use them* in their writing? Is it a good idea for student writers to use adjectives or other modifiers of nouns plentifully?

Procedure

1. Duplicate the following three example paragraphs. All are nonfiction, but they vary in other dimensions. The first is a (largely) narrative paragraph from a family history, the second is a persuasive paragraph from a book about writing, and the third is a descriptive paragraph from a memoir. All were chosen randomly from the work in which they appear. In each example, I have italicized the true adjectives and most of the other single-word modifiers of nouns, excluding determiners and numerals.

2. The students' job is to discuss
   1. How frequently the authors use adjectives and other modifiers of nouns
   2. How unique and vivid these modifiers are
   3. Why the passages are effective

Note: I have added a few comments on these questions after each selection.

Example 1: From Ian Frazier's *Family* (p. 255)

(*Note:* Where noun modifiers are repeated in the same context–*new*, *Hawaiian*—I have italicized them only once.)

When we lived in Cleveland Heights my father used to walk the half mile or so from our house down the hill to his *research* lab on Cornell Road, waving off colleagues who slowed to offer him a ride. When the lab moved to a *new* building in a suburb and we moved to Hudson, my father drove to work in *various off brand foreign* cars—"lawnmowers with roofs," a colleague called them. My mother made him *Hawaiian* shirts in *bright abstract* patterns and he took to wearing them winter and summer. He almost never wore a coat. Even on the *snowiest* day he left for work with nothing over his Hawaiian shirt but his *little* car. The new lab had plenty of room for the staff of over a hundred scientists, technicians, and others. A *high-ceilinged* room near my father's office held *car* and *truck* engines mounted on columns. The engines ran at *high* speed day and night, testing oils and fuels. In another room was a *sealed* chamber mounted on tracks on the floor and ceiling, for experiments which might blow up. (Things occasionally blew up at the lab.) My father roamed the halls a lot; he said he did his *best* thinking while walking. Then he would return to his desk and pull out its *small, dangerous* shelf and sit with his feet up on it. When people asked me what my father did for a living I said that he sat with his feet on his desk.

[Word count, 252; modifiers of nouns, 20]

Discussion: A modest number of modifiers of nouns is used here (7.9%), but one would hardly call them unique or vivid. Indeed, most of them are dishwater common—*new, bright, little, high, best.* Nevertheless, the *paragraph* is interesting, even colorful and vivid. These qualities seem to be achieved by concrete details related to the quirkiness of the character himself, details largely expressed in ways other than by using modifiers of nouns.

Example 2: From Donald Murray's *A Writer Teaches Writing.* (*Quoted* from *Purposes and Ideas*, David A. Jolliffe, ed., p. 150)

Departments of English ought to develop a curriculum which allows the student to concentrate on one phase of the discipline at a time under the direction of a teacher who is prepared to teach that *particular* specialty. We must develop *English* teachers who specialize in teaching language, others who prefer to teach literature and still others who are *expert* in teaching writing. We should not expect the student to go through a *repetitive English* course year after year which has a dibble of *language* study, a dollop of composition and a dabble of literature. Neither should we expect the teacher to be equally prepared to teach the *entire* curriculum. The discipline of English will not be well taught until we devise *new* ways of encouraging our students to learn. We cannot continue to blame our students for being bored by English when the courses are *repetitive*, and we cannot continue to blame teachers for boring their students when the faculty is expected to teach *diverse* subjects and to teach them in one *rigid* manner. Writing will not be taught efficiently until we develop *faculty* members experienced in the teaching of writing who are given the authority to design a climate in which students can learn to write.

[Word count, 207; modifiers of nouns, 12]

Discussion: The percentage of modifiers of nouns here is only 5.8. Moreover, there are only six different true adjectives (*expert, repetitive, entire, new, diverse, rigid*). The effect of this lengthy paragraph therefore cannot possibly depend on its use of these modifiers. It depends mainly, I think, on the power and interest (to its intended audience) of creative, clearly expressed ideas.

Example 3: From Frances Mayes (1997), *Under the Tuscan Sun* (pp. 185–186)

How Italian will we ever be? Not very, I'm *afraid*. Too *pale*. Too *unable* to gesture as a *natural* accompaniment to talking. I saw a man step outside the *confining telephone* booth so he could wave his hands while talking. Many people pull over to the side of the road to talk on their *car* phones because they simply cannot keep a hand on the wheel, one on the telephone, and talk at the same time. We never will master the art of everyone talking at once. Often from the window, I see groups of three or four strolling down our road. All are talking simultaneously. Who's listening? Talking can be about talking. After a *soccer* game, we'll never gun through the streets blowing the horn or drive a scooter around and around in circles in the piazza. Politics always will passeth understanding.

[Word count, 143; modifiers of nouns, 8]

Discussion: The modifier count here is 5.6 percent, about the same as the Murray, and after its first few lines—which contain undistinguished adjectives at best—there are no true adjectives for the rest of the passage. Yet the paragraph is quite entertaining and very well written. Its power comes from good concrete examples, which make the point that the author wishes to make: that native Italians are different from Americans.

The total use of modifiers of nouns in the three nonfiction passages is only 6.6 percent (40 divided by 602). Yet this is the kind of writing we most expect students to do in secondary schools, presumably because it is the kind of writing most likely expected of them in college and the larger world. Modifiers of nouns appear to play a very small role in that world.

LESSON EXTENSION

You may wish students to do their own studies of the density of modifiers of nouns. If so, I suggest that they select well-unified passages of at least a hundred words, excluding dialogue. I further suggest that they do not count numerals or determiners. (The reason is that writers do not consciously choose these, as they may choose other modifiers of nouns.) The modifier density is calculated by dividing the number of adjectives and other modifiers of nouns by the total number of words.

Still Another Type of Adjective—the Specifier or "Restrictive Adjective"

A good experiment to demonstrate that our mind knows many more rules than can be found in our textbooks is to ask students which one of the italicized words in the following sentence means "fussy":

> Both Nick and Corey are particular (i.e., fussy) students, but the *particular particular* boy I am referring to is Corey.

Are both "particulars" adjectives? Some might say so, but if they did, they would be obscuring a difference that the mind responds to as it interprets this sentence. We *know* that the second *particular* means "fussy," and is a true adjective, and that the first is a *specifier* of some sort.

Although the number of words in the specifier class—Quirk calls them "restrictive adjectives"—is relatively limited, they are not unusual. Some others are *chief, main, principal, same, only*, and *specific*. *Very* also belongs to this class, in phrases like "the very person I was speaking of." Note that this *very* is not the same word as the *very* that typically premodifies adjectives. Note furthermore that specifiers cannot be premodified by the intensifier *very*. That is, something can't be "very chief" or "very main."

The voice distinguishes the two words by placing stress on the specifying *very*. Compare the pronunciation of these two sentences:

> Marcia is the VERY person I had in mind.
> She has a very personal approach to problem solving.

Adverbs

Several of the identifying clues for adverbs are identical to those for adjectives and thus they are somewhat limited in value. Here are some others:

Adverb Clues

- Does the word contain the adverb-forming derivational endings, *-wise* or *-ward*?
- Is the word formed by adding the derivational ending *-ly* to an *adjective*? (If *-ly* is added to another part of speech, the result is usually *not* an adverb. *Friendly*, for example, is an adjective.)
- Can the word be moved to other parts of the sentence? (Unlike other parts of speech, most adverbs have *moveability*.)
- Does the word fit into the test sentence: "The batter hit the ball ____"? (Any other subject–transitive verb–object sentence will serve; e.g., "She drove the car ____.")

In addition to these clues, be sure that when students are searching for adverbs they use the questions listed in Chapter 2 (page 33). They are extremely effective for purposes of adverb identification.

Adverbs and Time

In grammar class, we speak as if verbs were the chief indicators of time in English sentences, but in fact, adverbs do as much or more to convey real time. Here are two simple illustrations:

> The train arrives tomorrow.
> The doctor will see you now.

Arrives is a present tense verb, but the sentence is clearly future (equivalent to "the train will arrive tomorrow"). It's the adverb *tomorrow* and not the verb that truly indicates time. In the second example, the so-called future tense (*will see*) is contradicted by the adverb *now*, which indicates that the time is truly present.

Here's a real-life example from an e-mail I wrote to a friend, expressing my disappointment at not being able to say goodbye upon a certain occasion: "Perhaps we weren't meant to say goodbye." This sentence is ambiguous. It can be read in either of the two following ways:

> We weren't meant to say goodbye *that night*.   (true past)
> We weren't meant to say goodbye *ever*. (timeless present)

The adverbials—*that night* and *ever*—can be used to disambiguate my sentence, illustrating that they and not the verb are true indicators of time.

Structure Words: Pronouns, Prepositions, Conjunctions, Determiners and Numbers, Auxiliary Verbs, Intensifiers

Contemporary traditional school grammars recognize three types of structure words: pronouns, prepositions, and conjunctions. Some older traditional grammars—such as Lowth and Murray—also recognized the *article* (*a, an, the*) as a distinct part of speech. In keeping with more modern practice, we have added several new categories.

Pronouns

There is sufficient material relating to how to identify this part of speech in Chapter 2. However, we are adding here an extension of Activity 2–1 and some additional pronoun activities.

Extension of Activity 2–1. (See page 23.)

A. Point out that, at one time, English had separate forms for the singular of *you*. You might try to elicit these forms from your students, prompting them if necessary by asking how commandments are often phrased (*Thou* shalt not kill, for example). I usually find a few students who can fill in *thou, thee, thy, thine,* and *thyself.* (Note the parallel between *thine* and *mine.*) The form *ye*—which students may know from the town crier's call, "Hear Ye," or from the Christmas carol, "Oh, Come All Ye Faithful"—is a plural form, historically, an alternative to plural *you.*

B. Discuss with students whether it would have been better to have kept the distinction between singular and plural *you.* (You might also point out that *you* was originally a plural form and thus anytime it is used as a singular, it is technically *wrong.*) Then you might ask students if they are familiar with the fact that some speakers do maintain a distinction between singular and plural in the second person. In my home state (Pennsylvania), *youse* is heard in the southeast and *you-uns* (pronounced variously) in the southwest. In the state just below us, *y'all* is common in some places. The personal pronoun chart—which shows that all singular and plural *you* forms but one are identical—makes it easy to see why people use such regional plurals.

 Usage note: The use of *-self* pronouns in compounds ("Write a letter to the mayor and myself") and as a type of emphatic ("To myself, mountains are the beginning and end of all natural scenery") is frowned on by some purists, who would replace the reflexive with *me.* However, to quote an *American Heritage Dictionary* usage note: "These usages have been common in the writing of reputable authors for several centuries." Indeed, the quote about the mountains comes from John Ruskin.

Activity A–7: Synonyms or Pronouns: What's the Difference?

Goal: To demonstrate that words other than pronouns regularly fit the pronoun definition.

Procedure

Often, we make too much of labels in the grammar classroom, when the real action is elsewhere. Try substituting for *author* in my Chapter 2 example:

The author	wrote a new novel.
The writer	wrote a new novel.
The novelist	wrote a new novel.
She	wrote a new novel.

Writer, novelist, she—all "take the place" of the noun *author*. Which one you use likely depends on factors other than pronoun versus noun. Do you want the alliteration of *writer wrote?* Is *novelist . . . novel* pleasing or unpleasing? Consider the following passage. Ask students how they might improve it.

> The novelist Anne Tyler has written a new novel. She said that she hoped that this novel would be "different" from her earlier novels but she sensed that it was "just another family novel."

Yes, *novel* is repeated too frequently, but the passage may be made less monotonous by replacing nouns with *synonyms*, not necessarily pronouns:

> The *author* Anne Tyler has written a new novel. She said that she hoped that this *book* would be different from her earlier *works* but she sensed that it was "just another family novel."

Activity A–8: Proforms

Goal: To teach a new type of word that "takes the place of a noun."
Pronouns replace noun phrases, but there are other words that act similarly to replace adverbial and adjectival phrases (that is, words or word groups that function in sentences as adverbs or adjectives). Linguists call these *proforms* (or *pro-forms*). Consider the following examples. Notice how the boldfaced proforms replace the antecedent italicized words.

Proform

Michelle must have felt *lazy*, but she didn't seem **so**.

Proform

Michelle lives *in Chicago*, and her son also lives **there**.

Proform

We arrived *late last Monday*, and they too arrived **then**.

So takes the place of the adjective *lazy*; *there* replaces the prepositional phrase *in Chicago*; and *then* replaces the adverbial phrase *late last Monday*.

Even more interesting, the proform *so* along with the empty verb *do* can replace an entire verb phrase (a verb and all its modifiers/complements):

> Jack should have *cleaned up his room quite thoroughly*

Proform

> *before his date arrived*, but he didn't **do so**.

In answers to questions, a form of *do* acts as a replacement for an entire verb phrase:

Q: Did Jack *clean his room at all?*

      Pro-predicate

A: No, he *didn't.*

Sometimes teachers try to encourage students to "speak in complete sentences." They mean well by this advice, hoping to reinforce the idea that students should *write* in complete sentences and thus avoid fragments. However, as the examples of sentences with proforms show, this is unnatural. One does not normally answer a question like "Did Jack clean his room at all?" by "No, he didn't clean his room at all."

Proforms allow speakers or writers to avoid repeating words, just as pronouns do. If speakers—including the teachers themselves—were actually to follow the advice to speak always in complete sentences, their listeners would quickly tire of listening to them. In fact, in speech the natural unit is not the *sentence* at all, but the *utterance*.

Prepositions

As noted in Chapter 2, nine prepositions account for 92.6 percent of all prepositional phrases. Five of these nine words, however, are not always prepositions. Consider discussing some or all of the following additional uses of these words, depending on the grade level you teach:

by: adverb and *passive (agent) marker
      She walked right on *by.*
      The job was done *by* a plumber.

for: conjunction
      She received a detention, *for* she was late.

in: adverb, adjective, and noun
      Guess what the cat dragged *in?*
      Grace was part of the *in* group.
      The *ins* won the vote by a slim margin.

to: adverb and *infinitive marker
      She didn't come *to* until midnight
      I have a secret *to* tell you.

on: adverb and adjective
      Put the tea water *on.*
      The television is *on* all day in their house.

Passive by and infinitival *to* are not listed as separate parts of speech in traditional school grammars. However, these functions are quite distinct from the normal uses of *by* and *to*.

In addition to the simple prepositions, there is a relatively large number of complex (sometimes called *compound* or *phrasal*) prepositions. The largest class of these consists of a simple preposition plus a noun plus a second simple preposition; such as *in case of, by means of, on top of,* and *for the sake of.*

A second relatively large category consists of an adverb plus a preposition: *together with, up to, away from.*

FOR LINGUISTICALLY CURIOUS STUDENTS: ARE PREPOSITIONS FUNCTION WORDS?

Traditionally, linguists have classified prepositions as function words, seeing them as glue that binds other words together. But more recently some generative grammarians have insisted that prepositions have too much lexical content (dictionary meaning) to be so considered. Try the following "Be a Linguistic Detective" activity with your students to discover if they have an opinion.

Can you tell what the following sentence means?
The valentine was found, by the way, by noon by chance by the tree by Jane by Tarzan, by golly.
First, try giving students these questions:
Who found the valentine?
Where was it found?
How do you know the answers to these questions?

The fact that students can answer the questions shows that they have considerable "knowledge" of linguistic structure. (Tarzan found the valentine. He found it at the tree near or next to Jane.) Here are some additional questions and remarks.

Notice that the word *by* is used *seven* times. Is it the same word in each case? How could one *translate* it or tell how it functions in each case? In one instance, *by* is the passive (agent-marking) *by.* How can one tell which of the seven *by*'s serves that purpose? Notice the commas, which signal pauses in speech. What do they tell?

Determiners and Numbers

One hesitates to add to the "heap of terms" referred to by Matthew Arnold at the head of Chapter 2. (Arnold, by the way, spent most of his adult life as an inspector of schools.) But the term *determiner* is so widely accepted among linguists that an exception is necessary. The most commonly used determiners are the articles— *a, an, the.* Like other determiners, they introduce noun-headed phrases:

Determiner	Adjective	Modifying Noun	Head Noun
a	wonderful	career	choice
an	interesting		job
the	best		answer
their		school	bus
those	friendly	police	officers

Any word that fits into the *determiner* position in noun phrases like these is considered a determiner. This would include possessive nouns.

Martha's	wonderful	career	choice

In addition to *a*, *an*, and *the*, the most commonly used determiners are the following:

- *this, that, these, those*
- *my, your, her, his, its, our, their*
- *every, each, no, either, neither*
- *some, all, any, few, enough, both, many, several*

Some linguists put numbers, both cardinal and ordinal, in a class by themselves. If they are not treated as a distinct part of speech, they could also be considered determiners.

her	*two*	wonderful	career	choices
her	*second*	wonderful	career	choice

Auxiliary Verbs

The English verb system is quite complex, but native speakers have a fairly good grasp of its fundamentals, at least where the oral language is concerned. Nevertheless, it is useful to distinguish at least a few subcategories of the verb. Whether they should be treated as separate parts of speech is a moot issue.

Quirk et al. (1972) specifically divide predicates of sentences into auxiliaries and main verbs. Auxiliaries are further divided into two major subcategories:

- Primary (*be, have, do*)
- Modal (*can/could, will/would, shall/should, may/might, must*)

All three of the primary auxiliaries can also be main verbs.

- I *am* the captain of my ship.
- We *have* many friends.
- They *do* homework every night.

The italicized words in the preceding three sentences are clearly not auxiliary verbs, since no main verb follows them.

Some modals have main verbs that are spelled identically:

- They *can* peaches every summer.
- I *willed* my estate to my favorite charity.

Activity A–9: Generating the Modal Auxiliaries

Goal: To demonstrate that native-speaking students have an intuitive grasp of modal auxiliaries

Procedure:

Give students a sentence like the following:

> The athletes _____ have received their awards.

Ask them to fill in the blank space with as many words as they can, words that do the same kind of work as *may*. It may take some prompting, but I have always managed to have students generate a complete set of the modals, thus proving that they "know" this part of speech.

Activity A–10: A Hot Tip—Modals to the Rescue

Goal: To provide student writers with a handy way of getting around some knotty subject-verb agreement problems.

Even people who write well and have a sound knowledge of English grammar sometimes have difficulty settling some matters of subject-verb agreement. Consider these three examples:

1a. Bacon and eggs (is? are?) my favorite breakfast.
2a. The stars and stripes (moves? move?) me to tears.
3a. No one but eight-dollar-an-hour test correctors (sees? see?) your essay.

We can talk about whether *bacon and eggs* and the other subjects of these sentences are conceived of as a unit or as two separate things, or whether *it* or *they* is the better pronoun substitute, but many students are still left uncertain. However, since no agreement is required when a modal auxiliary heads a verb phrase, the problem can be solved efficiently simply by inserting one:

1b. Bacon and eggs *may* be my favorite breakfast.
2b. The stars and stripes *can* move me to tears.
3b. No one but eight-dollar-an-hour test correctors *will* see your essay.

Of course, one would not add a modal at the cost of distorting meaning, but often an added modal does not do that; indeed, I have found that, in some cases, it may even express my intended meaning more precisely.

Intensifiers

A small number of words stand before adjectives (and some adverbs) and serve to increase or *intensify* their degree. Here is a brief list:

very	quite	somewhat	rather
really	pretty	more	most
too	a lot	very much	a good deal

Writing teachers sometimes object to the use of these words, and it's probably true that their overuse should be avoided in writing. But if you listen to people speaking, you are sure to hear them quite often (I've just used one myself), and they are much more common than one might imagine, even in very well written prose (there I go again).

Activity A–11: Using Intensifiers to Distinguish Parts of Speech

Goal: To help students distinguish adjectives and adverbs from nouns and verbs. Intensifiers stand before adjectives and adverbs. They do *not* stand before nouns and verbs. For example, you can say that someone is "very manly" (*manly* is an adjective), but you wouldn't say someone was "very man" (*man* is a noun).

Some verbs and adjectives are spelled the same way. *Entertaining*, for example, can be either a verb or an adjective. If you can put *very* in front of it, it's an adjective; if you cannot, it's a verb. Compare these sentences:

The clown was entertaining the children.
The clown was always entertaining.

In the first sentence, *entertaining* is a verb; it tells what the clown is doing. Notice that you could *not* say, "The clown was very entertaining the children." In the second sentence, *entertaining* is more likely an adjective describing the clown. You *can* say, "The clown was very entertaining."

References

Andrews, Larry. 1998. *Language Exploration and Awareness: A Resource Book for Teachers*. Second Edition. Mahwah, NJ: Laurence Erlbaum Associates.

Ash, John. 1785. *Grammatical Institutes: or, an easy Introduction to Dr. Lowth's English Grammar: Designed for Use in the Schools*. Philadelphia, PA: Joseph Crukshank.

Austen, Jane. 1950. *Pride and Prejudice*. New York: Random House.

Ballator, Nada, Marisa Farnum, and Bruce Kaplan. 1999. *NAEP 1996 Trends in Writing: Fluency and Writing Conventions* (NCES 1999-456). Washington, DC: National Center for Education Statistics.

Berlin, James. 1984. *Writing Instruction in Nineteenth Century American Colleges*. Carbondale, IL: Southern Illinois University Press.

Blair, Hugh. 1853. *Lectures on Rhetoric and Belles Lettres*. A New Edition. London: William Tegg.

Blau, Sheridan, Peter Elbow, and Don Killgallon. 1998. *The Writer's Craft*: Grade 11. Evanston, IL: McDougal Littell.

Braddock, Richard. 1974. "The Frequency and Placement of Topic Sentences in Expository Prose." *Research in the Teaching of English* 8: 287–302.

Braddock, Richard, Richard Lloyd-Jones, and Lowell Schoer. 1963. *Research in Written Composition*. Urbana, IL: National Council of Teachers of English.

Brosnahan, Irene T. 1976. "A Few Good Words for the Comma Splice." *College English* 38: 184–88.

Bullokar, William. 1977. *Booke at Large* (1580) and *Bref Grammar for English* (1586). Introduction by Diane Bornstein. Delmar, NY: Scholars' Facsimiles & Reprints.

Byatt, A. S. 1996. *Babel Tower*. New York: Random House.

Chomsky, Noam. 1986. *Knowledge of Language: Its Nature, Origin, and Use*. Westport, CT: Praeger.

Connors, Robert J., and Andrea A. Lunsford. 1988. "Frequency of Formal Errors in Current College Writing, or Ma and Pa Kettle Do Research." *College Composition and Communication* 39: 395–409.

Crowley, Sharon. 1998. *Composition in the University: Historical and Polemical Essays*. Pittsburgh, PA: University of Pittsburgh Press.

Crystal, David. 1988. *The English Language*. London: Penguin Books.

Dreifus, Claudia. 2001. "A Conversation with John McWhorter: How Language Came to Be, and Change." *The New York Times*, October 30, 2001, Science, F 3.

Fitzhugh, Will, ed. 2001. *The Concord Review* 12 (2).

Flood, James, Julie M. Jensen, Diane Lapp, and James R. Squire, eds. 1991. *Handbook of Research on Teaching the English Language Arts*. Sponsored by International Reading Association & National Council of Teachers of English. New York: Macmillan.

Fowler, H. W. 1965. [1926] *A Dictionary of Modern English Usage*. Second Edition. Revised by Sir Ernest Gower. London: Oxford University Press.

Frazier, Ian. 1994. *Family*. New York: Farrar Straus Giroux.

Fries, Charles C. 1940. *American English Grammar*. New York: Appleton-Century-Crofts.

Gass, William H. 2002. *Tests of Time*. New York: Knopf.

Goodlad, John I. 1984. *A Place Called School: Prospects for the Future*. New York: McGraw-Hill.

Graves, Donald H. 1983. *Writing: Teachers and Children at Work*. Portsmouth, NH: Heinemann.

Hacker, Diana. 1994. *The Bedford Handbook for Writers*. Fourth Edition. Boston: Bedford Books of St. Martin's Press.

Hairston, Maxine. 1981. "Not All Errors Are Created Equal: Nonacademic Readers in the Professions Respond to Lapses in Usage." *College English* 43: 794–806.

Hartwell, Patrick. 1985. "Grammar, Grammars, and the Teaching of Grammar." *College English* 47: 105–27.

Hausmann, Brock. 2001. "Recreating Grammar in the Language Arts Curriculum." Paper presented at Annual Meeting of the NCTE, 16 November. Baltimore, MD.

Hepworth, Brian. 1978. *Robert Lowth*. Boston: Twayne.

Hillocks, George, Jr. 2002. *The Testing Trap: How State Writing Assessments Control Learning*. New York: Teachers College Press.

Hodges, John C. 1941. *Harbrace Handbook of English*. New York: Harcourt, Brace and Company.

Hodges, John C., and Mary E. Whitten. 1982. *Harbrace College Handbook*. Ninth Edition. New York: Harcourt Brace Jovanovich.

Hodges, John C., Winifred Bryan Horner, Suzanne Strobeck Webb, and Robert Keith Miller. 1998. *Harbrace College Handbook*. Revised Thirteenth Edition. Fort Worth, TX: Harcourt Brace College.

Hopkins, Edward M. 1912. "Can Good Composition Teaching Be Done under Present Conditions?" *English Journal* 1: 1–8.

James, Henry. 1881. *The Portrait of a Lady*. New York: Random House.

Jespersen, Otto. 1938. *Growth and Structure of the English Language*. Ninth Edition. Garden City, NY: Doubleday Anchor Books.

Johnson, Samuel. 1775. *A Dictionary of the English Language*, in two (folio) volumes. London: W. Strahan. Reprinted 1967. New York: AMS Press.

Kael, Pauline. 1986. "The Current Cinema." *The New Yorker* 62: 77–80.

Kantz, Margaret, and Robert Yates. 1994. "Whose Judgments? A Survey of Faculty Responses to Common and Highly Irritating Writing Errors." Paper read at fifth annual conference of the NCTE Assembly for the Teaching of English Grammar, 12–13 August, Illinois State University, Normal, IL.

Kemper, Dave, Patrick Sebranek, and Verne Meyer. 2001. *Writers INC*. Wilmington, MA: Great Source Education Group.

Kennedy, X. J., Dorothy M. Kennedy, and Jane E. Aaron. 1997. *The Bedford Reader*. Sixth Edition. Boston: Bedford Books.

King, Stephen. 2000. *On Writing: A Memoir of the Craft*. New York: Scribner.

Kingsolver, Barbara. 1995. "Stone Soup." In *The Bedford Reader*. Sixth Edition, by X. J. Kennedy, Dorothy M. Kennedy, and Jane E. Aaron, eds. Boston: Bedford Books.

Kirkham, Samuel. 1843. *English Grammar in Familiar Lectures*. One Hundred and Fifth Edition. Baltimore, MD: John Plaskitt.

Klink, Anne L. 1998. "Unravelling the Comma Splice." *The English Journal* 87: 96–98.

Kohn, Alfie. 1999. *The Schools Our Children Deserve: Moving Beyond Traditional Classrooms and "Tougher Standards."* Boston: Houghton Mifflin.

———. 2000. *The Case Against Standardized Testing: Raising the Scores, Ruining the Schools*. Portsmouth, NH: Heinemann.

Kolln, Martha. 1998. *Rhetorical Grammar: Grammatical Choices, Rhetorical Effects*. Third Edition. Boston: Allyn and Bacon.

Kozol, Jonathan. 1992. *Savage Inequalities: Children in America's Schools*. New York: Harper Perennial.

Leonard, Sterling. 1929. *The Doctrine of Correctness in English Usage, 1700–1800*. Madison, WI: University of Wisconsin Studies in Language and Literature, No. 25.

Little, Gretta D., 1986. "The Ambivalent Apostrophe." *English Today* 8: 15–17.

Lloyd, Donald. 1952. "Our National Mania for Correctness." *The American Scholar* 21: 283–89.

Lowth, Robert. 1762. *A Short Introduction to English Grammar: With Critical Notes*. London: J. Hughs. (1967. Menston, England: The Scholar Press Limited.)

———. 1775. *A Short Introduction to English Grammar*. Philadelphia: R. Aitken, Printer. Facsimile Reproduction. Delmar, New York: Scholars' Facsimiles and Reprints.

MacLean, Marion S., and Marian M. Mohr. 1999. *Teacher-Researchers at Work*. Berkeley, CA: The National Writing Project.

Maittaire, Michael. 1712. *The English Grammar: or, an Essay on the Art of Grammar, Applied to and Exemplified in the English Tongue*. London. Reprinted by The Scholar Press Limited: Menston, England, 1967.

Mayes, Frances. 1997. *Under the Tuscan Sun*. New York: Broadway Books.

Mayher, John S. 1990. *Uncommon Sense: Theoretical Practice in Language Education*. Portsmouth, NH: Boynton/Cook.

McArthur, Tom. 1986. "The usage industry." *English Today* 7: 8–12.

———, ed. 1996. *The Concise Oxford Companion to the English Language*. Oxford: Oxford University Press.

McCarroll, Christina. 2001. "To Learn to Write in College, Write a Lot." *Christian Science Monitor*, August 7.

McQuade, Finlay. 1980. "Examining a Grammar Course: The Rationale and the Result." *English Journal* 69: 26–30.

McWhorter, John. 2001. *The Power of Babel: A Natural History of Language*. New York: Times Books, Henry Holt and Company.

Melville, Herman. 1851. *Moby Dick*. Pleasantville, NY: The Reader's Digest, 1989.

Merwin, W. S. 2002. *The Mays of Ventadorn*. Washington, DC: National Geographic.

Michael, Ian. 1970. *English Grammatical Categories and the Tradition to 1800*. Cambridge: Cambridge University Press.

———. 1987. *The Teaching of English: From the Sixteenth Century to 1870*. Cambridge: Cambridge University Press.

————. 1993. *Early Textbooks of English: A Guide*. Colloquium on Textbooks, Schools and Society. Reading, UK: University of Reading.

Monaghan, Charles. 1998. *The Murrays of Murray Hill*. Brooklyn, NY: Urban History Press.

Morenberg, Max. 1997. *Doing Grammar*. Second Edition. New York: Oxford University Press.

Murray, Donald. 1968. "The Climate for Writing." In *Purposes and Ideas*. Second Edition, D.A. Jolliffe, ed. Dubuque, IA: Kendall/Hunt.

Murray, Lindley. 1795. *English Grammar*. York, England: Wilson, Spence, and Mawman.

————. 1981. *English Grammar* (1824). A Facsimile Reproduction with an Introduction by Charlotte Downey. Delmar, NY: Scholars' Facsimiles & Reprints.

————. 1827. *Memoirs of the Life and Writings of Lindley Murray: In a Series of Letters, Written by Himself*. Second Edition. With a Preface and a Continuation of the Memoirs by Elizabeth Frank. York, England: Longman.

Nicholson, Margaret. 1957. *A Dictionary of American-English Usage*. New York: Oxford University Press.

Noden, Harry. 1999. *Image Grammar: Using Grammatical Structures to Teach Writing*. Portsmouth, NH: Boynton/Cook.

Noguchi, Rei R. 1991. *Grammar and the Teaching of Writing: Limits and Possibilities*. Urbana, IL: National Council of Teachers of English.

Norris, Kathleen, ed. *The Best American Essays, 2001*. Boston: Houghton Mifflin.

O'Connor, Patricia T. 1996. *Woe Is I: The Grammarphobe's Guide to Better English in Plain English*. New York: Riverhead Books.

Odell, Lee, Richard Vacca, Renee Hobbs, and John E. Warriner. 2001. *Elements of Language*. Sixth Course. Austin, TX: Holt, Rinehart and Winston.

Ohanian, Susan. 1999. *One Size Fits Few: The Folly of Educational Standards*. Portsmouth, NH: Heinemann.

Orwell, George. 1946. "Politics and the English Language." In *The Bedford Reader*, X. J. Kennedy, Dorothy M. Kennedy, and Jane E. Aaron, eds. Boston: Bedford Books.

Parker, Francis Wayland. 1873. Quoted in Charles Weingartner, "Mutterings: Basic Backwardness." *The English Journal* 65: 12–14.

Parkes, M. B. 1993. *Pause and Effect: An Introduction to the History of Punctuation in the West*. Berkeley/Los Angeles, CA: University of California Press.

Pinker, Steven. 1994. *The Language Instinct: How the Mind Creates Language*. New York: William Morrow.

———. 1999. *Words and Rules: The Ingredients of Language*. New York: Basic Books.

Pooley, Robert C. 1957. *Teaching English Grammar*. New York: Appleton-Century-Crofts.

Prentice Hall Writer's Companion. High School. 1995. Englewood, NJ: Prentice Hall.

Puttenham, George. 1589. *The Arte of English Poesie*. Menston: Scolar Press, 1968.

Quindlen, Anna. 1988. "Homeless." In *Living Out Loud*. New York: Random House.

Quirk, Randolph, Sidney Greenbaum, Geoffrey Leech, and Jan Svartvik. 1972. *A Grammar of Contemporary English*. Essex, England: Longman.

———. 1985. *A Comprehensive Grammar of the English Language*. Essex, England: Longman.

Radford, Andrew. 1988. *Transformational Grammar: A First Course*. Cambridge: Cambridge University Press.

Reid, James M. 1969. *An Adventure in Textbooks, 1924–1960*. New York: R. R. Bowker.

Rich, Susanna. 1998. *The Flexible Writer: A Basic Guide*. Third Edition. Boston: Allyn and Bacon.

Romano, Tom. 1992. "Evolving Voice." In *Teacher as Writer: Entering the Professional Conversation*, Karin L. Dahl, ed. Urbana, IL: National Council of Teachers of English.

———. 1995. *Writing with Passion: Life Stories, Multiple Genres*. Portsmouth, NH: Heinemann.

Sapir, Edward. 1921. *Language*. New York: Harcourt, Brace, and World.

Schuster, Edgar H. 1985. "Let's Get Off the Mythmobile." *The English Journal* 74: 40–43.

———. 1999. "Reforming English Language Arts: Let's Trash the Tradition." *Phi Delta Kappan* 80: 518–24.

———. 2000. "Language Arts Standards and the Possessive 'Apoxtrophe'." *Commentary*. *Education Week* 19: 45, 48.

Shaughnessy, Mina. 1977. *Errors & Expectations: A Guide for the Teacher of Basic Writing*. New York: Oxford University Press.

Simmons, Sue Carter. 1995. "Constructing Writers: Barrett Wendell's Pedagogy at Harvard." *College Communication and Composition* 46: 327–46.

Sipe, Rebecca Bowers. 2001. "Academic Service Learning: More Than Just 'Doing Time'." *The English Journal* 90: 33–38.

Sledd, James. 1996. *Eloquent Dissent: The Writings of James Sledd*. Richard D. Freed, ed. Portsmouth, NH: Boynton/Cook.

Sloan, Gary. 1990. "Frequency of Errors in Essays by College Freshmen and by Professional Writers." *College Communication and Composition* 41: 299–308.

Sommers, Nancy. 1982. "Responding to Student Writing." *College Communication and Composition* 33: 148–56.

Steinbeck, John. 1990. *Journal of a Novel: The East of Eden Letters.* New York: Penguin Books.

Strong, William. 2001. *Coaching Writing: The Power of Guided Practice.* Portsmouth, NH: Heinemann.

Strunk, William, Jr., and E. B. White. 1959. *The Elements of Style.* New York: Macmillan.

———. 2000. *The Elements of Style.* Fourth Edition. Boston: Allyn and Bacon.

Thill, John V., and Courtland L. Bovée. 1996. *Excellence in Business Communication.* Third Edition. New York: McGraw-Hill.

Thoreau, Henry David. 1849. "Civil Disobedience." In *The American Tradition in Literature.* Sixth Edition. George Perkins, Sculley Bradley, Richmond Croom Beatty, and E. Hudson Long, eds. New York: Random House.

Tieken-Boon van Ostade, Ingrid, ed. 1996. *Two Hundred Years of Lindley Murray.* Munster, Germany: Nodus Publikationen.

Trimmer, Joseph, and Maxine Hairston. 1981. *The Riverside Reader.* Volume 1. Boston: Houghton Mifflin.

———. 1983. *The Riverside Reader.* Volume 2: Boston: Houghton Mifflin.

Troyka, Lynn Quitman. 1999. *Simon & Schuster Handbook for Writers.* Fifth Edition. Upper Saddle River, NJ: Prentice Hall.

Tyack, David, and Larry Cuban. 1995. *Tinkering Toward Utopia: A Century of Public School Reform.* Cambridge, MA: Harvard University Press.

Wallace, David Foster. 2001. "Tense Present: Democracy, English, and the Wars over Usage." *Harper's Magazine* 302: 39–58.

Warriner, John E. 1946. "Hurdling English Mechanics." *The English Journal* 35: 447–450.

———. 1948. *Warriner's Handbook of English.* Book One. New York: Harcourt, Brace.

———. 1951. *Warriner's Handbook of English.* Book Two. New York: Harcourt, Brace.

Warriner, John E. and John H. Treanor. 1959. *Warriner's English Grammar and Composition: Grade 8.* New York: Harcourt, Brace and Company.

Warriner, John E., and Francis Griffith. 1977. *Warriner's English Grammar and Composition.* Fourth Course. New York: Harcourt Brace Jovanovich.

Weaver, Constance. 1996a. *Teaching Grammar in Context*. Portsmouth, NH: Boynton/Cook.

———. 1996b. "Teaching Grammar in the Context of Writing." *English Journal* 85: 15–24.

Webster, Noah. 1800. *A Grammatical Institute of the English Language, Part II*. Sixth Connecticut Edition. Hartford, CT. 1980. Delmar, NY: Scholars' Facsimiles & Reprints.

Wheeler, Rebecca S. 2001. "Grammar Alive: Discovery Learning in the Classroom." Paper read at Annual Meeting of the NCTE, 16 November. Baltimore, MD.

Williams, Joseph M. 1981. "The Phenomenology of Error." *College Composition and Communication* 32: 152–68.

———. 1995. *Style: Toward Clarity and Grace*. Chicago, IL: University of Chicago Press.

———. 1997. *Style: Ten Lessons in Clarity and Grace*. Fifth Edition. New York: Longman.

Zinnser, William K. 1976. *On Writing Well*. New York: Harper & Row.

Index

"A lot" / "alot," 79
Achieve, 140
Adjectives
    activities, 31–32, 203–206
    adjectival, 202
    adverbs, confusion with, 56
    definition, 30–31
    identification of, 201–202
    nonfiction writing, use of,
        203–206
    predicate, 41
    prepositions used as, 210–211
    restrictive, 206
Adverbs
    activity, 34
    adjectives, confusion with, 56
    adverbial, 34, 42–43, 207
    definition, 33–34
    identification of, 206–207
    prepositions used as, 210–211
    time and, 207
"Advise" / "advice," 77
"Affect" / "effect," 77–78
"Ain't," 57–58
American Dictionary (Webster), 50
American English Grammar (Fries),
    35, 183–184
American Heritage Dictionary, 57,
    69, 79, 208
American Scholar, 90, 121, 171,
    190
Andrews, Larry, 63
Angela's Ashes (McCourt), 32–33
"Anyways," 58
Apostrophe. See also contractions
    activities, 186–189
    contractions, 189–191
    history of, 183–185
    nonpossessive, 188–191
    possessive, 183–188
Apoxtrophe. See apostrophe
Appositives
    activity, 37–38
    definition, 37
"Are" / "our," 79

Arnold, Matthew, 19, 212
Arte of English Poesie
    (Puttenham), 172
Articles, 31–32, 212
"As" / "like," 71
Ash, John, 189
Assembly for the Teaching of
    English Grammar
    declares grammar a "broken
        part of the curriculum,"
        20–21
    website, 21, 77
Atlantic Monthly, 163, 191
Austen, Jane, 93, 133
Authority, quest for
    academies, 49–50
    dictionaries, 50–51
    foreign languages, 52
    ipse dixit, 52
    reason, 52–53
    standard English, 53–55
    usage, 51–53

"Back to Basics" movement, 17,
    46
Barthelme, Donald, 158
Bay Area Writing Project, 89
Bedford Handbook for Writers
    (Hacker), 129, 178, 185
Bedford Reader (Kennedy), xvi,
    120
Berlin, James, 92
Best American Essays 2001
    (Norris), 105, 121, 136, 171,
    190
Bible, The, 10–11
Blair, Hugh, 96
Blau, Sheridan, 177
Bovée, Courtland, 177
Braddock, Richard, 102, 136–137,
    140
"Brake" / "break," 79
Bref Grammar (Bullokar), 18
Brosnahan, Irene, 117–118
Brown, Goold, 52

Bullokar, William, 7, 18

COIK (Clear Only If Known),
    35–37
"Capitol" / "capital," 79
Case Against Standardized Testing,
    The (Kohn), 101
Catton, Bruce, 158
Cawdrey, Robert, 47, 50
Caxton, William, 54
Chaucer, Geoffrey, 56, 71
Chomsky, Noam, 4
Churchill, Winston, 7
"Cite" / "site" / "sight," 79
"Civil Disobedience" (Thoreau),
    106
Coaching Writing (Strong), xiv, 20
Cold Mountain (Frazier), 173
College English, 117, 191
Collins Cobuild Corpus, 77–78,
    86
Collyer, John, 33
Colons
    activities, 162, 165
    capitalization after, 164
    problems with traditional uses,
        163–165
    tool of compression, as a, 165
    usage, 161–162
Color of Water (McBride), 170
Comma splice
    activities, 118–119
    definition, 114–115
    usage, 116–118
Commas
    activities, 32, 203
    clarifying, 155–156
    contrary, 157–158
    courtesy, 156–157
    parenthetical, 158–159
    throwback, 159
Commonly confused words,
    77–88
Complements
    activity, 43

definition of, 41–43
direct objects, 41
indirect objects, 41–42
objective complements, 42
predicate adjectives, 41
predicate nouns, 41
"Compliment" / "complement,"
80
*Comprehensive Grammar of the
English Language* (Quirk et.
al.), 32–33
*Concise Oxford Companion to the
English Language, The*
(McArthur), 8, 38, 54, 61,
164, 184
Concord Review, The, 98
Conjunctions
activity, 36
definition, 36
prepositions used as, 210
Connors, Robert J., 68, 96,
114–115
Contractions
formal writing, use of, 190–191
usage, 80–81, 189–191
"Could of," "would of," etc., 80–81
"Council" / "counsel" / "consul,"
81
Crane, Stephen, 167
"Crazy" (Nelson), 199
Crystal, David, 132
Cuban, Larry, 6
Cunningham, Michael, 173

Dahl, Karin, 104
Dashes
activity, 167–169
usage, 166–167
"Dear Harper" (Price), 173
"Debris of Life and Mind"
(Stevens), 109
Defoe, Daniel, 50
DeLillo, Don, 173
Descriptive rules. *See* rules of
grammar
Determiners, 31–32, 212
Development houses, 69–70
Dialects
activity, 63–64
nonstandard, 62–63
Dickinson, Emily, 166
*Dictionary of American English
Usage* (Nicholson), 106
*Dictionary of Modern American
Usage* (Garner), 71

*Dictionary of Modern English
Usage, A* (Fowler), 69, 73
Dictionary of the English Language
(Johnson) 7, 50
Dietrich, Paul, xiii–xiv
"Different from"/ "than," 70–71
Dillard, Annie, 191
Dionysius Thrax, 33
Doing Grammar (Morenberg), 42
Double comparisons, 56, 62
Double negatives
activity, 53
French, use of, 52, 61
in nonstandard English, 56,
60–62
used by Johnson, Chaucer,
Shakespeare, 56
Doublespeak Awards, 68
Dowd, Maureen, 171

Educational Testing Service, xiv,
xviii
Elbow, Peter, 21, 177
Elements of Language (Odell), 17,
28, 51, 120, 122, 135
Elements of Style (Strunk and
White)
"be" verbs, use of, 107
comma splice, 116
contractions, 190–191
dashes, 166
"have got," 74
paragraphs, 143
passive voice, 124
semicolons, 172
sentence fragments, 110–111
split infinitives, 72
Eliot, T.S., 60
*English Exercises, Adapted to the
Grammar* (Murray), 12
English Grammar (Murray)
adjectives, 13, 31
compared to Lowth's *Short
Introduction to English
Grammar*, 10–11, 13–15
nouns, 13, 26
paragraphs, 144–145
parsing, 14
parts of speech, 13, 18
prepositions, 74
pronouns, 13
publication of, 9, 11–13
punctuation, 152
syntax, 14
verbs, 13, 28

*English Grammar in Familiar
Lectures* (Kirkham), 15
English Grammar, The (Maittaire),
1
*English Grammatical Categories and
the Tradition to 1800*
(Michael), 7–8, 18
English Journal, 90, 163, 190
English Language, The, (Crystal),
132
English Reader (Murray), 12
Errors
as a sign of growth, xiv
consequences of focusing on,
94–96
fear of, causing poor writing,
xiv, xv, xix
Harbrace, emphasis on, 17,
66–68
Jonathan Edwards Syndrome,
92–95
Lowth's "no errors are so triv-
ial," 1, 10, 95
status-marking, 55–56, 80
treatment of students', xiii–xiv,
92–96
Warriner's emphasis on, 68
Errors & Expectations
(Shaughnessy), 66
"Essay upon Projects" (Defoe), 50
Evans, Bergen, 61
Evans, Cornelia, 61
*Excellence in Business
Communication* (Thill and
Bovée), 177–178
"Except" / "accept," 81–82

Fadiman, Anne, 171
Family (Frazier), 204
Favorite writer test, xii–xiii
Feedback from students, xvi
"Fewer" / "less," 75–76
Fitzgerald, F. Scott, 74
Fitzhugh, Will, 98
Flexible Writer: A Basic Guide
(Rich), 178
Flood, James, 153
Flower, Linda, 191
Foreign languages and English
grammar, 43–46
Form class words, 194–195
"Formal" composition, 190–191
Forster, E.M., xv
Fowler, H.W., 69, 73, 106
"Fox," 108–109

Frazier, Charles, 173
Frazier, Ian, 204
"Frequency and Placement of
    Topic Sentences in
    Expository Prose"
    (Braddock), 136–137
Fries, Charles, 35, 183–184, 186

Garner, Bryan A., 71
*General Principles of English
    Grammar* (Collyer), 33
Gerunds, 198–200
"Girl" (Kincaid), 173
Glaser, Joe, 171
Glossary of Bêtes Noires and
    Mythrules, 70–76
Glossary of Commonly Confused
    Words, 77–88
Goodlad, John, 6
Gowers, Ernest, 69, 73
Grammar. *See also* rules of gram-
    mar, and traditional school
    grammar (TSG)
    "broken part of the curricu-
        lum," 20–21
    definition, xi
    reasons for teaching, 6–7
*Grammar and the Teaching of
    Writing* (Noguchi), 20, 115
Grammar instruction. *See also* tra-
    ditional school grammar
    reasons for, 6–7
    terminology used in, 19–23
Grammar of Contemporary English
    (Quirk, et. al), 155
Grammar of Grammars (Brown), 52
"Grammar of schooling," 6, 46
Grammatical Institutes (Ash), 189
Graves, Donald, xiv, 94, 100, 102
Gray, James, 89
Great Gatsby, The (Fitzgerald), 74
*Growth and Structure of the English
    Language* (Jespersen), 50
Guth, Hans P., 59, 70

Hacker, Diane, 178
Hairston, Maxine, 55, 80, 105,
    115
*Handbook of Research on Teaching
    The English Language Arts*
    (Flood, et. al.), 153–154
Harbrace College Handbook
    (Hodges)
    appositives, 37
    colons, 161, 163

commas, 155
contractions, 189–190
dashes, 166
"different from" / "than," 71
errors, emphasis on, 17, 66–68
fused sentences and comma
    splice, 115–116
negative attitudes in, 66–67
nouns, 26
paragraphs, 141
parentheses, 169
prepositions, 74
publication of, 17–18
semicolons, 173–174, 178
sentence fragments, 110
sentence openings, 120–122
sentences, 39
topic sentences, 136
verbs, 28
"you," avoidance of, 106
Harper's Magazine, 190
Hartwell, Patrick, 35
Harvard, 9, 91, 98
Hausmann, Brock, 20
"Have got," 73
Hemingway, Ernest, 157
Hillocks, George Jr., 101, 104
Hodges, John C. *See also Harbrace
    College Handbook*, 17–18
"Homeless" (Quindlen), 137–140
"Hopefully," 69, 71–72
Hopkins, Edwin, 90
Hornberger, Theodore, 70
Hours, The (Cunningham), 173
Howards End (Forster), xv

"I," avoidance of in writing,
    105–106
Image Grammar (Noden), 20
Infinitives
    activity, 200–201
    definition of, 198–199
    prepositions used to mark,
        210–211
    split, 72–73
Intensifiers, 214
"Irregardless," 58
"It's" / "its," 82

James, Henry, 73, 167
Jefferson, Thomas, 106
Jespersen, Otto, 19, 46, 50
Johnson, Samuel. *See also
    Dictionary of the English
    Language*

disagreement with Webster, 50
double negatives, 56
English syntax, 7, 14,
    standards established by, 50–51
use of "have got," 73
Jonathan Edwards Syndrome,
    92–95

Kael, Pauline, 144
Kantz/Yates Survey, 77, 86–88, 115
Kelly, Walt, 152
Kemper, David, 177
Killgallon, Don, 177
Kincaid, Jamaica, 173
King, Stephen, 124
Kingsolver, Barbara, 107–108
Kirkham, Samuel, 15
Kittredge, George Lyman, 47, 52
Klink, Anne L., 117–118
"Know" / "no" and "knew" /
    "new," 82
Kohn, Alfie, 46, 101
Kolln, Martha, 131
Kozol, Jonathan, 19–20, 157,
    179–180

Language (Sapir), 1
Language acquisition, xiv, 3–6
*Language Exploration and
    Awareness: A Resource Book
    for Teachers* (Andrews), 63
Language Instinct, The (Pinker), 4
"Learn, leave, or be beaten," 9, 93
*Lectures on Rhetoric and Belles
    Lettres* (Blair), 96
"Led" / "lead," 83
Leonard, Sterling, 51–52, 72, 75
"Less" / "fewer," 75–76
"Let's Get Off the Mythmobile"
    (Schuster), 190
Lewis, Mark, 18
"Like" / "as," 71
Lily, William, 7, 13
Lincoln, Abraham, 15, 106
Lloyd, Donald, 90
"Loose" / "lose," 83
Lowth, Robert. *See also A Short
    Introduction to English
    Grammar*
    authority of usage cited by, 51
    comparison with Hodges, 17
    comparison with Murray,
        10–11, 13–15, 69
    contractions, opinion of, 185
    education of, 8–9, 69

Lowth-Murray tradition, 15
Swift's proposal, reaction to, 50
Lunsford, Andrea A., 68, 96, 114–115

MacLean, Marion S., xvii, 159
"Mail" (Fadiman), 171
Maittaire, Michael, 1, 2, 18
Maxwell, William, 71
Mayes, Frances, 170, 205
Mayher, John, xv, 104
Mays of Ventadorn, The (Merwin), 172
McArthur, Tom, 47
McBride, James, 156, 170
McCourt, Frank, xi, xvii, 32–33
McQuade, Finlay, xvii–xix
McWhorter, John, xii, 61–62
"Me and," 58–60
Melville, Herman, 96, 184
Mersand, Joseph, 16
Merwin, W.S., 172
Meyer, Verne, 177
Michael, Ian
   conjunctions, 36
   countertradition, 18
   difficulty of definitions, 19, 28
   history of grammar texts, 7, 10, 13
   number of Lowth's editions, 9
   punctuation in traditional grammar, 10
Mid-continent Research for Education and Learning, 140
Minimal Essentials Test (MIMS), 21–22, 26, 174
Moby Dick (Melville), 96
Modal auxiliaries, 78, 80, 213–214
Modern English Usage (Fowler), 106
Modifiers of nouns. *See* adjectives
Mohr, Marian M., xvii, 159
Monaghan, Charles, 11–13
Morenberg, Max, 42
Morrison, Toni, 156
Murray, Donald, 21, 204–205
Murray, Lindley. *See also English Grammar*
   comparison with Lowth, 10–11, 13–15, 69
   doctrine of usage, writing on, 84
   education of, 11, 69
   Lowth-Murray tradition, 15

textbooks by, 12–13
Murrays of Murray Hill, The (Monaghan), 13
Mythrules. *See* rules of grammar

NAEP. *See* National Assessment of Educational Progress
NCTE. *See* National Council of Teachers of English
Nation at Risk, 17
National Assessment of Educational Progress, 100, 103, 115
National Council of Teachers of English, 68, 77, 104, 191
National Writing Project, 89
Nelson, Willie, 199
New Yorker, 71, 144, 173, 190–191
New York Times, The, 27, 37, 47, 54, 58–59, 111, 144, 159–161, 171, 191
Nicholson, Margaret, 69, 106
Noden, Harry R., 20, 159
Noguchi, Rei R., 20, 115, 157
Nonstandard English, 55–63
Nonstandard speech, 62–64
Noun phrases
   activity, 196
   identification of, 195–196
   substitution by pronouns, 22–23
Nouns
   activities, 27–28, 196, 201
   as verbs, 201
   compound, 196
   definition, 26–27
   identification of, 195
   predicate, 41
   prepositions used as, 210
Numbers, 31–32, 212
Nystrand, Martin, 157

Objects, direct and indirect, 41–43
O'Connor, Patricia, 47
Ohanian, Susan, 101
On Writing: A Memoir of the Craft (King), 124
On Writing Well (Zinsser), xiii
One Size Fits Few (Ohanian), 101
"Only look and connect," xv, 54, 177
"Only," placement of, 75
Orwell, George, 107–108, 124

PSSA. *See* Pennsylvania System of School Assessment
Paragraphs and paragraphing
   activities, 144–145, 146–149
   art, not science, 142–144
   definition, 140–141
   five paragraph themes, 145–146
Parentheses
   activity, 171–172
   usage, 169–171
Parker, Dorothy, 89, 96–97
Parker, Francis Wayland, 90
Parkes, M.B., 151, 154, 181
Participles, 198
Parts of speech. *See also individual parts of speech*
   form, or lexical, classes, 193–195
   intuitive understanding of, 3
   Lowth and Murray on, 13
   part of language acquisition, 4–6
   structure classes, 193–194
   traditional teaching of, 1–3
   updated treatment of, 193–214
Passive voice
   activities, 125–129, 131–135
   legitimate uses of, 130–131
   traditional injunctions against, 124–125
"Past" / "passed," 83
Pause and Effect: An Introduction to the History of Punctuation in the West (Parkes), 154
Pennsylvania System of School Assessment (PSSA), 94, 102, 119, 173,199
Pequod [ship], 184
"Phenomenology of Error" (Williams), 96
Pinker, Steven
   double negatives, 61
   language instinct theory, 4
   "me and," use of, 59–60
   nouns as verbs, 201
   words and parts of speech, 5
"Pogo," 152
"Politics and the English Language" (Orwell), 107–108, 124
Pooley, Robert C., 52
Portrait of a Lady, The (James), 73
Positive reinforcement
   teaching writing using, xiv
   learning language through, 4

Possessive apostrophe. *See* apostrophe, possessive
Power of Babel, The (McWhorter), 61
"Precede" / "proceed," 83–84
Prepositions
  activities, 35, 211
  additional uses, 210–211
  as function words, 211–212
  complex, 211
  definition, 34–35
  ending sentences with, 74–75
Prescriptive rules. *See* rules of grammar
Price, Reynolds, 106, 166, 173
Pride and Prejudice (Austen), 133–134
Priestley, Joseph, 11, 50
"Principle" / "principal," 84
Priscian, 13, 33, 36
Problem-Solving Strategies for Writing (Flower), 191
Proforms, 209–210
Pronouns
  activities, 23–26, 208–209
  definition, 21–23
  first person, avoidance of, 105–106
  incorrect, 56
  indefinite, 23
  second person, avoidance of, 106–107
Pronunciation, 5, 66
Proposal for Correcting, Improving and Ascertaining the English Tongue (Swift), 50
Proulx, E. Annie, 173
Punctuation. *See also individual marks*
  activity, 181–182
  antiquated marks, 183
  changing conventions of, 151–152
  conventional vs. unconventional, examples, 181–182
  internal marks in contemporary American prose, 159–161
  Parkes's position that it's a personal matter, 151, 154, 181
Puttenham, George, 172

Quindlen, Anna, 137–140
Quinn, Jane Bryant, 164
Quirk, Randolph, 46
  adverbs, 33

colons, 163
comma, 155, 157
comma splice, 116
numerals, 32
sentences, 38–39
split infinitives, 72
verbs, 212–213

Radford, Andrew, 194
"Real" / "really," 58
Reflective teachers
  conduct research, xv–xix
  encourage students to examine, break rules, xv
  seek feedback from students, xvi
Reid, James M., 16–17, 70
Research by teachers
  discovering what students already know, xvi–xvii
  Finlay McQuade's on outcomes, xvii–xix
  soliciting feedback from students, xvi
  teacher-researcher groups, xvii
  value of, in testing traditional rules, xv–xvi
Research in the Teaching of English, 191
Rhetorical Grammar (Kolln), 131
Rich, Susanna, 178
Riverside Reader (Trimmer), 105, 120
Romano, Tom, 21, 104
Rousseau, Jean Jacques, 8, 14
Rubba, Johanna, 64
Rules of grammar
  bedrock rules not to be broken, xi
  creativity undermined by overemphasis on, xv
  descriptive rules, 48–49
  dialect, use of, 63–64
  Glossary of Bêtes Noires and Mythrules, 70–76
  inadequacy of traditional teaching, xvii–xix, 6–7
  intuitive understanding of, 49
  learned with language acquisition, 3–6
  learning before breaking, xiii–xv
  mythrules, breaking of, xii–xiii
  not followed by educated speakers, 55

not followed by professional writers, xii–xiii, xvi, 105–113, 116–125, 136–140, 144
not followed by textbook writers, xv, 140–142, 176–179
prescriptive rules, 48
self-confidence undermined by overemphasis on, xiv–xv
Ruskin, John, 73

Safire, William, 111, 144, 191
Sanders, Michael S., 169
Santayana, George, xix
Sapir, Edward, 1, 6
Savage Inequalities (Kozol), 20, 179 180
Schools Our Children Deserve, The (Kohn), 46
Schuster, Edgar, 190
Sebranek, Patrick, 177
Self-confidence and writing, xiv–xv, 94, 96
Semicolons
  activities, 175–176, 180–181
  before conjunctive adverbs, 176–179
  difficulty teaching, 174–175
  heavy comma, 179–181
  light period, 174–179
  recommended but not used by text editors, 176–179
  student use of, 173–174
  usage, 172–175
Sentences
  activities, 40, 111–113, 123–124
  clincher, 135–136
  definition, 38–40
  fragments, 40, 110–111
  fused, 114–116
  openings, xvi, 120–123
  rambling, 114–116
  topic, 136–140
Shakespeare, William, 7, 10, 50–51, 56, 60, 62, 74, 136, 172, 185
Shaughnessy, Mina,
  difficulty of writing well, 96
  errors, 89
  nonstandard speech, 63, 66
  semicolons, 175, 179
  sentences, 115
Shipping News (Proulx), 173
Short Introduction to English Grammar, A (Lowth)

adjectives, 13, 31
apostrophe, 185
comparison with Murray's
    English Grammar, 10–11,
    13–15
double negatives, 60
intention and influence of, 9
nouns, 13
parsing in, 11, 14
parts of speech, 13
prepositions, 74
pronouns, 13
publication of, 8–9
punctuation, 151–154
semicolons, 172
verbs, 13, 28
Simon & Schuster Handbook for
    Writers (Troyka), 178–179,
    185
Sinatra, Frank, 61
Sipe, Rebecca Bowers, 163
Sledd, James, 89, 91, 100, 149
Sloan, Gary, 97
Sobel, Dava, 170, 180
Social Contract, The (Rousseau), 8
Some Landmarks in the History of
    English Grammar (Kittredge),
    47
Sommers, Nancy, 91
Spelling, teaching of, 6
Standard English. *See also* Well-
    Edited American Prose
activity, 76
definition of, 53–55
difference between written and
    spoken, 55, 75–76
Standards. *See also* authority,
    quest for, standards move-
    ment, xvi, 20
state standards, 173–175
Staples, Brent, 159
"Stationery" / "stationary," 84
Steinbeck, John, 97
Stevens, Wallace, 109–110
"Stone Soup" (Kingsolver),
    107–108
Strong, William, xiv, 20, 92
Structure words, 207
Strunk, William. *See Elements of*
    Style
Style: Toward Clarity and Grace
    (Williams), 47, 191
Subject–verb agreement/disagree-
    ment, 56, 64–66, 213–214

Subjects
    activity, 41
    definition, 40–41
    sentence openings, using,
        121–122
Suffixes, knowledge of, 202
Swift, Jonathan, 10, 50, 73
Synonyms, 22, 208–209

Table Alphabeticall of Hard Usuall
    English Words (Cawdrey), 47,
    50
Tannen, Deborah, 156
Teacher as Writer (Dahl), 104
Teacher-researcher group, xvii
Teacher-Researchers at Work,
    (MacLean and Mohr), xvii
Teaching a Stone to Talk (Dillard),
    191
Teaching Grammar in Context
    (Weaver), xiv, 6
Teaching of English, The
    (Michael), 19
"Teaching of Grammar"
    (Jespersen), 19
Terminology, problem, 19–21
Testing Trap, The (Hillocks), 101
Textbooks, grammar
    collaborative authorship, 69–70
    comparison of Lowth's and
        Murray's, 31–14
    Latin and Greek roots of, 13
    pressure to keep them simple,
        185–186
"Than" / "then," 84–85
Thesis statements, 136–140
"They're" / "their" / "there,"
    85–86
Thill, John V., 177
Thoreau, Henry David, 106
"Threw" / "through," 86
Thurber, James, 158
Tinkering Toward Utopia (Tyack),
    6
Tooke, Horne, 33
Topic sentences, 136–140
Traditional school grammar
    (TSG). *See also* rules of
    grammar
    "broken part of curriculum," 20
    countertradition, 18
    definitions inadequate as used
        in, 15, 19–23, 26, 30–31, 33,
        34–43

errors, emphasis on, xii–xiv, 15,
    66–68, 92–96
faults of, 2, 15, 45–46, 191–192
Latin and Greek roots of, 7, 13
Lowth-Murray tradition, 15
negative attitudes of, 66–68
paradigm for teaching, 21
reliance on rules, xiii–xv, 48,
    68
vs. traditional scholarly
    grammar, 46
Trimmer, Joseph, 105
Troyka, Lynn Quitman, 116,
    178–179, 185
Twenty-seven Commonly
    Confused Words, 77–88
"Two" / "too" / "to," 86
Tyack, David, 6

Under the Tuscan Sun (Mayes),
    170, 205
Underworld (DeLillo), 173
"Unravelling the Comma Splice"
    (Klink), 117–118
Updike, John, 156
"Usage Industry" (McArthur), 47
Usage texts, 68–70

Verbs
    activities, 29–30, 43, 109–110
    auxiliary, 212–214
    "be," 107–109
    complements and, 41–43
    definition, 28–29
    identification of, 197
    nonstandard forms, 56
    nouns used as, 201
    state of being, 28–29
    traditional school grammar,
        instruction in, 1–3
    transitive/intransitive, 43, 197
    verbals, 198–199
    vivid / "be" verbs, 107–109
Vonnegut, Kurt, 172

WEAP. *See* Well-Edited
    American Prose
Wallace, David Foster, 164
Warriner, John E. *See also*
    Warriner's Textbooks, 15–18
Warriner's textbooks
    authorship, 16–17, 69
    clincher sentences, 135
    comma splice, 115–116

contractions, 190
drills, use of, 16, 21
errors, lists of, 68
nouns, 26
paragraphs, 140
prepositions, 35
pronouns, 21
semicolons, 177
verbs, 28
Weaver, Constance, xiv, xviii, 6, 115
Webster, Noah, 15, 50–51
Well-Edited American Prose (WEAP), xi–xii, 54–55, 60, 111, 152, 157, 159
Wellesley, 98
"We're" / "were" / "where," 87
Wheeler, Rebecca, 64
White, E.B. *See Elements of Style* (Strunk and White)

Whitten, Mary, 16
"Who's" / "whose," 87
Williams, Joseph M.
    "arbitrary nature of our judgments," 47
    coherence, 122
    contractions, 190–191
    errors in students' writing, 96
    favorite writer test, xii–xiii
    passive voice, 131
    rules, value of, 68, 70
    topic sentences, 140
Winchester, Simon, 163, 170
Winchester College, 8, 10, 93
Woe is I, (O'Connor), 47
Woolf, Virginia, 173
"Write" / "right," 87
Writer Teaches Writing, A (Murray), 204–205
Writer's Craft (Blau et. al), 177

Writers INC (Sebranek, et. al.), 35, 115, 135, 177
"Writers on Writing" series, 160–161
Writing
    activity, 98
    difficulty of, 96–98
    helping students improve, 104
    teaching by positive reinforcement, xiv
    testing, not conducive to good writing, 100–103
    topics assigned in, 101–104
Writing With Passion (Romano), 104

Yard, The (Sanders), 169–170
"You," avoidance of in writing, 106–107
"You're" / "your," 87–88